The Record of Global Economic Development

The Record of Global Economic Development

Eric Jones

Melbourne Business School, Australia
and University of Reading, UK

Edward Elgar
Cheltenham, UK • Northampton, MA, USA

Published by
Edward Elgar Publishing Limited
Glensanda House
Montpellier Parade
Cheltenham
Glos GL50 1UA
UK

Edward Elgar Publishing, Inc.
136 West Street
Suite 202
Northampton
Massachusetts 01060
USA

A catalogue record for this book
is available from the British Library

Library of Congress Cataloguing in Publication Data

Jones, E.L. (Eric Lionel)
   The record of global economic development / Eric Jones.
     p. cm.
   Includes bibliographical references and index.
     1. Economic development. 2. Economic development — Social aspects.
   3. Economic development — Environmental aspects. 4. Globalization
   — Environmental aspects. 4. Globalization — Economic aspects. I. Title.

   HD75 J664 2002
   338.9 — dc21
                                         2001051131

ISBN 1 84064 806 6

Printed and bound in Great Britain by MPG Books Ltd, Bodmin, Cornwall

Contents

List of tables

Preface and acknowledgements

In this volume I deal with themes relating to economic development and cultural, institutional and structural change. My aim has been to illustrate historical and modern patterns, and to some extent integrate them. Behind this purpose lies another, which is to show that plain economic history can help to pick out the more durable of the arrangements that favour growth. To do so involves trying to restore historicity to modern topics and modern interest to historical investigations. The conditions that favour long-term growth are essentially political ones. They include contestable markets (including information markets), free trade, and decentralized institutions. This lesson is well known yet is in constant danger of being ignored or obscured, as witness the ceaseless efforts to roll back free trade – efforts that seem to be swelling as one millennium gives way to the next.

My work on economic history has flowed readily enough into the modern topics dealt with in this book. Present-day East Asia has proved especially fertile ground for someone already interested in its past and able to compare its unfolding with Western development. Just as current globalization (and, one fears, the protectionist reaction to it) is a re-run of the first globalization boom of 1870–1914, so recent attempts at cultural explanations of East Asian development replay unsatisfactory Weberian-style analyses of the European Miracle. The fit between past and present can never be exact and is easily over-strained, but, with due precautions against self-serving analogies, comparisons can be very suggestive.

The main themes of the book are indicated by the part titles. Slightly rephrased, they are long-run world economic history, the check to growth from protectionism, the East Asian Miracle and Crisis, and adjustments to global competition. There are two further topics and many more cross-links than will at first appear. Agriculture is the first additional topic; it receives special notice in both the world history and Protectionism sections. Culture is the second such topic, it is discussed in the chapters on the significance of East Asian development and Asian Values, as well as in comments on cultural protection in Chapter 10. The subject of Protectionism spills over from the part devoted to it, for example to material on early agricultural protection in Chapter 4, to Japanese legal protection in Chapter 3, to the defence of Australian supermarkets inspired by protectionist complaints from small grocers in Chapter 11 and to a discussion in Chapter 12 of the current anti-globalization backlash.

The impetus to assemble and prepare the material for this book was an invitation to lecture in Japan. One of the topics on which I was asked to speak was the 'relevance' of my book, *The European Miracle*. At first I jibbed at this part of the assignment, being a little gun-shy as the result of criticisms that had been aimed as much at me as at the book. Most people seemed to like the *Miracle* but a small number of noisy anti-European or anti-Western ideologues most definitely did not. Since I had never intended to imbue my economic history with political significance, and have not met these people, their animosity rather took my breath away. While I believe that economic history can be used to throw light on the present, this has to be done sensitively. In the *Miracle* and a subsequent volume, *Growth Recurring*, I went out of my way to caution against the dangers involved in transposing conclusions about the past into the present and tried to clinch the point by identifying some of the facile transpositions in the literature.

In any case, when I wrote the *Miracle* my philosophical viewpoint would not necessarily have endorsed the type of conclusion that critics purport to have found in the text. Of course I cannot answer all of their points because I have never held some of the views ascribed to me, for instance that Europe is 'permanently superior'. In so far as such a statement means anything it is the diametrical opposite of my views about the long-run dynamics of economic systems. Another critic claimed that I argue by 'mentality' – again that Europeans were in some way superior. Stephen Mennell has already dealt with that: as he expressed it in the introduction to a book that he, Joop Goudsblom and I jointly authored, 'we share a suspicion of all forms of mentalistic explanation, where culture, religion, or ideology is seen as the main engine of history'.[1] With regard to assaults on anything that can be passed off as 'Eurocentric', I am content for Joel Mokyr to frame the debate; his title is 'Eurocentricity Triumphant'.[2]

Notwithstanding the polemics with which world economic history has become suffused, the question of whether economic history can help us understand the present (whether one period helps to explain the next) remains an interesting topic and deserves to be aired. On second thoughts, then, I decided to accept the challenge with which my Japanese hosts had confronted me. Even the title of the visiting position, which incorporated the term 'economic dynamics', implied a challenge. Economic Dynamics is not a clear-cut subject but it invites, and in this case was intended to invite, investigations of the relationship between economic history and contemporary economic change. I doubt that a comparable opportunity to address this would be offered in the Western world, where other subjects are being encouraged to crowd economic history right out of the syllabus. I learned with interest that this is not so in Japan. The government there intends courses on history to constitute one-third of undergraduate work in faculties of economics and business in the national universities, on the grounds that the subject is the proper foundation of social science. This is the opposite of current opinion in the West.

Nevertheless, although they are shallow, Western attitudes are not wholly misguided. There are reasons for avoiding purely historical treatments. Historians, including economic historians, typically claim too much for the 'genetic' approach – that is to say for explaining the present in terms of the past. Current structural forces need to be taken into account too. They affect what is chosen from the menu, so to speak, which history hands us.[3] History is only half the equation. Nevertheless it is still an indispensable half, a point that is neglected by those in adjacent disciplines who have appropriated the resources formerly devoted to history and who prefer to dodge the mastering of historical material (a prejudice easily communicated to students). I do not spend any further time in the present volume scolding the anti-history movement but I hope to show by illustration that it has overshot the mark.

PART I LONG-TERM ECONOMIC DEVELOPMENT

The first part of the volume deals with *very* long-run economic development, largely taking the form of re-evaluations of *The European Miracle* and *Growth Recurring*. It was especially appropriate for me to reconsider these works because a Japanese edition of the *Miracle* had been published in August 2000 by the University of Nagoya Press, in a translation by Professors Minoru Yasumoto and Kohei Wakimura. *Growth Recurring* also reappeared in 2000, with a long new introduction, in the University of Michigan series, 'Economics, Cognition, and Society'. Because these books were actually written in 1979 and 1986–87 respectively, and could draw only on literature available at those dates, I found it interesting to consider how their theses had fared in the light of subsequent research and debate.

Accordingly, in the first three chapters I offer some comment on later work and the more serious criticisms. Where research has shown that Asian economies were more advanced than the literature disclosed when the books were written, the early advantage held by Europe will obviously have been less than I thought. But to the extent that this is correct, it makes the European achievement of rapid growth *more* remarkable, not less. Those who are overcome by Euro-envy can avoid this conclusion only by denigrating the practices employed by Europeans in the course of economic growth. That means arguing that the Rise of the West was at the expense of the decline of somebody else, as if history were a zero-sum game. Subsequent experience – all the borrowings from the West and all the income gains that have ensued – shows this to be untrue.

The entire East–West dispute is hardly science, or social science; it involves distorting scholarship in order to fight again archaic battles of the 'Clash of Civilizations' type. When other civilizations achieve stable growth, the interest of non-Westerners in these old intellectual conflicts will die away. What will happen to Western scholars who dislike their own societies enough to make careers of denigrating them past and present, I cannot imagine. Doubtless the personally disgruntled will find fresh targets.

I was drawn into these disputes willy-nilly, as will be apparent from Chapter 3. The point I add in this volume is that, whether or not Europe's institutions were first designed for the common good (and clearly many were not), they often possessed a quality of openness that has enabled their benefits to be extended to wider and wider social groups. These groups include non-Europeans, since institutions as well as technologies have been adopted elsewhere, while the basis of much international law and many international organizations is European or at any rate Western. It is a historical fact that the West 'got there first'. A mature attitude does not involve rejecting the Western legacy but grasping its beneficial aspects with both hands. Plenty of non-Westerners are willing to do so, though, as usual with cultural transfers, they find it easier to adopt technologies than ideas that might disturb existing power structures.

An analogy that may make clearer what I have in mind is with veterinary medicine. Until the era of antibiotics, science was often helpless in the face of animal infections. As late as the 1920s there were 'wise men' in England who counselled farmers to meet calamities among their cattle herds, such as Bedfordshire disease, by burning frogs in the farm gateway. The sickness is a deficiency disease, readily cured by providing the cattle with mineral licks. As someone commented, few minerals are released by burning a frog. Yet a scientific veterinary profession had come into existence and, even if there was little it could do at first, it knew enough not to burn frogs. Fortunately research was on the brink of important advances. Vets assimilated the findings as they emerged, translated them into practice, and spread the word among the farm community. Was it not better – a stupendous act of faith, if you like, but a heartening one – to have ready a trained veterinary profession than not to have had such a profession in the first place?

In a similar vein, European history happened to create institutions that were capable of universally benign results once political circumstances generalized them. This was not the case in systems that were, and sometimes remain, in the hands of undemocratic political elites. China is clearly the largest remaining unmodernized polity. Smaller historical cultures could also be self-referential, in contrast to the boundless curiosity displayed by Europeans. Thus Peter Munz notes that the Maori were so fixated on perpetuating their patriarchal social order that they were uncomprehending of anything that did not seem to bear on it, even the threat implied by the arrival of the Europeans.[4] The quality of openness, rooted in the polycentric nature of Europe's society, gave Europeans options for growth and expansion seldom inherent in societies with more static hierarchies.

The fourth chapter in Part I complements the earlier ones. It uses a supply and demand framework to put order into the *very* long-term history of agriculture. When the whole world was poor, output and consumption remained in long-term equilibrium. Production seldom ran far ahead of consumption, and for obvious reasons consumption could not run far ahead of production. How did things change? It was not always via demand-pull in which the growth of population neatly created the pairs of hands needed to feed the extra number of mouths. We can infer from the big demographic cycles in world history that there were periods when the growth of supply did overtake demand. Usually this drew human numbers up with it and, as it were, cancelled out the gains in real income per head. In other words, population growth typically consumed the additional food produced by the stellar episodes when major new practices were spread.

What was needed was an increase in supply that would outpace population growth and bring the price of food right down, putting pressure on producers to switch into petty manufacturing or leave farming for more productive occupations. Fresh land in the neo-Europes certainly helped with this, supplemented by industrial inputs to agriculture and better institutions to diffuse improved methods. Labour productivity in agriculture rose dramatically, but not fast enough to maintain farm incomes, especially as European peasants often moved to better land in other continents. The accelerating increase in supply pushed farm incomes down, contributing to industrialization but also to the perverse response discussed in Part II.

PART II   PROTECTIONISM

Part I is on Growth but Part II is on Anti-Growth. Whereas the first part considers the conditions under which past economic growth took place, the second recognizes that growth is fatally easy to slow or stop. Protectionism is one of the main threats and this part consists of two chapters dealing with the familiar case of agricultural protection and the less familiar case of language protection. Complementary material on language appears later in the book, in Chapter 10, while Chapter 11 was inspired by yet another protectionist challenge, in this case to supermarkets.

As to agricultural protection, the farm sector usually reacts to downward pressure on its incomes by intensifying production. A familiar paradox is involved. Individual farmers can maintain their own incomes by expanding output and reducing unit costs, but when all of them are striving in the same direction the result can only be a further squeeze on prices. This tends to be good for consumers but not for farmers themselves. A frequent alternative is therefore for them also to seek protection against foreign competition.

Chapter 5 begins by describing the phases in English agricultural history when events conspired to give farmers the protection for which they clamoured. Taxpayers in the developed world have been surprisingly willing to subsidize agriculture but support for still further increases in output is simply not affordable. A clever twist has thus been found to add to the arguments for protection. This is to claim that farmers should be paid for functions other than producing commodities, such as safeguarding the environment. The name bestowed on the creation of these previously unpriced benefits – which an already well-fed, high-income population may now be supposed to want from the land – is 'Multifunctionality'. The main thrust of Chapter 5 is to examine the case for this by looking at the record of farming in Lowland England. My interest arose from over 50 years' observation of the landscape as a hobby naturalist and from prolonged, though peripheral, involvement with the farm sector. As someone once said, all the best social science is autobiographical. Observation had made me sceptical of the claims of farmers to provide significant environmental and other benefits as a side effect of commodity production. On examining the record I was even more surprised at the extent of agriculture's negative impact.

The other chapter in Part II deals with language protection. My interest in this less familiar topic arose when my wife took a degree in Linguistics. She found herself in the Department of Linguistics at La Trobe University with other keen, hard working, adult women and a staff capable of arousing genuine intellectual excitement. The study of language requires few props and is readily discussed over the dinner table. In order to keep up my end in the conversations, I took to glancing through the books and articles. Fascinating though they were, it was apparent that none of the authors had ever heard of economics, though they sometimes contrived to give the impression that, had they done so, they would have been against it! Rather like farmers, linguists talk as though the taxpayer owes them a living, though both occupations live so enclosed in their own professional cultures that they are probably unaware how they sound to outsiders. Linguists are inclined to speak as though funds without limit should be forthcoming to record and preserve each and every language on the planet. This assumption of the essential rightness of preservation chimes with the wishes of cultural producers who employ minor languages and of course with the politicians who, in response, pontificate so fatuously about the sacredness of language. There may be a scientific case for language preservation as there is for research into languages but it is taken as axiomatic rather than expounded. The opportunity cost of preserving languages for their own sake is seldom taken into account.

PART III EAST ASIAN DEVELOPMENT

The most striking alteration in world economic geography in modern times, perhaps at any period, has been the rise of East Asia. Thirty years real growth rates of 6 or 8 per cent per annum in many countries in the region reasonably enough justifies the label of the East Asian Miracle. The pace, even more than the enormous scale, of this achievement eclipsed all previous episodes of growth. Contrary to recent assertions, this does not invalidate comparisons with European experience.[5] What can be 'predicted' from history in detail may be moot but I urge that Asia is not exempt from the general pattern of development found earlier in Europe.

Asian exceptionalism is simply not persuasive. The only possible exceptionalism, at least in the 1990s, was that of the United States, where types of production and consumption were being created that all other countries were adapting to, either by trying to catch up or by striving to exclude the influence of the 'Great Satan'.[6] *Mutatis mutandis*, evolving demographic structures and rising real incomes produce comparable results everywhere. Income-related patterns of consumption in East Asia have already followed a path not unlike that in Europe and North America. Most striking of all is the shift of attention in the more developed parts of Asia from bread-and-butter issues to non-material demands already familiar in the West, such as for environmental clean-up and legal freedoms. This spillover from lives of mere shopping, as it were, to politics was to be expected once a sufficient number of people felt secure in their new level of material comfort.[7]

But in 1997 the East Asian Miracle faltered and in some countries went into reverse, though (it is important to note) nowhere to the extent of wiping out all the gains over the previous generation. This downturn proved embarrassing, not least to those who had triumphalist books and articles scheduled for publication that year or the next. There was a great deal of back-pedalling and even more attempts to claim that events were actually vindicating whatever position a given writer had previously taken. Only a few authorities were candid enough to admit that they had grossly exaggerated the strength of Asian economies.

I pretend neither to have predicted the Asian Crisis nor to have been wholly exempt from the bullish mood of the times. I do claim however to have been enough of a contrarian to have insisted that the institutional foundations of Asian growth would turn out to be rickety. No one at the time was interested in scepticism and some were scornful of it. Before the Crisis my annual lecture on corruption was condemned by occasional students who had failed to grasp the pains I was taking to show that corruption is not specifically an Asian problem: surely no citizen of the European Union could have dared suggest that! Thus I was braced for trouble when an Indonesian student came up after a class and asked whether I had said that Transparency International's (the premier body surveying and fighting corruption) index listed his country as number one. I replied 'yes' and he said, 'I think it should be number one, number two and number three!'

Since the Crisis audiences have indeed been much more willing to consider the fragility of Asian political and institutional arrangements. My version of the Crisis in Chapter 8 is that it was 'premature' in the sense that, had the system of fixed exchange rates not crashed, a more general institutional crisis would have surfaced within a few years. This would probably have taken the form of political conflict within Asian societies over issues of governance that few publicly questioned during the years of rapid growth.

Readers can judge the cogency of this argument for themselves, since Part III contains pieces written in 1991 and 1997 as well as one written in 2000. The pieces tackle institutional and cultural aspects of the Asian experience. Chapter 7, written in 1991, suggests that whenever growth starts to speed up in other regions we will find that commentators respond by extolling the positive features of their cultures too.

They will celebrate the merits of features that have hitherto been dismissed as obstacles to growth. I was amused to note that, once Indian growth began to accelerate in the 1990s, Amartya Sen discovered 'the fact that India has perhaps the longest accounting tradition in the world has now been dusted up and presented as a causal explanation' of the new-found dynamism.[8] Hinduism is a prime candidate for being transformed from growth impediment into growth propellant, like Confucianism before it and Christianity earlier still. We should not take such arguments in terms of over-generalised value systems very seriously. Chapters 8 and 9 also question the salience of cultural explanations of the East Asian Miracle.

PART IV   ADJUSTING TO GLOBAL CHANGE

In order to sustain economic growth, all economies have to face up to continual alterations in their industrial structure. Whether they like it or not they are embroiled in permanent revolution, or what a McKinsey Report called the 'race without ending'. It is the challenge of structural change that makes free trade seem so threatening, because it brings in international as well as local competitors. This calls out the Protectionist fire brigade which is always on stand-by. In reality more of the challenge comes from technological

innovation than from imports, but either way the effect can be to stir up
Schumpeterian gales of creative destruction. One cannot argue that in the short
run such changes are Pareto optimal, with no one worse off and at least one
person better off. Some businesses and whole industries are always going to
be washed away in the process. Economists are too glib about the lag before
the people involved can be redeployed. The appeal of economic change can
only be to the greatest good of the greatest number, the point being that the
destruction *is* creative, with new firms, new industries, and new jobs arising.
There are net gains as capital and labour shift to higher-earning occupations.
Society no longer supports makers of crinolines or hansom cabs, nor should it
do so. But it cannot be denied that some people will suffer while waiting for
the new equilibrium.

Much the biggest set of structural changes that the world has seen was that
accompanying industrialisation. New industries, using machinery powered by
steam and housed in factories, out-competed traditional handicraft ones
formerly carried on in dwellings or small workshops. Industrial employment
as a whole expanded while agricultural employment shrank. Hence an
advanced economy used to be defined by a percentage of the labour force in
agriculture low enough to be counted on the fingers of one hand. By the end
of the twentieth century a second and quite distinct wave of structural change
was taking place. This was the expansion of tertiary (service) occupations at
the expense of manufacturing. Episodes that have been called 'the second
industrial revolution' – any number of phases have attracted this label – turn
out to have been little more than changes within subdivisions of manufacturing. The transition from manufacturing to the service industries, which *The
Economist* once described as producing 'things you cannot drop on your foot',
is of an entirely different order. A great impetus has been given to this shift by
the adoption of the computer. Although the computer has breathed new life
into some manufacturing industries, its most promising effect has been to
generate an information revolution underpinning the rise of the tertiary sector.

The American economy has adjusted best to this new phase of structural
change. Returns to shareholders by major corporations in the United States are
said to have been half as high again as in Europe and almost three times as
high as in Australia. Other economies have not merely often failed to meet
American standards but have performed below what it is reasonable to think
of as their own potential. Chapter 10 discusses the Australian case. The costs
of limited structural change there have been obscured by self-congratulation
about the high rate of growth in the 1990s, much of which is catch-up on
earlier periods when Australia lagged behind Europe or the States. As the new
millennium begins many of Australia's largest companies are contemplating
moving their headquarters overseas and listing on the stock exchanges of the
United States or United Kingdom. The young native-born and people with

MBAs are leaving the country at an increased rate and although some will undoubtedly return no one can be sure that the most creative will do so. Australia is in danger of exporting the creative people and companies that would help it look outwards. Certainly the country is hampered by a tiny domestic market; its problem is less the 'tyranny of distance' than the tyranny of small market size. Nevertheless there are deficiencies that could be remedied by bolder policies. Chapter 10 concentrates on internal difficulties of adjusting to structural change.

One of the areas where competition within Australia is intense is retailing. But the very fact elicits a chorus of demands for protection, in this case from small grocers who fear the competition of the supermarket chains. Chapter 11 gives a history of retail grocery in Australia throughout the twentieth century that I prepared as background to the submission by the supermarket chain, Coles Myer, to a joint parliamentary enquiry into retailing in 2000. The United Kingdom has held a very similar enquiry. Before writing the history there is no doubt that I fell into the category known to market researchers as 'the reluctant shopper'. However I became converted to the supermarket case after contrasting supermarkets with the family groceries in which I spent so many dreary hours queuing as a small boy and after contemplating the extended range of products and lower prices supermarkets have offered to consumers since the Second World War.

Retailing is a topic where popular opinion is sure it knows best in condemning the supermarket chains for offering tough competition to smaller grocers, but I am sure the public mistakes its own interests. Indeed this is made clear by 'revealed preference', which means noting what consumers do instead of what they say. What consumers do is patronize the supermarket while talking up the corner store. In the long run, protection of less efficient shops would serve the interests of their owners and no one else.

Chapter 12 offers some general conclusions about globalization.

ACKNOWLEDGEMENTS

Over half the text of this book consists of material written especially for it or that has appeared only in the half-light of discussion paper series. The remainder consists of studies prepared for my programme of lectures in Japan and intended to complement the earlier material. The whole reflects the development of my interests in recent years, involving themes such as the rise of East Asia, Protectionism, and cultural, institutional and structural change, approached from different angles but all informed by my original professional perspective as an economic historian.

In 2000 I was appointed seventh Distinguished Visiting Professor in

Economic Dynamics at Osaka Gakuin University, following Williamson, Ranis, Adelman, Fogel, Mathias and Temin. This annual visiting programme was initiated by Professor Yasukichi Yasuba and supported by the President of the University, Mr Yoshiyasu Shirai. I wrote the necessary lectures during the summer for delivery during my visit to Japan in the autumn. At the host university I delivered the lectures printed here as Chapter 3, 'The European Miracle and its Relevance' (the Phoenix Lecture), Chapter 5, 'Multi-functionality', and Chapter 9, '"Asian Values" and cultural explanations'. I gave 'Environment, State and Economic Development' (Chapter 2) at Meiji University, Tokyo, as the Special Lecture to the annual meeting of the Japan Socio-Economic History Society. Other lectures were delivered at the universities of Kyushu, Osaka, Tohoku, Tokyo (Institute of Oriental Culture) and Waseda, and at the Kansai Center of Economic Research, Osaka.[9]

The courtesy, hospitality and attention that my wife and I received at every place we visited in Japan were memorable. Professor Yasuba deserves pride of place among the many people to whom we owe thanks, not only for conceiving of the programme in the first place but also for making the administrative arrangements, doing the lion's share of translating where that was required, and for great personal generosity during our visit. Other colleagues who were outstandingly kind and helpful included Professors Kunio Katayama and Masamichi Mizuhara at Osaka Gakuin University, Kiyoshi Sakimaki and Yoh Kawana at Tohoku University, Yoshio Fujii at Kyushu University, and in Tokyo, Minoru Yasumoto.

The remaining chapters have more diverse origins. Chapter 4, on world agriculture, was written for this volume to supplement the long-run histories in the first section and act as a bridge to the following section on Protection. Chapter 7 on the 'Ultimate Significance of East Asian Development' was a Discussion Paper of the School of Economics and Commerce at La Trobe University in 1991. Chapter 8 is the third incarnation of a paper on the East Asian experience which, at the invitation of Dr David Gress, I gave to the Danish Institute of International Affairs at Copenhagen, in October 1997, reworked for a joint session of the Max-Planck-Institut and the Department of Economics of the University of Jena, Germany, in November, and gave finally in the seminar series of the Institute of Advanced Study at Berlin, where I was a Fellow, in December. The Asian Crisis was unfolding that autumn, obliging me to update the talk for each occasion. The (third) version here appeared in the *Lectiones Jenensis* series of the Max-Planck-Institut in 1998. Chapter 10 on Australia's response to structural change appeared as a Pelham Paper of the Centre for the Practice of International Trade at Melbourne Business School in 1999; I was persuaded to turn to this matter by Professor David Robertson, then the Centre's Director. I was encouraged to write Chapter 11 on the history of retail grocery by Kerrina Watson and Chris Mara of the Government

Affairs Department at Coles Myer in Melbourne; acknowledgements to others who helped me to understand retailing are made in the chapter itself. Chapter 12 was written for this volume.

I am, as always, deeply in debt to my wife for attending to so many of the household jobs while I sat at my desk and for her editorial work on this volume, as well as for a lifetime of interesting conversations about the issues raised here and many, many others.

NOTES

1. Stephen Mennell, 'Introduction: Bringing the Very Long Term Back In', in Johan Goudsblom, Eric Jones and Stephen Mennell, *The Course of Human History: Economic Growth, Social Process, and Civilization* (Armonk, New York: M.E. Sharpe, 1996), p. 6.
2. J. Mokyr, 'Eurocentricity Triumphant', *American Historical Review*, **104** (4) (1999), at http://www.historycooperative.org/journals/ahr/104.4/ah001241.html (10 January 2001).
3. K. Basu, E. Jones and E. Schlicht, 'The Growth and Decay of Custom: The Role of the New Institutional Economics in Economic History', *Explorations in Economic History*, **24** (1987), 1–21.
4. Peter Munz, 'The Two Worlds of Anne Salmond in Postmodern Fancy-Dress', *The New Zealand Journal of History*, **28** (1), 1994, 61–2.
5. Walter Russell Mead, 'The End of Asia', *Foreign Affairs*, (November-December), 2000, 156–61.
6. Eric Jones, 'Globalism and the American Tide', *The National Interest*, **53** (Fall 1998), 18.
7. See e.g. Liu Junning, 'Classical Liberalism Catches on in China', *Journal of Democracy*, **11** (3), 2000, 48–57; William McGurn, 'The Gang of Three: Mao, Jesus and Hayek', *Policy*, **16** (3), 2000, 35–7; and Eric Jones, 'Asia's Fate: A Response to the Singapore School', *The National Interest*, **35** (Spring 1994), 18–28.
8. Amartya Sen, 'Asian Values and Economic Growth', in UNESCO World Culture Report, *Culture, Creativity and Markets* (Paris: UNESCO, 1998), 41.
9. Chapters 2 and 3 are to appear in Japanese in *Shakai-Keizaishi-Gakkai* (*Socio-Economic History*, the journal of the Japan Socio-Economic History Society) and the Economic Journal of the Faculty at Osaka Gakuin University respectively. The lecture at the Kansai Center is not reprinted here but was published (in Japanese) as Eric L. Jones, *Australia's Economic and Strategic Prospects* (Osaka: Kansai Economic Research Center, 2000).

PART I

Long-term economic development

1. Very long-term economic growth and its implications

INTRODUCTION: SCHOOLS OF THOUGHT

Studying the *very* long term has never been fashionable among general historians and even less so among economic historians and economists. During the 1950s and 1960s scholars concerned with possible lessons for developing countries concentrated any historical investigations they did make on the British industrial revolution and the industrialization of follower countries, of which Meiji Japan was then the sole non-Western example. But these studies did not teach many lessons that could be applied directly to very poor countries with weak institutions. Historical processes had in any case been too slow to appeal to people living through the early stages of development. They wanted to jump to the present. Eventually the interest petered out. History almost vanished from economics syllabuses.

During the 1980s and 1990s, interest has however again been displayed in economic change over long periods, over wide regions, and indeed at the global level. The rise of international economic integration may now seem to add legitimacy to work on these large topics, but in reality it preceded public discussion of globalization. As far as economic history is concerned, I would date the first signs as being books by John Hicks and Douglass North in 1969 and 1973 respectively.[1] Their initial aim was not to find theorems immediately applicable to specific economies, the exercise was closer to pure scholarship. Nevertheless, as they thought, it may shed some light on the growth process as a whole. There may be a useful side effect in persuading economists to extend the time frame with which they concern themselves and also to return to studying institutions, as the founding fathers of the discipline did.

Although studying the long term remains a minority interest, some relatively distinct schools of thought have begun to emerge. I will mention four. The first school, the old, internalist, British industrial revolution one, persists in some quarters but has lost much of its impetus. Fewer students from the Third World are probably told nowadays that knowing about spinning jennies and canal boats will help them to revolutionise their home economies. The other schools are in more expansionary phases. They include a (rather loose) group of world historians and another of quantitative economic historians, as well as a less coherent number of writers, usually from outside the history professions and often entirely from outside academe, who are interested in long-period change on virtually the scale of the entire human species.

The second school, the world historians, tends to be aggressively ideological and strongly anti-Western. Its adherents – we cannot quite call them members – typically incline to believe that growth began early, say in the sixteenth century. They usually think that it resulted from Europeans exploiting other peoples or at least other peoples' territories. The latest twist is to attribute the Rise of the West to chance, to the 'accident' that Europeans were in a unique position, by virtue of the location of their homelands on the surface of the globe, to acquire the resources of the Americas, or to the 'accident' that William of Orange secured the English throne in 1688, but only by accepting limited monarchy and in practice permitting groups eager for economic growth to share power.

The third school, the quantifiers, is defined by method rather than ideology and therefore does not spend much time engaging with the world historians. They are so sure that there was no significant growth before the 1820s (rather than the typical 1760 start of industrial revolution studies or the much earlier dates selected by the world historians) that they dismiss earlier periods as of little interest. Typically they show no interest in regions other than the West. They devote themselves to periods when statistics become prolific. This enables them to employ their professional tools. The tools of economics tend to abstract from institutions, even from the greatest institution of all, the state. The professional bias of people trained in economics is in any case away from the documentary research required to investigate periods lacking in predigested statistics.

This categorization into schools is by no means watertight. Individual scholars try to differentiate their product, though chiefly away from the arguments of their fellows in the same camp. It is almost like the situation with respect to trade: there is far more trade among the regions within any one country than among separate countries. For example, Angus Maddison, the leading producer of long-run series, alludes to three or four centuries of slow pre-industrial growth in the West, with no Asian equivalent.[2] Other quantifiers seldom acknowledge the significance of this, almost as if growth arose out of nothing early in the nineteenth century.

To my mind, the world history school occupies the more interesting ground, but the quantifiers, although somewhat blind with respect to the origins of growth, are the more serious reasoners. The world historians are too driven by an unprofessional desire to engage in the enterprise that David Landes has called de-legitimizing the West.[3] The quantifiers ignore Bob Clower's observation that it is easy to work on economies once they have differentiated but the real task is to explain differentiation in the first place.[4]

The fourth category of writers on long-term change is more heterogeneous. It includes natural scientists like Jared Diamond or Robert Wright.[5] Wright's book, *Nonzero*, has the revealing subtitle, *The Logic of Human Destiny*. In so far as writers of this type do display a central tendency, it is to think in terms of the history of the whole human species and to try to explain its 'success', relative (say) to other species or very early times. This is an ambitious genre: 'ancient history in a nutshell', as Wright states, 'onward and upward' (p. 118). The triumphalism of the West or the triumphalism of industry is here replaced by the triumphalism of our species. Over many decades there has been a trickle of writings along these lines by biologists.

The grand generalizing approach has merits and defects. It does seek patterns in the mass of evidence and usually avoids being buried in superfluous detail; on the other hand it can incautiously homogenize rather distinct types of phenomena. In my view, biologists, though fascinated by archaeology, seldom deal with the complex movements of the last few centuries in a credible way. Some scientists and economists who write about human history are almost as careless or unscrupulous as Marxist world historians about attributions and the interpretations they place on the work of other scholars. There is a tendency in the whole field to strip explanations down to their bare logic and, by de-emphasizing contexts, to get things slightly wrong or at any rate to infuriate specialist historians (especially by arguing that detail does not matter or that numerical estimates 'in principle' are acceptable substitutes for numbers warranted by actual documents).

We are dealing with shadowy matters about which we have too much still to learn to prize our own tentative ideas so much. Fresh perspectives have emerged since my own first major foray into this field, which was when preparing to write *The European Miracle* in the 1970s. They are the result of an accumulation of new findings rather than blinding flashes of discovery. They relate, as much as anything, to an understanding that parts of East Asia were becoming much more interconnected by trade than any accessible literature previously acknowledged. The implications of this may be that it was closer to touch-and-go that Europe would be the first area to make the transition into sustained growth. It was still first. If we discount the 'accidental' school of world historians who want to believe that Europe's rise depended on no internal factors, merely chance or a seizing of resources elsewhere, the puzzle of European growth becomes, if anything, greater than it has always seemed.

Except that I concentrate more narrowly than most of these writers on the economy, and naturally hope to avoid the errors mentioned, my own work can perhaps be placed in the fourth, eclectic category. By this I mean *Growth Recurring* and more particularly my chapters in Goudsblom, Jones and Mennell, *The Course of Human History*.[6] My aim has been to grasp what humanity's long-term economic experience has been like, with special reference to what early episodes of growth may tell us about the origins of growth in general, that is, not necessarily just in Europe or during the industrial revolution. We possess so few cases of new starts to growth that we cannot afford to waste the opportunity of learning from all of them. The quantifiers' insistence on the importance of the *scale* of nineteenth-century growth seems exaggerated. How something grows matters less than how it started growing, and in any case the story of nineteenth-century industrialization is perfectly familiar. For economic historians to refrain from searching for, or utilizing, earlier instances of growth – however transient – is as if palaeontologists were to decline to study fossils on the grounds that some of the organisms they represent are now extinct.

ASSESSMENT AND MEASUREMENT

Real per capita GDP is the best single standard for comparing economies, as well as for comparing their performance in different periods. This is not to say that material well-being is the highest human goal, nor even that real income is a perfect guide to welfare, but it is hard to deny a close relationship with these things. Using it as an index is less confusing, ambiguous or contentious than using other measures – or than switching among different criteria, as so easily happens. Of course, we can seldom *measure* the level or rate of change in per capita GDP, given the almost empty universe of long-run historical statistics. After all, even modern data are poor for less-developed or authoritarian countries. Statisticians are willing to accept almost any government's figures for convenience when, quite frankly, the data are often not robust enough to support serious comparisons. Even so, per capita GDP does offer a consistent standard in principle. One advantage is that it is neutral with respect to so-called 'structure snobbery', and gets us away from assuming that we should necessarily be searching for the start of industrialization rather than for signs of growth in whatever form it appeared.

Rising real income per head is called *intensive* growth and we should thus look first for the occasions when whole economies achieved it. Later, I shall introduce the complication that, in any economy which succeeded, the set of institutions present during the transition was also immensely important. The reasons for thinking this are at least two-fold: first, some other matters such as liberty and the security of the individual, which are not always precisely captured by trends in income, are at least as important; secondly, certain types of institution are vital if growth is to be sustained over the long run. Income gains may sometimes be secured in dictatorial regimes, but such regimes are not very stable and, arguably, the gains are at greater risk than in regimes where the institutions are more securely grounded in public support.

Before we turn to transitions to *intensive* growth, which is what we think of as economic growth today, we need to examine how the world economy functioned in the long, long periods that preceded them. My suggestion is that the world economy was almost always expanding and was therefore characterized by *extensive* growth. The point is a simple one, which may be why it is not usually emphasized or even mentioned. In contrast to common assumptions about a virtually unchanging past, the economy was not static. This matters, because when total GDP was growing economies could more easily have been transformed into ones with rising GDP per capita than if they had really been stagnant. Indeed, we will see that it would have been surprising had this transition not happened, and more than once. Admittedly, it might be almost as surprising if we could detect early transitions, given the lack of anything approaching regular economic data and the limited interest of most historians and pre-historians in the systematic study of the economy. The rates of growth involved were undoubtedly low by modern standards and very vulnerable to being reversed, so that episodes of *intensive* growth would have been short and hard to detect. There are, nevertheless, three major candidates for early transitions to *intensive* growth to which we will come in a little while.

Extensive growth means growth in total GDP but not in GDP per capita. In other words, the growth of output or income keeps pace with the growth of population but does not exceed it. The data and estimates we have on world population, for instance in the compilation by McEvedy and Jones (1978), show that it has been growing for millennia. The total at the end of each century was almost always greater than the total at the end of the previous century. Since we can reasonably assume that the world began, at some remote date, with incomes sufficient only for bare subsistence, there is no room for output to have fallen or the population would simply have starved. At a minimum, therefore, growth of the *extensive* type must have taken place if population grew: total world output and income went up without (necessarily) raising output or income per head. Thus the very long-term economic experience has at least been one of expansion, though seldom one of deepening.

'EXTENSIVE GROWTH PLUS'

In reality, the average long-term human experience has been a fraction more than merely expansionary. We may call it '*extensive* growth plus'. The reason for thinking along these lines is that the quality of capital and productivity of technology improved over time. We are constantly made aware of additional finds of tools and other artifacts by archaeologists and medievalists. If much of this early equipment seems of minor significance, for example the replacement of the distaff by the spinning wheel, the reason is that we are misled by the expectations that modern machinery arouses. The *proportionate* social savings made possible by changes in handicraft technology or agricultural technology in a poor world may have been just as great as later gains from industrial technology. Some people may urge that if the slow stream (actually an intermittent trickle) of new implements did not raise income per capita, this only goes to show that the forces suppressing *intensive* growth were so powerful as to stifle all change of interest before the period of industrialization, perhaps as late as the nineteenth century. But, although we definitely need to examine what did frustrate transitions to *intensive* growth most of the time, to urge that there was no interesting change would be to miss the significance of *extensive* growth or '*extensive* growth plus'.

Consider the possible indicators of economic expansion, which, though not linear, was in a sense cumulative. Population growth is an indicator by definition. There are a few fragmentary data on life expectancy that suggest it rose in the long term. The elite, non-agricultural percentage of the population supported by the peasantry also edged up. The few actual calculations (made by the late Raymond Goldsmith) relate to the elites of individual empires and differ among them, but we can discern a faint general trend.[7] This may of course derive from better tax gathering rather than productivity gains. However, the fact of productivity gains in farming is believable when we take into account that the peasantry was also able to support a slowly rising proportion of the population in towns. The structures of towns themselves are a biased record because the more authoritarian regimes celebrated themselves with the biggest, most solid buildings and monuments. Peasant communities that lived well are the hardest of all to detect.

The overall record of economic expansion discernable through all the ambiguities and gaps in the evidence indicates change that must seem to modern eyes to have taken place in slow motion. The significance of expansion, albeit slow, is that it required innumerable business decisions, innumerable decisions to create infrastructure, and even innumerable efforts to invent new technology. In the classical world of Greece and Rome, methods of producing glass, olive oil, pottery and iron were all improved and slowly diffused after 450 BC.[8] Roman villas were heated by under-floor hypocausts. Roman Gaul (France) had a mechanical reaper for grain. Many remarkable stone arches were built in Roman times, including long aqueducts to conduct water into towns. In north-western Europe, beyond the *limes* or bounds of the Roman empire, even the barbarians of the time devised better ways to make barrels, trousers, shirts, stockings, laced boots, and the fibulae which were the precursors of safety pins. New products such as soft soap and wagons were invented. And, as is well known, the technological record of some other civilizations was very creditable, especially that of early China, which in many respects anticipated and out-classed Europe.

The pre-modern world was simply not static. Where so much positive economic activity took place merely to keep output abreast of population growth, we are obviously looking at systems with an inherent potential for growth. Yet mostly they did not lead on to *intensive* growth. Well known crop diffusions, for example, like the 'Arab Agricultural Revolution' that brought new crop species from India as far west as Spain, or the 'Columbian Exchange' that diffused American crops like maize, peanuts and potatoes to Europe, Africa and China, did not obviously sustain rises in per capita GDP. It seems almost perverse that so much agricultural improvement, slight as it may now appear, was not sufficient to tip economies into *intensive* growth.

STOCK AND FLOW APPROACHES

Growth did not begin in the 1820s from nothing. In Britain and Europe, promising structural change in the economy (signalled by a declining share of the workforce in agriculture), predated the classic industrial revolution by a century or more. Europe meanwhile absorbed overseas resources, such as from the Americas. While these resources did without doubt take a long time to produce much measurable growth – this is a point the quantifiers make against the world history school – they may nevertheless have prevented an actual *deterioration* in returns to labour relative to returns to land-ownership. The fact that the response was delayed does not mean that there was no impact at all, nor that Adam Smith was necessarily wrong to describe 1492 and 1498 as turning points in world history. Does an oak tree grow only from the sapling and not from the acorn? The really interesting point is however that, despite the relative sterility of the Spanish and Portuguese economies, much of Europe was already capable of utilizing overseas resources without merely squandering them.

Moreover the institutions gradually accumulating in Europe, especially in Britain, were significant for the market economy that in the nineteenth and twentieth centuries was to raise incomes so very much higher. Clearly many of the institutions were originally designed to benefit elites. The opening sentence of David Gress, *From Plato to NATO*, proclaims that 'liberty grew because it served the interests of power'.[9] Magna Carta (1215), the Provision of Oxford (1258) and the Statute of Marlborough (1266) are cases in point, but it is even more to the point that the gradual removal of restrictions on royal and arbitrary power, of limitations on the independence of the law, together with the slow lifting of press censorship and so forth was all generalizable. The scope of beneficial institutions could eventually be extended to wider and wider circles of the population, in ways that some other traditions still do not readily permit. They had a lot of latent potential to foster growth, whether or not they quickly produced system-wide increases in the flow of income.

Let me offer an analogy. The BBC correspondent, John Simpson, who lived in South Africa under the apartheid regime, makes it clear that, for all its evils, this was not remotely like the other dictatorships from which he has reported.[10] The principle of the rule of law, though desperately perverted, did survive and was there to be revived in a cleaner form when apartheid ceased. If we consider British law in the early nineteenth century we can see that it, too, was abused. Thousands of people were executed, or transported to Australia, for offences that would scarcely be treated as crimes today. Yet in the longer term it was better to have an apparatus of law that might some day be softened and extended than to start with no functioning legal system or tradition at all. This is surely evident from the struggles of some less-developed countries to establish independent legal systems today. In other words, the stock of institutions can possess or retain the potential to operate usefully even if it is not currently doing so or long before its scope has been widened to encompass the whole population.

The quantifiers take a 'flow' view, which is a central part of our interest, as I noted when discussing the search for changes in per capita GDP. That approach offers consistency but by itself it is too narrow. We shall understand better why this increased where and when it did if we add a 'stock' view, recognizing the role of the accumulation of cultural capital, contract law, information markets, and so forth, as a prelude to nineteenth-century growth and as a major factor in sustaining economic performance.

SUPPRESSANTS OF INTENSIVE GROWTH

Rather than searching solely for forces that 'pushed' Britain or Europe into industrialization, we need to decide what it was that blocked transitions everywhere throughout most of history. Given the fact of very long-term economic expansion without much by way of *intensive* growth, this ought to be our first task. I do not mean to suggest that we should ignore the small number of successful transitions that can be identified; far from it, we will shortly come to them.

Thus, instead of searching for 'push forces' (such as Max Weber's Protestant Ethic) to account for European change, we should examine suppressants as general phenomena, and then, and only then, look for the means whereby they were eroded in history's rare cases of *intensive* growth. The idea that there was indeed a widespread tendency towards economic growth, suppressed or not, requires a somewhat contentious assumption – that a fraction of the population would always try to improve its standard of living by something more definite than putting a little extra effort into routine work. To modern economists such an assumption will seem uncontroversial, even banal: we tend to assume that people are rational maximizers. Yet to everyone except economists the assumption apparently seems outrageous. The resistance is mostly ideological and relates to people's so-called 'model of man'. The aim of maximizing material wealth or income is flatly denied as a description of historical behaviour, of pre-capitalist behaviour; and is sometimes denied as a goal at any time. Actually my assumption is a very mild one: it is that in any large population some people will always try to improve their material lot. This justifies asking the question, what was it that stopped them from making efforts that, taken together, would have sufficed to convert omnipresent *extensive* growth into society-wide *intensive* growth?

I have no defence against the ideological objections, which spill over into asserting that even now people 'really' want to maximize other objectives. That seems to me a confusion: it is as if people do not usually have all sorts of non-material or cultural goals as well as conventional material ones. They do, but it stops few people from trying to acquire extra income. More interesting are objections to the notion that income maximization, raised to the societal level by some principle of composition like Adam Smith's invisible hand, is not an accurate description of historical behaviour.

Let me repeat, therefore, the point that positive investment, inventive and innovative behaviour were common features of pre-modern times. Without them continual population growth on the observed scale could not have been sustained. This surely shows that some – many – people did have materialist goals alongside the other aims we all possess: spiritual, aesthetic, social, family goals and so forth. One might indeed expect that poverty-reducing aims would be prominent, even dominant, when societies were poor and the costs of poverty were so hideously apparent. Recent work in psychology has set out four principles of social relations: communal sharing or group solidarity; authority ranking or hierarchy; equality matching or egalitarianism among peers; and market pricing (exchange relationships determined by pricing or utility).[11] All children learn to balance *and use* all four properties, which are held to be universal properties of both the individual mind and society. In the circumstances it seems quite reasonable to reassert my 'recurrent growth' hypothesis – that a drive towards *intensive* growth was present historically – and to turn without further ado to what so often frustrated its economy-wide realization.

Given that average incomes were always very small in the past, that most communities were rural, and any positive rate of growth was low, it is easy to believe that growth may have been literally eaten away by population increase. Conceivably the population response was so automatic that it constantly reduced living standards to the same bare minimum. The observable technological innovations may have generated no *net* gain in incomes, especially if their effect was to increase food supplies. The process need not have been Malthusian, with the population pruned back because agricultural technologies were unable to feed the increase; it need only have been Boserupian, with output matching population growth but never overtaking it for long enough to turn *extensive* into *intensive* growth.

Shocks like natural disasters and armed conflict may also rather easily have derailed any incipient upturn. With low life expectancies, planning horizons would have been short, though that may have been offset by the settled nature of rural communities which we know had the confidence to put up buildings and plant trees for a distant posterity. Another suppressant often mentioned in the literature is cultural or religious values hostile to growth. A concern with the afterlife was widespread, though not universal, and this resulted in the building of temples, churches and cathedrals that had limited positive implications for material prosperity.

I am not persuaded that either the lack of a growth ethic or the existence of values actually hostile to growth is a primary explanation of so much growth-less history. Are values really as permanent as they appear? Had growth been brought about by some other circumstances, would cultures not have adapted and religions become more worldly (as many since have)? Cultures do adapt; it is their organizational forms, like churches, and their terminologies that often persist for long periods and so give a false impression that their practical force is unchanged. Older persons may never escape the conditioning of their youth, but youth itself is flexible in the presence of new incentives or when old restraints are lifted. The best case that religious values can suppress public discourse about innovation is the one made by Timur Kuran with respect to Islam and it may be that values can act as more of a suppressant than I am inclined to think.[12] Yet although Islam is a world religion it was not the religion of the world. Other religions and cultures were demonstrably adaptable. In any case Islam itself did not wholly lack periods of intellectual and scientific flowering.

A possible conclusion about suppressants is that in different societies different obstacles blocked growth. In other words there were multiple equilibria, with societies held below the *intensive* growth threshold by various forces. Yet this multiple equilibria explanation of so much non-growth in so many societies and civilizations over such an immense time span is very untidy. A more general explanation seems called for. I am inclined to accept the suggestion of Freeman and Lindauer, writing about under-development in Africa: 'we hypothesize that there is a lexicographic ordering of the determinants of growth and that first and foremost is political stability and security of property'.[13] Turning this on its head, they conclude that, 'there is no single recipe for achieving economic growth, but there is one way to prevent growth: through instability and absence of property rights'.

The most general, almost universal, suppressant is a political one of the type Freeman and Lindauer indicate. After all, the political organization of past societies was almost invariably one of rule, not representation, just as many poor countries suffer corrupt or dictatorial governments today. The rulers or ruling elite were rent-seekers. They extracted a general levy called 'rent-cum-taxes'. The very failure to distinguish between the concepts of rent and taxes shows that rulers thought of the countries or populations over which they presided as belonging to them. They believed that their power was divine and based it on the theory which in early seventeenth-century England was called the 'divine right of kings'.

No pre-modern ruler offered much by way of services in return for the resources he took, other than internal order and external defence, which were in his own interests anyhow. More regimes were lethargic rather than outrageously grasping and they tended to be inefficient at levying taxes; they suppressed growth partly because they provided poor conditions in which it could emerge, notably by failing to offer independent law that applied to rulers and ruled alike. That failure raised the costs of exchange and restricted the size of the market.

TRANSITIONS TO INTENSIVE GROWTH

Yet we have a vast stretch of time to work with, and during that time an enormous number of societies were unconsciously experimenting with forms of economic organization. Despite all the odds, growth did sometimes happen. Almost certainly it occurred on many occasions, though mostly transiently and without leaving a clear record; we shall find more cases only if we specifically look for them. There were three major cases to which I want to draw attention. They were Song China (between the tenth and thirteenth centuries AD), Tokugawa Japan, and seventeenth- and eighteenth-century Europe. Describing these episodes as phases of *intensive* growth rests on a number of criteria. I have relied on the consensus of sober professional opinion, which has the more validity because so few general historians are seriously interested in the economy: what their opinions reveal, almost inadvertently, is mostly free from conscious attempts to depict real growth. I have also set the standard at reports of growth over at least 100 years, in order to eliminate the more transient and debatable episodes.

More precisely, the criteria include reports of large investments in infrastructure, especially communications; noteworthy and well-diffused improvements in productive technology (remembering that we are dealing with what were still mainly agricultural economies); marked urbanization; and structural change via the withdrawal of labour, or labour time, from farming into cottage industry (which implies rising farm productivity). We have to be sure that tax gatherers were not merely extracting a larger surplus at such periods and producing a false impression of growth via conspicuous consumption by the elite. The largest percentage extraction for which we have an estimate was the Ottoman empire, where the top one-thousandth of families secured 15 per cent of output in 1550, besides what they received and spent maintaining their retainers.[14] I have not included it because it does not obviously satisfy the other criteria.

The expansion of cities is particularly important because it implies that agriculture was supporting an increasing proportion of people who no longer had to grow their own food. It also means that communications and methods of distributing or marketing food were well advanced. The expansion of rural domestic industry implies that labour in some parts of the countryside was increasingly making commodities like textiles, furniture, and various petty goods, which were traded against food produced by others who concentrated on food production. The fact that there was more trade along rivers, canals, coastal routes and roads, together with investment in these modes of communication, implies that incomes were rising above subsistence levels. The full-time farmers were mostly in areas of better soil and hence had lower costs per unit of output. Farmers in such districts were able to 'import' handicraft items of better quality than they, or their village craftsmen, were likely to make and which cost them fewer resources to acquire. This is a trade model of rural domestic industrialization; it points to a growing regional division of labour, with associated income gains. We can detect this in the cases of Song China, Tokugawa Japan, and Europe (or at any rate, north-western Europe) in the seventeenth and eighteenth centuries.

I do not want to enter into describing these early phases of *intensive* growth in any detail. More evidence is gradually coming to light of the income gains in each case. Maddison claims that GDP per capita in the West grew at twice the rate of the remainder of the world between AD1000-1997; he has even made an estimate for AD1000 on which to base this calculation.[15] He also makes a point that is at odds with the views of some other quantifiers, but with which I agree. This is that the innovations of the industrial revolution were not what originated Western growth. What did that was a slow economic ascent over the three or four centuries preceding industrialization, for which he finds no Asian equivalent. Industrialization was the result of *intensive* growth rather than its cause. Maddison is right to stress that the fundamental change in Europe was 'recognition of the capacity to transform the forces of nature through rational investigation', rather than any particular set of inventions. Technology may seem to offer free lunches but when we look at the very long term we can see that the crucial matter is what types of society and what institutions best enabled inventions to appear and be utilized. These things required a longer genesis. But I think Maddison overlooks the significance of the Song and Tokugawa cases. East Asian growth need not have been continuous to have been real.

MECHANISMS FOR GENERATING INTENSIVE GROWTH

Let us accept that the cases mentioned did satisfy the criteria and therefore constitute periods of *intensive* growth that lasted for some time in each of three major societies. Why were these societies the ones that achieved growth? What was special about them? There seem to have been two main mechanisms. The first was 'emergency marketization', to which the Song more or less conforms. The point with respect to 'emergency marketization' was that a ruler had to spot the possible revenue gains from encouraging market expansion. This meant lifting various restrictions, providing institutions that supported market activity, and above all refraining from taxing away any additional product. Two assumptions are necessary: one that the ruler was facing a sudden need for resources to defend his territory against a military threat – the Song were being pressed by steppe invaders. The other assumption is that, if they are permitted to retain the bulk of anything extra they produce, people will respond quickly. Most rulers lacked the wit or nerve to free the market in the face of a threat: they reacted by squeezing out any resources they could lay their hands on. Only an exceptional individual could see the greater benefits of releasing market forces. The counter-intuitive nature of 'emergency marketization', its unfamiliarity, the risk and the slight delay involved, explains why it was so rare. This is not to say there were no examples other than the Song; Alfred the Great's Wessex (southern England) in the ninth century AD was one.[16]

The second growth mechanism was 'elite settlement', which was also rare. It requires the ruler and the other powerful figures contending with him for control of a country to come to terms and engage in implicit power sharing. I say implicit because face-saving devices were always adopted to make the titular ruler seem more powerful than he was. Some authors think 'elite settlement' is inherently unlikely to occur, but Eggertsson correctly remarks that the type of constitutional equilibrium involved can reflect 'a real balance of power or fortuitous convergence of interest among social groups spontaneously created by historical circumstances.'[17] Japan at the start of the Tokugawa period and England after the 'Glorious Revolution' of 1688, when William III was obliged to compromise with diverse interest groups, are cases in point. The Tokugawa may have seemed powerful, running as they did the so-called 'potted plant' system that redistributed the *daimyo* (lords) and insisting (in the *sankin kotei* – alternate residence – system) that the *daimyo* spend part of each year and much of their rent-roll in Edo. But in reality this was a compromise. Lordships were reallocated but not all the land was seized and given to Tokugawa followers. The *han* operated substantially independent economic programmes. The Japanese case was actually a double compromise. The shogunate did not do away with the Imperial line but kept it for symbolic purposes, and the Tokugawa shogunate did not completely dominate or expropriate all the lands of those *daimyo* who had been its enemies.

The Tokugawa had won in Japan's civil wars; they had come to power by violent means. But they pacified Japan rather than incur the costs of eradicating all their enemies, like some Khmer Rouge. England, too, was well aware of the high costs of conflict, after 50 years of civil wars and previously unsustainable solutions to the problem of royal succession. The economic systems that resulted in Japan after 1600 and England after 1688 were not fully centralized. In neither place was the ruler or central government quite in a position to take from the elites as much by way of taxes as was typical in more genuinely autocratic states and empires. Nor was the nobility quite as free to exploit the peasantry. In parts of continental Europe, where overlapping jurisdictions were not uncommon, it was well known that the powerful could be played off against one another.[18] Moreover, rulers sometimes tried to undermine the power and revenue base of the aristocracy by appealing to the peasantry over their heads with the offer of tax concessions and legal safeguards, the policy called *Bauernschutz*. But only rarely did political compromises (or stalemates) enable countries to settle down and the market really to flourish.

THE LONGER-TERM PROSPECTS OF PRE-MODERN GROWTH

Accordingly, the final question that arises concerns the further evolution of *intensive* growth in pre-industrial circumstances. Even when scholars accept that growth of this type did occur, they tend to dismiss it on the grounds that it was merely ' Smithian growth', which is to say allocative growth capable of reaping only a once-off gain. There was no guarantee, they say, that Smithian growth would automatically evolve into 'Promethean growth' based on cumulative advances in technology. Perhaps not. Nothing is guaranteed.

Yet, in the already complex economies of seventeenth-century England and Japan, the chances of Smithian growth transforming itself into Promethean growth were really quite good. So far from either society having attained static allocative effficiency or static technical efficiency, there was plenty of room for further Smithian growth. Resources were not optimally allocated nor was the best-practice technology of the day widely installed. Existing methods continued to be improved well into the nineteenth century.[19] Furthermore, any society that could generate Smithian growth on the scale of England or Europe and Japan was surely capable of a feedback effect that would see growth bringing about institutional change and raising up new social classes with an interest in seeing growth continue. Before the nineteenth century, industrialization did not require much science. Even in East Asian countries which did not share Europe's Scientific Revolution, it is not impossible that the comparatively elementary science involved could have been brought into being by the needs of industry itself. We should not assume that because something did not happen, it could not have happened. We should not take mere snapshots of dynamic processes. Given the right conditions, any society could advance, and certainly that includes old, complex societies like those of East Asia. What was needed was political stability, the rule of law, good information markets, and property rights that offered incentives for enterprise. The implications of very long-term economic growth turn out to be political ones.

NOTES

1. John Hicks, *A Theory of Economic History* (Oxford: Oxford University Press, 1969); Douglass C. North and Robert Paul Thomas, *The Rise of the Western World: A New Economic History* (Cambridge: Cambridge University Press, 1973).
2. Angus Maddison, in Ian Castles (ed.), *Facts and Fancies of Human Development* (Canberra: Academy of Social Sciences in Australia, Occasional Paper 1/2000), pp. 11 *et seq.*
3. David Landes, *The Wealth and Poverty of Nations* (New York: W.W. Norton, 1998).
4. Robert Clower, 'Snarks, Quarks, and Other Fictions', in Louis P. Cain and Paul J. Uselding (eds), *Business Enterprise and Economic Change* (Kent, Ohio: Kent State University Press, 1973), p. 8.
5. Jared Diamond, *The Rise and Fall of the Third Chimpanzee* (London: Vintage, 1993), Robert Wright, *Nonzero: The Logic of Human Destiny* (London: Little, Brown, 2000).
6. E.L. Jones, *Growth Recurring: Economic Change in World History* (Ann Arbor, Michigan: University of Michigan Press, 2000, edition with new introduction), and J. Goudsblom, E. Jones and S. Mennell, *The Course of Human History* (New York: M.E. Sharpe, 1996).
7. Raymond Goldsmith, *Premodern Financial Systems: A Historical Comparative Study* (Cambridge: Cambridge University Press, 1987).
8. Cf. Jones, *Growth Recurring*, p. 57.
9. David Gress, *From Plato to NATO: The Idea of the West and its Opponents* (New York: The Free Press, 1998).
10. John Simpson, *Strange Places, Questionable People* (London: Pan, 1999).
11. In Lawrence Harrison and Sam Huntingdon (eds), *Culture Matters: How Values Shape Human Progress* (New York: Basic Books, 2000), p. 147.
12. Timur Kuran, 'Islam and Underdevelopment: An Old Puzzle Revisited', *Journal of Institutional and Theoretical Economics*, **153** (1997), 41–71.
13. Richard B. Freeman and David L. Lindauer, *Why not Africa?*, NBER Working Paper 6942, February 1999 (Cambridge, Mass.).
14. Goldsmith, op. cit., p. 235. The equivalent or even larger concentrations of wealth which

Goldsmith records for ancient Attica and medieval Florence may have been secured by trade.

15. Maddison, loc. cit., p. 11.
16. S.R.H. Jones, *Economic Growth and the Spread of the Market Principle in Later Anglo-Saxon England*, University of Auckland Working Papers in Economics, no. 48 (1988).
17. Thrainn Eggertson, *Norms in Economics*, Discussion Paper, 10-99, 1999, Jena: Max-Planck-Institut, p. 14 n. 13.
18. E.L. Jones, *The European Miracle: Environments, Economies, and Geopolitics in the History of Europe and Asia* (Cambridge: Cambridge University Press, second edition, 1988), p. 91.
19. Cf. Jones, *Growth Recurring*, op. cit., p. 26.

2. Environment, state and economic development in the history of Europe and Asia

INTRODUCTION

The subject of this chapter is uncomfortably broad. It requires anyone who tackles it to offer, or at least pretend to offer, a simultaneous solution to innumerable interlocking puzzles in economic history. I would beg to be excused from this enormous task had I not given a hostage to fortune 20 years ago by writing *The European Miracle*.[1] No one can dream of employing primary sources to cover such a sweep of the past as the long-run development of a whole continent, against a background of the experience of other continents. When I wrote the book even the potentially relevant secondary sources were already far, far too large in number for anyone to read all of them. The only hope of making sense of the field was to suggest a model that would incorporate and codify the more plausible-seeming of the available interpretations. What might constitute a satisfactory 'model' is however a matter of opinion, and opinions about methods and approaches are often dogmatically expressed. This means that the literature of world economic history ranges from works in which the analytical bare bones are submerged in the flesh of endless minute description to others that contain logical concepts supported by little more than stylized facts.

My own approach was intended to be, and remains, a middle-of-the-road one. It was and is meant to contain an economic logic for those with eyes to see, but enough detail, or at any rate enough references to telling details, to ground the work in historical reality. I wanted to put some order into the material on European economic history and find some clues in the experience of other continents or civilizations as to why Europe became the first among them to achieve sustained economic growth. This has since been misrepresented as a kind of European triumphalism by a number of authors whose aim, open or covert, is what David Landes has called delegitimizing the West.[2] I can only say that I deplore the misrepresentation and do not think that chauvinism, nationalism, ideology or methodological intolerance have any place in economic history. Nor do I accept that we cannot make a reasonable effort at allowing for our own biases when writing about the big issues of the subject.

In my book I tried to synthesize ideas about European and Asian economic history that were to be found in the English-language literature up to the end of the 1970s. Despite the size of the literature, world economic history as a specific field of study was unfashionable at that time, and the relatively small proportion of authors trying to draw together what was then known seldom referred to one another. The field was not yet a coherent one. Subsequent interest has generated a more connected history in which alternative interpretations are brought into contention with one another. For this reason, and because a Japanese edition of *The European Miracle* was published in 2000, by the University of Nagoya Press, in a translation very kindly made by Professors Minoru Yasumoto and Kohei Wakimura, it is particularly appropriate for me to restate my thesis. This will enable me to respond to the most recent criticisms and try to draw out salient implications of Europe's initial economic success. Some of the more recent alternative views are sufficiently radical (and, in my opinion, sufficiently misleading) to encourage me to think that responding to them may actually deepen our understanding of the problems of long-run economic development.

First, there is the question of my book's title. This was intended to echo a phrase found here and there in the literature. It was meant to draw attention to the primacy and in some senses the improbability of Europe's achievement, given that continent's previously rather marginal position in world trade and development. Europe was simply the first continent, or if one prefers the term, civilization, to achieve sustained economic growth and industrialization, just as Japan was the first country in Asia to achieve these things. For all the denigration of everything Western by so many modern scholars, and a recent comment to the effect that Meiji Japan was really only catching up with China, the awkward fact (for these critics) is a matter of record: Britain, Europe, the United States, and Japan really were first.

What the title does not mean is that there was anything supernatural about the European achievement, although that is what the term 'miracle' has been taken to imply by some literal-minded native English speakers. Some of them have suggested that I am contradicting my own title in trying to explain an achievement that, by definition, must be beyond rational explanation. But apart from the symbolic use of 'miracle' to emphasize the improbability of the outcome, the word in English also means 'marvel'. Anyone who does not agree that the start of a process that raised real incomes so very far above previous historical levels was truly 'marvellous' is beyond reasoning. These semantic issues are however far less interesting than the question of how the miracle actually came about.

THE LATE PRE-INDUSTRIAL 'EURASIAN' CONTEXT

During recent centuries the world's most populous and complex societies or civilizations lay in Europe and Asia. The received view is that the main civilizations were more or less on a par as regards technology, both in agriculture and handicraft or workshop industry. Similar problems of production had apparently elicited comparable solutions. In addition there had undoubtedly been over the centuries some degree of diffusion of 'best practice' techniques. The question is, why was it Europe (a relatively small player on the edge of the Old World) that broke away from the slow elaboration of methods common to the great agrarian civilizations? As soon as this issue is raised, it becomes apparent that we need to decide the period at which this happened, and whether it was a gradual process or the type of rapid event that old accounts of the British industrial revolution suggest. History and geography are inextricably entwined, and to talk about the issues at less than encyclopaedic length will require us to make very bold generalizations and sweep many regional differences out of sight.

Other civilizations than the European one had experienced marked early spells of economic and technological advance. We are not dealing with a stagnant pre-industrial world and not really with one where change had always taken place at the same pace everywhere. The technological record of early China appears to have utterly outclassed anything Dark Age Europeans could manage. Song China (between the tenth and thirteenth centuries AD) was even more advanced, with a water-powered spinning machine for hemp and an output of iron per head seemingly not matched in Europe until about 1800.[3] Islamic North Africa had a flowering of its science during the centuries of the European Middle Ages, though this did not last. The Ottoman Empire ceased to be as expansionary, or successfully expansionary, as it had been at first, and became increasingly resistant to the adoption of better technologies from elsewhere, meaning Europe. As for India, it hardly seems possible to detect economic or technological change of a high order and, certainly, the Mughal Empire rather quickly lost its initial impetus.

Thus these societies did not continue to develop at the same rate as during some early phases. Several Asian societies reportedly experienced a 'turning inwards' during the fifteenth century. This seems to have been a coincidental downturn in dynastic cycles; the important point being that it pre-dated any European colonial intrusion. Accordingly, if we are to understand what was special about Europe, we need to grasp how its political and economic life differed, or came to differ, from the internal dynamics of the empires that were the characteristic organizational forms of large Middle Eastern and Asian societies.

At any one time, all Old World societies contained advanced and less-developed regions. Nor was a lack of internal uniformity confined to Asia. Eastern Europe always lagged behind Western Europe, though its history was punctuated by convulsive efforts at catching up. A striking case was the Petrine Reforms in Russia. Peter the Great made his Grand Tour as far west as England in the 1690s and tried to import as much new technology, and hire as many artisans, as he could. Stalin described this as 'a peculiar attempt to jump out of a framework of backwardness'. The clock was set back, however, under Peter's successors, until the next jerky effort by the Tsarist state to drive growth forwards.

All I will say by way of comment at this point is that the pattern of regional change within the western half of Europe seems to have been exceptionally fluid. Europe, especially seaboard Europe, was early linked up in something approaching a single market. There was competition among regions from the Baltic to the Mediterranean, as well as a good deal of complementary trade along coastal routes, meaning that different areas could trade on their comparative advantage. The speed of adjustment may have been sluggish by modern standards but on a historical timescale there was a perceptible sequence of regional rises and falls.[4] The decline of Venice in the late seventeenth century was accompanied by the rise of the Low Countries, in fact Venice's decline was partly caused by an inability to cope with that rise. The decline of the Netherlands in the eighteenth century coincided with the rise of Britain. No single political authority could halt the process of competition and regional adjustment because there was no single authority. Just as noteworthy was the fact that so-called 'declines' were only relative ones. They meant little more than losing a few leading industries to some competing region, and seldom involved losses in absolute income.

I do not say that similar adjustments took place nowhere else, but they did not occur everywhere, and the increasing flexibility of early modern European commerce was particularly apparent. The *scale* of trade may have been larger in a few other areas, notably in China, while bulk trade around the Japanese coast was well developed, but Europe's bulk trade in everyday commodities and its commercial institutions were rapidly evolving. There was no overall decline in the European system and while Asia was 'turning inwards', Europe was turning outwards. Very soon it was to add full-blown factory and steam-powered industrialization to commercial expansion and the intensification of its agriculture.

To the possible objection that industrialization happened in only one, eccentric, offshore society, Britain, and was not a pan-European feature, I would make two points. First, much more of Britain's development involved borrowings from various mainland European neighbours than has usually been recognized; the most prominent aspect was that industrialization arose from the fusion of French science and British artisanship.[5] Second, the capacity of a number of countries in the north-western quadrant of Europe to adopt British methods and equipment within a few short decades suggests that Europe was already a highly interconnected system with something approaching a single market for information, despite efforts by the British government to prevent the export of technologies and technologists. The institutions and business forms in many European countries, as well as in Britain's offshoot, the United States, were either similar to those of Britain, or represented acceptable enough substitutes for industrialization to diffuse quite fast. Diffusion was slower in southern and eastern Europe and desperately slow elsewhere, until we reach the second half of the nineteenth century and distant Japan.

POSSIBLE CAUSES OF EUROPE'S PRIMACY

(a) The Environment

There are five main categories of explanation of the European miracle: environment, culture, technology, market and political structures. We have to be careful when discussing these categories: they are broad, we are implicitly contrasting them with conditions in a diverse set of Asian societies, and each situation has to be sketched in a few sentences. Moreover, the categories are not in reality quite as fixed as they appear. Take the environment.[6] It is probably futile to argue for or against the special suitability of Europe's resource endowment when we know that resources are a function of technology and that trade is a substitute for resources. In other words, resource advantages or constraints are not likely explanations of either growth or nongrowth in the long run. And if this applies to Europe, it applies elsewhere. We should probably be looking instead at entrepreneurial and technological responses as more vital sources of growth.

An environmental argument might be rescued, as I tried to do in *The European Miracle*, by pointing to advantages in the way the resources of Europe were distributed, and its advantages with respect to waterborne transport. Europe was favoured in these respects over some parts of Asia, but not obviously over all parts. Another rescue might be attempted by referring to the different disaster profiles in Europe and elsewhere.[7] Europe may have been favoured in this respect too. Disasters were hard to hedge against in the absence of insurance markets. On the other hand, certain governments, and not merely European ones, did offer substitutes for part of the marketplace: they tried to 'insure' against famine by intervening in grain markets, as the Tokugawa did in an effort to stop some of the *han* from retaining all their own grain in years of poor rice harvest. The best-known case was China's system of ever-normal granaries. It is not clear whose mix of intervention and market was best in the long run, though Japan had occasional severe famines into the nineteenth century and the Chinese system seems to have deteriorated after about 1810. Administrative reforms, higher output and more trade in grain do seem to have created a special resilience against famines in Europe during the eighteenth century. In addition, both European states and the Qing Empire compensated peasants for losses of animals in cattle plagues but it was only in Europe that a proportion of the value of losses rather than a flat payment was offered.

The most vexed 'environmental' question relates to the acquisition of overseas resources, notably those from the Americas. Was Europe's growth significantly stimulated, even made possible, by this influx?[8] The 'world historians' usually argue that what they portray as a resource grab was indispensable, but they tend to skirt two crucial points: first, that it was, after all, Europe which reached out to the New World rather than, say, China, and second that European markets were sufficiently mature to put any resources so gained to productive uses, rather than squandering them in either conspicuous consumption or mere population growth. It is perhaps surprising that vessels from tiny European countries succeeded in venturing to the Americas and Asia. The much larger Ming Empire had sent large junk fleets as far afield as Africa in the early fifteenth century. But China halted such activities and explicitly decided not to renew them in the latter part of that century, just before the first European voyages round Africa to India.

No such central power as the Ming court existed in Europe, not even the Pope in Rome (who had tried to divide the outer world into separate Portuguese and Spanish spheres of influence). In Europe's decentralized states-system it was less easy to block economic activity on political grounds. What was forbidden in one state might be allowed in another. Columbus himself 'shopped around' for support for his voyages to the supposed Indies until he found the Spanish queen willing to back him. This may further suggest that the issue was not resources in the first instance. Instead the crucial point was that Europe possessed an unconscious, but fundamental advantage in a political decentralization that permitted the release of economic energies. This is a point to which we will return.

(b) Culture

Another category of explanation that is often mentioned is culture, including differences in religious values. This seems to me another trap for the unwary, because while differences in attitudes, values and behaviours are readily visible at any one moment – in cross-section, as it were – they change via dynamic processes.[9] Cultures are likely to remain fixed if there is no incentive to alter them. A better way to express this may be to say that they are unlikely to be altered if there is no actual disincentive to keeping things as they are. If one's upbringing makes one comfortable with a given cultural practice, a strong stimulus will be needed before one changes it. But incentives do change or history would be totally unvarying and uniform. There is thus little case for talking as though cultures are fixed, independent variables. Admittedly, despite all the newspaper talk about globalization, there is even now no single world 'market' for cultural ideas, at least not in the sense that every young person, everywhere, is presented with a menu of alternative cultural elements from which to choose. Instead, we are all conditioned from birth to accept without much thought the values of the society around us. But society does not condition each generation alike, hence the disagreements that many young people have with their parents. Another example of the mutability of culture appears in the work of Thomas Sowell, who explains the different behaviour of Japanese immigrants in California and Brazil by pointing out they left Japan at different periods and had been conditioned in quite different ways.[10]

Cultures are extremely contingent phenomena. They are altered by feedback effects from the economy – yet economic life is precisely what culture is supposed to be explaining. Adamant statements to the effect that 'culture matters' or 'makes all the difference' seem to be over-enthusiastic responses to the fact that we can observe conspicuous cultural differences at any one moment. Despite the enthusiasm about their supposed explanatory power, it is hard to find consistent explanations of cultural change in the literature about world history. I will make only two points. One is that most major societies across Europe and Asia have experienced phases of considerable positive economic activity, with a good deal of technological change and even real economic growth. In so far as culture offers an explanation of these phases, we can only suppose that each culture switched for a time to emphasizing the promotion of growth, only to become conservative again and choke off that growth. The outcome is ambiguous and it is at least as likely that economic or political change drove cultural change as the opposite.

The second point is that the leading cultural explanation of Europe's rise, the birth of Max Weber's Protestant Ethic, has long been cast into doubt. It seems more likely that Protestantism, and the values of thrift and hard work involved, arose out of prior economic growth in masterless, proto-industrial regions, like the borders of the Low Countries and parts of England, than that Protestantism *caused* growth in the first place. The supposed Protestant virtues – on a broader view, hardly confined to Protestants or even to Europe – may have been adaptations to greater, but scarcely guaranteed, opportunities to prosper. All in all, cultural explanations of the great movements in the world economy are slippery and unconvincing. It is especially surprising to find that historians, who should be most aware of the changes in cultural variables which hide behind the unchanging names and labels for these things, are so persuaded of culture's permanency.

(c) Technology

A third category of explanation is technological. The staple argument of the industrial revolution school was that key inventions made in late eighteenth-century Britain were the pivot on which all economic history turned. More recently, it has been shown that the inventions of any great economic significance were largely confined to the textile and iron industries and did not yield their full results until well into the nineteenth century, as was certainly true of steam power. Innovation is more relevant to the productive system than the mere fact of invention. Even more important, I would say crucial, is the emergence of societies in which both invention and innovation can flourish.[11] It may be a little extreme to urge that any needed technologies will follow almost automatically from the creation of conditions in which inventive and innovative activity can take place, but it is hardly an extreme proposition to note that without encouragement, or more to the point without the removal of discouragements, technological change will be hampered.

The central requirement is a lifting of disincentives, assisted perhaps by the actual creation of supportive institutions like venture capital markets. Direct government involvement in science and technology is beside the point, in the long run it tends to interfere with creativity and distort the directions in which change occurs. Despite the excessive claims made for state-supported science in late nineteenth-century Germany, this was not a major part of the European experience. It is in any case more important to concentrate on how Europeans managed to learn how to raise the rate of invention and innovation than to dwell on the history of particular clusters of inventions in particular industries. What was vital, to repeat, was the emergence of types of society in which technological activity was not discouraged. In this process the decentralized political structure of Europe again played a large role.

The technological category of explanation is probably a diversion. Technology is a sort of intermediate producer good. Once a society possesses advanced technologies it does have the opportunity of surpassing its neighbours and outdoing its own previous record. But the coming into being of new technologies like steam power, capable of multiplying Europe's productive capacity, is part of what we are trying to explain in the first place. We should concentrate on the institutions and social and political organization that lay at the root of inventive responses.

(d) The Market

The expansion of the market is likewise part of what we need to explain. Certainly we can track the way in which markets replaced command and customary elements in the European economy. In that respect there were two signal developments greater than the sheer extension of commodity markets. One was the emergence of markets for factors of production, land and labour, and their freeing from the restrictions of custom. The other was the way countries began to trust international markets for food, something that was most marked in the case of the Netherlands. A willingness to rely on trade was a sign of maturity, both on the part of the international economy itself and on the part of decision-makers.

These two developments benefited economic life by allowing resources to be devoted to more productive uses. Yet I can scarcely reiterate too often that they remain phenomena which themselves have to be accounted for. They did not arise out of thin air; markets are not self-enforcing. Once again we will have to turn to deeper political and institutional features for an ultimate explanation. Before we do so, however, we need to deal with objections to the expansion of markets as any guide at all to the type of growth that flowed into industrialization. The objection made by those who think of the industrial revolution as lying across a divide that could be bridged only by technology is that market expansion was essentially, and only, 'Smithian'. They see market expansion as merely promoting one-off allocative gains that would soon run into diminishing returns. The gains would peter out. Only the increasing returns to technology could usher in the modern world of 'Promethean' growth. Yet as far as the eighteenth century was concerned there was a long way to go before 'Smithian' growth need have lost its impetus. Even in England the traditional sectors of the economy continued to grow and become more productive well into the nineteenth century. Allocative gains and the relatively simple technologies of the period had a lot of life left in them.

(e) Political Structures

Lastly we come to the nation-state and the states-system. I do not believe in any mono-causal explanation, certainly not of such a prolonged, large-scale and complex process as the European Miracle. Nevertheless one can see how growth may always be frustrated – by the absence of a degree of political security and secure property rights. It is certainly hard to see how the miracle might have come about in any recognizable form without fairly strong states in at least the north-western quadrant of Europe, and in the absence of competition among those states. European political units had been falling in number over a long period. Out of the feudal fragments, so to speak, emerged larger nation-states that were positively governed – so determinedly managed on occasion as to unify or create nations out of the people who happened to live within a state's borders. Moreover, European states were bonded in a 'stable state of division', and that was vital.

Rulers saw, or rather felt their way towards, growth because they responded to economic strength as the foundation of military strength. The way the process operated was more by default than by planning, but this was the more powerful because it was less arbitrary. Europeans lived in relatively small states and if they were badly treated – over-taxed, expropriated, or threatened with worse – it was physically possible for them to slip away over a frontier into a more tolerant country. This was not possible in anything like the same degree for merchants or entrepreneurs sealed, as it were, within the great Asian empires. No amount of sophistry can make the Asian political situation look as competitive.

European rulers came dimly to perceive, or inarticulately feel, the process going on. If they drove out holders of capital and individuals possessed of scarce skills, their states would suffer and the neighbouring states gain. This even happened across the outer borders of Europe, as when the Ottoman Sultan welcomed as wealth-creating an influx of Sephardic Jewish merchants who had foolishly been extruded by the Spanish monarchy. Later European rulers were more attentive, or at least less punitive, towards economically-productive minorities. European life was competitive in this way and yet at the same time remained, for reasons of its history, a functioning single market, particularly for ideas. The common use of Latin among the learned and French among the diplomats helped Europeans to exchange ideas even as the frontiers of the rising nation-states were beginning to solidify. No amount of sophistry can make the Asian intellectual situation look as unified. Europe had the dual advantage of more competition *and* more unity. A blind competitive process kept its economic development moving and, even within Europe, left the more authoritarian states lagging. Some of the efforts to replicate growth by statist means, notably the German attempt, were to imbue the twentieth century with its terrible pathologies of modernization.

ALTERNATIVE OPINIONS

Recently two otherwise separate sets of writers have converged on an interpretation of Europe's experience that dissolves away any explanation in terms of the internal dynamic of the European system during pre-industrial times. No 'privilege', as one of these groups would say, is to be credited to Europe that might elevate it – and therefore its politics and institutions – above other systems, especially Imperial China. There was no 'European Miracle'.

The first of these groups, the 'world historians', is ideological, anti-Western in tone, and decidedly Sinocentric. They believe that Europe's rise came about through chance. There is a certain amount of disagreement, one would have thought fatal disagreement, about what the fortuitous or chance event may have been. It was perhaps the military victory of William of Orange, who became William III of England after 1688.[12] His success (as an older Whig history used to say) established the Protestant ascendancy and the power of a number of associated, market-oriented interests. It may have been the 'chance' that Europe could seize and grow on the basis of resources from the Americas.[13] That occurrence is stridently portrayed as deplorable, on what by this late date must surely be simulated grounds of anti-colonialism. In one recent formulation, China's economy is depicted as equally or more advanced than that of pre-industrial Europe.[14] The corollary is that, had China happened to have the same good fortune, it would have grown too, presumably without the moral problem said to arise from Europe's seizure of resources from the indigenous inhabitants of the Americas. Another implication of the revaluation of Chinese economic history, much of which is no doubt acceptable as static description, is that Europe broke away from the common progress of Old World civilizations only very late. Whether China, or anywhere else, truly possessed the sort of dynamism that impelled Europe's growth seems to me, however, to be improbable.

The second group of writers, the 'quantifiers', takes a position that converges with the first one for very different reasons. They explicitly reject the overseas voyaging of the 1490s as a turning point in world history.[15] They emphasize instead the enormous income gains of the nineteenth century, which dwarfed all that had gone before. Hence they ignore earlier periods and the question of origins. One might think that the same reasoning would see twentieth-century growth as so dwarfing nineteenth-century growth as to render that, too, rather uninteresting. However, the nineteenth century did leave pre-digested statistics and is therefore an open field for the tools of modern economics. This brings it under the notice of the quantifiers when earlier centuries escape.

Both schools thus downplay the earlier experience of Europe, either its self-differentiation from other parts of the world before industrialization or its rate of growth before 1820. The European Miracle vanishes. To all intents and purposes, there were no positive developments internal to Europe, only the brutal seizure of resources from elsewhere. Additionally, any developments that did occur were trivial, because they did not generate growth on the scale of the nineteenth and twentieth centuries. The main dissenter from these positions is the chief quantifier, Maddison, who acknowledges that growth after 1820 did derive from three or four preceding centuries of slow Western ascension, but (in striking contrast to the 'world historians') with no Asian equivalent.[16]

What I propose to do here may perhaps be unexpected. I shall not try to contradict the opposing view that the internal evolution of Europe before the 1820s was of little or no account – let us call this the 'synthetic' view. Rather, I would like to explore the *implications* of accepting that there was, in essence, no European Miracle in the first place. My approach will be to consider the different interactions of growth with the institutions prevailing at its onset in different societies.

Ultimately, institutions are creations of choice and can be adapted to altered conditions. Alternatively, they may silently adjust. We face here the problem that exists with respect to culture, which is that institutional names and labels are likely to persist even when scope and function change. Functional dissimilarities among institutions around the world may be concealed by unconscious assimilation if their names are translated as something approximately similar: guilds are prime examples. Institutions may be captured by elites, in order to defend entrenched interests or secure a new advantage, but are likely to keep their old names.

It was historically rare for existing forms to be replaced wholesale rather than adapted. A striking exception was the way in which Arab Islam erased its precursors. According to Bernard Lewis, Islam's replacement of advanced and deep-rooted civilizations in Southwest Asia and North Africa was, 'one of the most successful cultural revolutions in human history'.[17] Ironically, the permanent Latinization of France, Spain and Portugal by the Romans was less remarkable because it replaced no pre-existing, advanced, literate civilization. On that time-scale, European civilization was a global latecomer. These early cultural shifts have of course had far longer to consolidate themselves than the non-Western world has had in which to accommodate industrialization and growth.

One of the implications of the 'synthetic' view of a late and externally induced European industrialization – the view that Europe's earlier developments were nothing special – is that almost any society in the world must have been 'close to growth'. In reality, growth has been slow to arrive or has not come at all in most of the non-European world, and where it has come the social costs of the attendant changes have often been appallingly high. Modernization still seems to challenge the identities and self-esteem of many in less-developed countries, and this has produced reactions such as Hindu fundamentalism and especially Islamic fundamentalism. Communism similarly embodied features inherited from earlier phases of history. It traded on apocalyptic visions like those of the European Middle Ages (showing the developed world the face of its past, as Marx might have said), and treated all human exchanges as zero-sum. Communism may have been invented in Western Europe but it was never practised there with the murderous ferocity that came from grafting it onto less developed societies.

The existing stock of institutions everywhere influenced, and often distorted, the path of development. Forced industrializations like the Soviet one exacted the highest price. Who dare say that the present miserable standard of living among ordinary Russians has been worth acquiring at the cost of millions of dead? For a long time the Soviet economic performance was grossly exaggerated by Western sympathizers. It is important to add that calculations of economic growth that do not set a price on freedom miscalculate in two ways. They run the risk of equalizing systems that may in the short run have similar living standards but only one of which also has individual freedom. In the longer run they neglect the role of freedom in sustaining growth. Individual freedoms mean noisy societies but ones in which policy mistakes can be pointed out and corrected, without debilitating conflict.

The polar case of under-development, even failed development, is sub-Saharan Africa. According to Chabal and Daloz in *Africa Works*, the continent is embroiled in a crisis of modernization *deeply rooted in its own history*.[18] There is chronic disorder. Wealth owners put 37 per cent of their capital outside the continent, compared with 17 per cent in Latin America and only 3 per cent in East Asia. Even the Western-educated elite accepts explanations of events in terms of witchcraft, which can be interpreted as hedging against abnormal uncertainty. African intellectuals are now among the fiercest critics of their own societies' failings. Disorder nevertheless offers opportunities to some, which means the same elites who robbed their states in the 1960s and 1970s. Their grasping is rational, given the absence of functioning institutions fitted to run modern states and economies.

Reform can certainly occur in societies that initially lack a stock of appropriate institutions. Take Turkey.[19] In 1918 Kemal Ataturk reinvented Turkey on the lines of a secular European nation-state. Yet Turkey got stuck. According to *The Economist*, the details of the Kemalist legacy are now defended by the elite which runs the country in such a way as to fossilize them: contrary opinion is resisted and even parliamentarians can be tortured. In 1950 average income was a little above Spain's or Portugal's, but these countries have rid themselves of authoritarianism and now have three or four times Turkey's average.

These cases suggest that institutions, and especially the stock of institutions at the start of modernization, are crucial. The quasi-modernity of Turkey has produced results far above Africa's, but is self-limiting because it does not replicate the underlying function of decentralized institutions. Such institutions include those conducing to political pluralism, independent law, and a free press. They presume security of property and security of the individual. Their latent function is to encourage self-correction in the system, so that misconceived policies may be exposed and replaced.

Clearly the forerunners of institutions of the relevant sort were intended to promote the interests of elites against the arbitrariness of rulers and of their own peers. But, in order to sense their value, we do not need to pretend anachronistically that European institutions at the time of industrialization served all of their modern purposes. A decentralized system like the European one, or at any rate like that of the first industrializer, Britain, was open-ended, not closed. Full political participation could be progressively extended to those outside the elite, first to all males, then to females as well. It would be easy to romanticize the system but praise for it is not false when set against the standards of most other systems. The institutions of the mainland Asian empires that existed during the centuries of Europe's growth offered little protection for property or the individual, not merely in practice, but in principle. Conquest dynasties thought themselves above the law and had no interest in providing independent law for their subjects.

We return, then, to the European Miracle. It seems to me miraculous, or if you like marvellous, that Britain and Europe were not only the first parts of the world to achieve sustained growth but possessed a stock of institutions that adapted fairly readily to the stresses of the process. The inheritance of a system of competing and complementary states helped to generalize growth in one part of Europe to other parts, on pain of falling behind. On second thoughts, though, all this seems less than coincidental. The stock of internal institutions combined with the external 'balance of power', as these things evolved in the pre-modern period, was deeply involved in bringing nineteenth-century growth about, spreading it, and warding off reverses. Even if rapid growth did not really start until the 1820s, it rested on centuries of accumulating institutional and political foundations. Their blind evolution was the true European Miracle.

NOTES

1. E.L. Jones, *The European Miracle: Environments, Economies, and Geopolitics in the History of Europe and Asia* (Cambridge: Cambridge University Press, 1981; second edition with new introduction, 1988).
2. David S. Landes, *The Wealth and Poverty of Nations* (New York: Norton, 1998), *passim*.
3. Cf. E.L. Jones, *Growth Recurring: Economic Change in World History* (Ann Arbor: The University of Michigan Press, edition with new introduction, 2000), especially chapter 4.
4. Cf E.L. Jones, 'Venetian Twilight: How Economies Fade', *Journal of Economic History*, **56** (3), 1996, 702–5.
5. This point is made most persuasively by Joel Mokyr, *The Lever of Riches* (New York: Oxford University Press, 1990).
6. On this topic, see E.L. Jones, 'Environment: Historical Overview' and 'Natural Resources: Overview', in Joel Mokyr (ed.), *The Oxford Encyclopedia of Economic History* (New York: Oxford University Press, forthcoming, 2001).
7. J.L. Anderson and E.L. Jones, 'Natural Disasters and the Historical Response', *Australian Economic History Review*, **XXVIII**, 1988, 3–20.
8. See for example the recent work by Kenneth Pomeranz, *The Great Divergence: China,*

Europe, and the Making of the Modern World Economy (Princeton: Princeton University Press, 2000).

9. E.L. Jones, 'Culture and Its Relationship to Economic Change', *Journal of Institutional and Theoretical Economics,* **151** (2), 1995, 269–85.

10. Thomas Sowell, *The Economics and Politics of Race* (New York: William Morrow & Co., 1985).

11. E.L. Jones, 'Technology, the Human Niche and Darwinian Explanation', in E.L. Jones and Vernon Reynolds (eds), *Survival and Religion: Biological Evolution and Cultural Change* (Chichester: John Wiley, 1995), pp. 163–86.

12. Jack Goldstone, *Europe's Peculiar Path: Would the World be 'Modern' if William III's Invasion of England in 1688 had Failed?*, mimeo, University of California, Davis, 2000.

13. An exponent of this view is Pomeranz, op. cit.

14. Ibid.

15. Kevin H. O'Rourke and Jeffrey G. Williamson, *The Hecksher-Ohlin Model Between 1400–2000: When It Explained Factor Price Convergence, When It Did Not, and Why*, NBER Working Paper No. W7411 (November 1999).

16. Angus Maddison, in Ian Castles (ed.), *Facts and Fancies of Human Development* (Canberra: Academy of the Social Sciences in Australia, Occasional Paper 1/2000), p.11 *et seq.*

17. Bernard Lewis, *The Multiple Identities of the Middle East* (London: Weidenfeld and Nicolson, 1998), p. 51.

18. Patrick Chabal and Jean-Pascal Daloz, *Africa Works: Disorder as Political Instrument* (The International African Institute/James Currey, Oxford, 1999).

19. Edward McBride, *The Economist* 'Survey of Turkey', 10 June 2000.

3. The European Miracle and its relevance

INTRODUCTION

This chapter is not simply about my book, *The European Miracle*, which was first published in 1981, but its 'relevance'.[1] The subtitle of the book is *Environments, Economies and Geopolitics in the History of Europe and Asia*. In the text I analysed and contrasted the economic histories of these two continents but did not link either history to the present day. As indicated in the previous chapters, I explicitly rejected the idea of 'relevance', in that I warned against equating the institutions of the past with those of the present.

In 1988 I repeated my belief in the virtues of pure scholarship in a second book, *Growth Recurring*, which has the subtitle *Economic Change in World History*. Economic history can help us draw maps of the processes of growth but we should not presume that paths through the forest of long-dead circumstances are a detailed guide to modern routes – the social landmarks have usually changed too much for that.[2] The second book supplements and to some extent corrects the first; for instance, it tries to incorporate the Tokugawa Japanese experience into my overall version of world economic history. A little more on Japan's remarkable early achievement appears in my chapters of a third book, written with Joop Goudsblom and Stephen Mennell, and called *The Course of Human History: Economic Growth, Social Process, and Civilization*.[3] These three books contain most of what I have had to say about world economic history.

THE ISSUE OF 'RELEVANCE'

Historical analogies are dangerous. For example, showing that certain developments improved life in the past does not and cannot constitute an endorsement of them today. I pointed out that the fact that European nation-states provided administrative and disease control measures superior to those which had been obtainable in the miscellaneous, small jurisdictions of the Middle Ages was not intended as a defence of nationalism. What nationalism did was force the coalescence of fragmentary political units and expand their size and intensify their coherence, but in an arbitrary way. Members of a nation or inhabitants of a nation-state have something in common, but it is an artificial something. Nineteenth-century European states were constructs; they went out of their way to promote unity, imposing national languages, establishing national school systems, focusing railways on their capital cities, and so forth. As one social engineer said at the time, we have made Italy, now we must make Italians.

The reverse side of this was that other quite similar people were left outside the nation, turned into more sharply-defined strangers, and made the potential objects of aggression. It is easy to think of nations and nation-states as deeply meaningful units if one comes from an island country like Britain or Japan but even these are historical amalgams, forged out of older, smaller units like the Saxon kingdoms and the *han*. I did not want my ideas on the earlier benefits of the nation-state to be mistaken for an endorsement of nationalism.

Similarly, in *Growth Recurring* I rejected the idea that the oriental empires were surrogates for modern China, Russia or (courtesy of the Ottoman empire) Islam. Modern governments offer more services and have far greater scope for political and social control than the ancient tyrannies. Likewise, I rejected the idea that the guilds were surrogates for trade unions. Guilds are popularly confused with labour unions but were actually quite different in membership, purpose and powers, as well as quite distinct within and without Europe. Such analogies are superficial, even false. They represent labelling errors, that is they treat the institutions of different periods as if they performed the same functions just because the same name for them has come down through time.

Labelling errors are sometimes compounded by translation errors, whereby approximately similar institutions in totally different civilisations are also called by the same name. Translators assimilate foreign concepts to ones with which they are familiar. Again, the guilds are a good example. Typically, guilds in independent European towns could set the price, quantity and quality of a product. By controlling the entry of apprentices and hiring of journeymen workers they could also restrict competition among firms, none of which was permitted to grow larger than the others. I do not find that the so-called guilds in the Ottoman empire or Imperial China could keep out competitors in this way. They were much more the instruments of states that had social order more in mind than income protection, and did not permit their guilds to exclude men from membership.

Yet the fact that I consciously disavowed the idea of lessons for the present does show that I was aware of what are called the 'uses of history'. No one who grew up during the Cold War could fail to have noticed that the Marxists, at least, seized every opportunity to rewrite history for their own purposes. They derided the idea that history could be written in a neutral fashion. They certainly went out of their way themselves to replace honest efforts at neutrality with sometimes open, sometimes covert, rhetoric. Much of this was designed, in David Landes' term, which bears constant emphasis, to delegitimize the West.[4]

I do not know whether right-wing writers have used the book, but some figures who would commonly, though incorrectly, be termed right-wing have certainly done so. These are the market liberals, often followers of Friedrich von Hayek. In an appendix to his *The Constitution of Liberty*, Hayek explains why he is not a conservative but someone who prefers openness and the discomforts of permanent competition to either the centralized dictates of socialism or the vested interests of conservatism.[5] The market liberals have found in my book a positive message about economic and political openness and competition which was not, however, consciously written into the text.

This only goes to show that the issues of long-run development and the associated governing institutions really are live matters today. I was perhaps naive in thinking that I could isolate my work from modern uses and abuses of the past. There is a phrase in Latin, one of the few remaining traces of the older Western educational system, which expresses the helplessness of authors faced with the use and misuse of their work: *habet sua fata libella*. This means that once one has published a book, the text takes on a life of its own and is interpreted the way others wish to interpret it. To that extent the 'deconstructionist' school of literary critics is correct: books turn into what readers choose to make them. As times change, and in different societies, meanings may be attached quite other than those the writer intended. And writers can set down things in an obscure way. I know, for instance, that *The European Miracle* presented Professor Minoru Yasumoto with several puzzles when he was kind enough to translate it.[6] The deconstructionists are not right, though, that there are no such things as authors, only readers who will understand the book in their own ways. I want to reclaim my own role as author here, and comment for myself on the implications of my book.

THE EUROPEAN MIRACLE AS ECONOMIC HISTORY

The title, *The European Miracle*, is meant to echo similar phrases used to describe the way in which early modern Europe, or its north-west quadrant, pulled ahead of other regions in Eurasia and became the first to achieve sustained economic growth. Nowadays the transition tends to be dated to the 1820s rather than to the former conventional starting date for the British Industrial Revolution of 1760. It is now claimed that since 1820 *world* per capita real income has risen 20 times as fast as it did in the preceding eight centuries, although, as we all know, the geographical distribution of growth has been most uneven and confronts us with many problems of interpretation.[7]

The explanation in *The European Miracle* is in layers. There is no seeking for a mono-causal solution to the puzzle of Europe's rise in the fashion either of older writers trying to account for the Industrial Revolution or of many economists trying to explain some phenomenon like the current under-development of Africa. I see no reason *a priori* to think economic processes are as simple as that. Without wishing to leave structure behind in favour of narrative, the way some general historians do, my view is that it may be the whole complex of changes that matters. Taking historical processes apart in a reductionist attempt to locate a single 'driver' seems neat and logical but may leave us, in a phrase from Goethe, holding all the pieces in our hand, but lacking the inner band that held them together. In other words, we may find that some historical mixes and sequences of factors proved viable and others did not. The philosophical principle of Ockham's Razor tells us not to multiply hypotheses but it does not assert that complex processes are in reality simple.

The explanation worked from the general to the particular and the early to the late. Each element underlay the next and probably continued to operate while its successor began to work. Incremental advantages compounded one with another. They included relative freedom from – or the ability to recover from – natural disasters that destroyed capital; cumulative advances in technology that were produced in multiple but interlinked centres; the genesis of mercantile societies able not merely to seek overseas resources (for example, in the Americas) but also able to use them productively rather than squander them in high living or more than commensurate demographic growth.

To some extent these various abilities were founded in an abnormally diverse environment. This is not to say that geological or topographical diversity *caused* long-term growth but it did reduce some costs and raise the probability of a positive outcome. Resources were scattered about the European continent. This encouraged trade to bring them together. The long, indented coastline and the many navigable rivers made it possible to move bulk products about more cheaply than where there were large, uniform landscapes. Numerous ethnic and language groups had been long settled in mountainous and densely forested country in Europe, where they had resisted being drawn into mainstream society. Conquering and managing sizeable areas or populations was expensive and tended to deter anyone who wished to unify Europe by force.

After the Fall of Rome in the fifth century AD there were from time to time attempts to bring the continent under a single rule, remembering always that Rome itself had never ruled the northern part of Europe. The emperor Charlemagne tried to unify the continent. He failed. The Habsburg Charles V tried. He failed too. Napoleon tried. Hitler tried. They also failed.

If we are to speak about relevance, the European Commission is making another attempt to bring about unification now. Its ambitions are grander than ever. They extend to including Turkey (an Islamic country, the heart of the Ottoman empire) and parts of the former Soviet bloc. Perhaps the EC will succeed. The danger along European Miracle lines is that a highly centralized, statist, *dirigiste* and bureaucratic EU may replace some markets and stifle some novelties, particularly institutional innovations that are not to the taste of the dominant French and German bureaucrats. It will be a test of the Miracle's conclusion that long-run strength lay in decentralization and competition. Or are circumstances more favourable for large units now? The counter-argument, which would diminish the relevance of *The European Miracle*, is that information markets are better integrated, while now that North America and East Asia exist as highly developed regions their external competition may provide the needed stimulus.

The central sections of the *Miracle* deal with the rise of the nation-state and a states-system. The idea is that Europe remained a single market for ideas at the same time as political and economic decisions were decentralized in ways that were suppressed in large land empires. Emperors usually took precautions to ensure that provincial governors did not take too many initiatives of their own or break away entirely. The many political units in Europe coalesced only slowly into nation-states. Each unit, and each state, made its own choices. But none did so in complete ignorance of what was happening in the others. The monarchies were much intermarried. Diplomats spoke to one another in French. Ideas were exchanged in Latin, which was the *lingua franca* of educated people. Exchanges of news and ideas were relatively easy when travel was not impeded by the need for passports. Scientists and merchants – sometimes they were the same individuals – travelled around and wrote copious letters to one another. They and their letters even crossed the Atlantic, helping to bond the entire Western world into a single culture or, more pertinently, to ensure that it remained a single market for information whatever the disputes in its internal politics.

The states increasingly, though slowly and without much premeditation, began to improve conditions for economic activity. They offered what we would today call business-friendly laws, flexible institutions and less arbitrary taxes. Citizens began to suggest 'growth programmes', that is plans for economic development, though often mercantilist ones. Some were not unlike Honda Toshiaki's list of the obstacles to growth in Tokugawa Japan; the difference may have been that his list went unpublished.

Mainly, however, the developmental process in Europe was a blind one. States, or their rulers, sensed that economic power was essential for military power. They began to compete with one another for capital and skilled labour, at least by refraining from the severe and unjust treatment of individuals with money or skill. In addition, there was a growing tendency for production to be privatized – by abolishing communal agriculture and industrial guilds – while social welfare became more a public function, at first in the forms of disaster relief and disease control.

As was recognized by the great French scholar, Marc Bloch, a central feature of the emergent system was the binding or taming of the ruler. Hitherto rulers had not been bound by their own enactments. In non-European systems they continued to be above the law, indeed to embody the law. Originally the land they ruled was deemed to belong to them and in a more primitive past they ruled by the supposed 'divine right of kings.' In very broad outline, the rise of states with continuity of purpose and an enlarged merchant sector gradually reduced European rulers to the role of presiding officers. Kings and other dignitaries were co-opted into the growth process, to become (as their personal temperaments or circumstances determined) company chairmen, presiding over a chief minister who was somewhat like the CEO or chief executive officer of the state.

Historians will be reluctant to recognize this. The panoply of courts and the ceremony surrounding elite figures looks very traditional, slow to change and devoid of immediate economic functions as we would conceive them today. I admit the business analogy is inexact and am aware of Paul Krugman's article insisting that a country is not a company.[8] But I am also aware of Wolfgang Kasper's work on competitive institutional innovation to attract capital and enterprise.[9] Whether a country intends it or not, it offers a specific bundle of institutions that affect the costs and operation of businesses within its jurisdiction. Beneath the surface of European history changes in government functions and eventually in economic performance were taking place.

The central tendency was thus for the nation-states to become more bourgeois in orientation. Unlike the great empires, the nation-states emerging in Europe began in some respects to look like a cluster of firms. They competed, colluded and created novelties at a faster rate than in earlier times or other places. Failing to provide suitable conditions meant falling behind, though the countries that did so lurched forward from time to time in attempts to import the latest apparatus of economic and technological activity

MODERN IMPLICATIONS OF THE EUROPEAN MODEL

Wolfgang Kasper has been kind enough to label the process of institutional competition the 'Eric Jones Effect'.[10] He has in mind the feedback from economic growth that persuades governments to provide more business-friendly institutions. Where some advanced states generated investors with capital needed by enterprises in less-advanced countries, the tendency was for conditions in the less-advanced places to be brought up towards the more advanced level. Investors wanted guarantees of low political risk for their loans or investments.

We can surely see a similar effect in the modern world. Even though Western banks proved scandalously poor at assessing political risk in the lead-up to the Asian Crisis, they have since become hesitant about returning to countries that have been slow to reform their financial and legal systems. Why, we may ask, were Western lenders so ready to take risks before the middle of 1997? Part of the answer is that if they had studied any relevant subject at university at all, it was economics; in a rush to become quantitative and seem 'scientific', modern economics has increasingly dropped those parts of the syllabus dealing with history and politics. We therefore have financial sectors staffed by people who lack understanding of the institutional context in emerging markets and have scarcely heard of previous financial crashes. I expect that we will see bursts of incautious investment in emerging markets in the future, just as in the past. Investment bankers are often too young to have any personal memory of an earlier crash. If this deficiency is not offset by the vicarious experience that comes from learning economic history, the chances of future crashes will be the greater. One should read Charles Kindleberger on the recurrent cycle of financial panics.[11]

To return to *The European Miracle*, I did not assert that a multi-centred states-system entirely accounted for Europe's growth, though the way it fostered competitive markets was an important part of the argument. The book as a whole built up layers of cumulative causation. My aim was not to recount the historical record in all its descriptive detail. Even with respect to the nation-states and states-system I was describing ideal types and trying to distil the underlying, latent, story. Economists are fairly happy with this approach; they tend however to be impatient with even such little detail and few complications as my rather short text does include. They do not like the fact that I decline to put my finger on a single trigger that separated Europe from the remainder of the late pre-industrial world. Economists often overlook the potential value of the redundancy in historical description, which may signal explanations and offer warnings that the more cut-and-dried approach of *a priori* modelling misses. Historians, of course, tend to dislike my approach for the opposite reason: they distrust any attempt to isolate key elements via a stylized framework rather than recounting concrete facts. It is the role of economic history to educate both of its parents.

Another element that has to be incorporated in the analysis of European economic history is the individualism and creativity of the continent. Part of this stemmed from a feature that was once again peculiarly European, the competition between the secular government and a largely independent church or churches. Ecclesiastical courts operated alongside royal courts and many early lawyers came from the ranks of the clerics who were in any case the main body of educated people. Civil law emerged in a slow, tortuous way from the competing jurisdictions of different states once rulers saw the advantage of offering their subjects independent courts in which disputes might be adjudicated.

Here Europe really differentiated itself from other systems. The Chinese emperors, who were often conquerors from Central Asia, never offered genuinely independent law and definitely did not wish to subject themselves to independent court rulings. Even today, despite efforts to develop international law in order to satisfy foreign business, the ultimate law-giving body in China is a political one: the National People's Congress. This is fundamentally different from the practice that grew up in Europe and which became embedded in the political principles whereby European and other Western states are governed. The independence of the judiciary and a crucial role for private lawyers in dispute resolution may have been carried to extremes, some would say to excess, in the United States. For all that, it is a major element in Western history, vitally affecting past and present economic performance.

Japan's different tradition is now causing some dismay. According to press reports, Japan has only one lawyer (*bengoshi*) per 7000 people, compared with one per 395 people in the United States.[12] France, whose Napoleonic legal system was closer to the origin of Japanese law than the English Common Law tradition which the United States followed, has four times the proportion of lawyers that Japan has. Even allowing for differences in the definition of legal functionaries, Japan thus does seem to be short of lawyers to deal with the contracts that international business, and increasingly domestic business, involves. A stigma may attach to taking disputes to court – yet the courts are reportedly clogged. At any rate, the *Keidanren* and big companies have been pressing the government to increase the number of lawyers. There seems to be Protectionism on the part of lawyers in Japan: foreign lawyers are banned, at least in the domestic sphere. Japan's bar association is lobbying against change.

There are admittedly difficulties associated with bringing about change. Any academic tends to be suspicious of promises to expand supply by lowering examination standards, modern Western societies have done too much of that in too many different fields. An excess of practitioners leads to an over-servicing that may be as serious as under-servicing. One would not wish to see Japan import the rent-seeking that clearly impels many of the actions taken to court by American lawyers, especially in 'class actions' where members of the group supposedly harmed by some action or other need not even know that the matter has been brought before the law.

Commerce does find ways around bottlenecks. A recent big acquisition of a Japanese supermarket chain by Mitsubishi was governed by English law, using English language documents! But it seems to me – and it follows from *The European Miracle*'s contrasting of European and Asian systems – that not having an independent, adversarial court system is a costly way of proceeding. The point is a significant one. A major feature of Western development has been the emergence of 'black letter' law, especially contract law, in which a mixture of written agreements and the precedents of earlier judicial rulings hold sway. There are big differences between the Common Law's reliance on precedents and the Napoleonic Code's emphasis on prior logic, but they are closer to one another than either is to systems of law governed by mixtures of politics and case-by-case negotiation.

I have already referred to the takeover of what had always been politicised law by the Chinese Communists. They introduced an ideologically new legal system but one still in the inherited tradition of Imperial law where the ultimate authority was not an independent judiciary. The legacy of Imperial legal arrangements was equally crucial outside mainland China. Consider the manner of doing business, or at any rate the stereotypical way of doing business, among the Overseas Chinese. They are commercially very important in Southeast Asia. Estimates of the share of GDP which the Overseas Chinese account for in each of the countries where they operate add up to a vast total. In Indonesia the Chinese, 3 per cent of the population, were under Suharto said to own 70 per cent of commercial assets. But they do not transact business in the European way.

The usual 'Chinese' approach to making deals is via *guanxi* (networking) rather than by impersonal contact and contract. In other words, networking is super-important and it is an essential part of the behaviour to establish closer and closer personal relationships. Why is there this difference from the impersonal – and more easily generalizable – approach of Western business? The answer seems to lie deep in the key divergence between the histories of Europe, and hence the West as a whole, and those of other societies, in this case China.

Europe developed contract law; Chinese business continued to be based on relationships. In practice, it is true, many deals in the West are actually struck on the basis of a handshake – there are studies of the acceptance of non-enforceable contracts. Westerners spend a lot of time and resources on their personal contacts, though not as much as the Chinese. Many, probably most, Western transactions nevertheless remain formally contractual ones. And behind the informal ones there does lie a regular legal system that can be turned to as last resort. Independent legal systems do exist nowadays in many Southeast Asian countries, but Overseas Chinese deals continue to be set up primarily through *guanxi*.

The Overseas Chinese inherited their expectations from the unreliable legal practices of the Qing empire. Some of them were refugees from Communist

China, some left China much earlier, but they were all the heirs of a tradition that substituted *guanxi* for legalism. The Qing were not willing to submit themselves to an overarching rule of law and did not supply China with universal codified law. In the circumstances, what were people to do? They faced the same problems in business as anybody else, but without the last resort of independent courts if things went wrong. Trust remained an issue. They still needed a means of sifting out the crooks. Hence the five levels of Confucian relationships and the forming of closer and closer personal ties with business acquaintances than most Westerners find comfortable. Of course, as I have indicated, Westerners do form networks to facilitate business; they still play golf with business acquaintances. But I think much of this is a search for information about prospects and commercial conditions rather than mainly a means of establishing trust.

In Qing China, one device for assessing the reliability of business contacts was to restrict dealings to people from the same native place. Information is easier to come by when the set of possible partners is limited and they are likely to know one another, or are able to find someone who does know the reputation of the other person. Notice, however, that I use the term 'restrict'; the negative side of the practice is that it limits the extent of the market. The practice, which the Overseas Chinese have to some extent continued, tends to restrict business to a sub-set of all possible deals.

The behaviour of the Overseas Chinese was entirely sensible. They had to find a means of determining trustworthiness when the state provided them with no appropriate service. Their resort to relationships rather than formal law was however a second-best option which was less reliable and tended to limit the market. The unreliability of informal procedures is evident in the extremely bitter quarrels over inheritance among the Overseas Chinese. Ways round the limitations of informality are increasingly being found because the opportunities of international business are now so tempting. Many of the younger Chinese have taken MBA degrees in Western universities and become familiar with Western practices. Yet reliance on relationships is still a limiting factor within the global market.

Western companies find it hard to explain informal dealings to their shareholders and it is now illegal in OECD countries for businesses to offer bribes when soliciting business. In the Chinese and other non-Western systems, gifts would not be seen as illegal. They would be seen as normal practice, though it is obvious (to a Westerner) that they are anti-competitive, enable some firms to obtain deals that their efficiency and prices do not warrant, and harm the interests of consumers.

An interesting sidelight is thrown on these matters by what happened recently to the Singaporean investment in a new town in Guangdong. The local authorities led the Singaporeans to think their project would go ahead but privately supported a competing project. Even Lee Kwan Yew was unable to resurrect the Singaporean scheme and it was eventually abandoned. Commentators said that Singaporeans are unable to cope with mainland Chinese practices: the Taiwanese understand 'Chinese' ways but the Singaporeans no longer do. They are shocked by this because they see themselves as an Asian culture, in practice a Chinese one, but in reality they have adopted 'Western' commercial standards. They have inherited a more regular legal system from another empire – the British empire. Indeed, Singapore has flourished not only because of its aggressive, clever, economic policies but at least as much because it offers all comers a court system that enforces contracts in a transparent, incorrupt way.

Part of the 'relevance' of *The European Miracle* thus lies in the message it contains about law-based systems and their greater long-term efficiency than relationship-based systems. Viewed in very long-term perspective, it was less important how quickly European societies raised the standard of living of their inhabitants than that they created institutions with better and sounder prospects for the future. Static, cross-sectional measures of living standards and other economic variables do not highlight the dynamic element that would eventually raise European incomes so much and permit readier recoveries from shocks. Among the standard ways of assessing economic systems, dynamic technical and allocative efficiencies are more significant for the longer term than static technical and allocative ones. The ability to recover from shocks is also important.

Large economies like mid-Qing China could at times be very effective. A recent book by Kenneth Pomeranz, *The Great Divergence*, shows this very plausibly.[13] His is explicitly a challenge to my book and will oblige us all to revalue the historical productivity of China. To my mind, Pomeranz greatly overstates his case when he goes on to interpret all the comparative evidence in favour of China. I have said in a review article that I do not find his descriptions of European practices at all convincing. That is less to the point, however, than the institutional dynamics of the European system. Development in Europe was more continuous and less easily set back than in China. And the individualism of Europeans supplemented this with a greater upsurge of technological inventions than occurred anywhere else. The inventions even of the British Industrial Revolution had widespread origins in the European continent, often being based on French science and involving individuals from many countries.

Whatever the early achievements in China, and they were especially considerable under the Song dynasty, it was in the end Europe and the West that achieved the 'Miracle' and industrialized first. Moreover it was Japan, not China, that was best able to copy this – even though I accept the point that Pomeranz and others are now making that China did not lag as much as we once thought. To my mind, the Japanese case reinforces the conclusion that deep social and political factors had major unintended consequences in readying societies for modern economic growth. In contradistinction to Pomeranz I do not think that Europe was merely lucky because it came across coal mines and seized the resources of the Americas at just the right time, when it was running out of other natural resources. The European Miracle lay less in supposedly chance events like that than in constructing a governmental, institutional and commercial framework that could capitalize on its opportunities. Beyond that, it lay in not stifling the creativity of its people. If anything has modern relevance it is the importance of open markets for information coupled with the opportunity for individuals to retain the rewards of their effort.

CONCLUSION: THE RELEVANCE OF HISTORICAL CHANGE

At the end, I wish to return directly to the matter of 'relevance' and thus to the problems of using long-run economic history for modern purposes. Any usable lessons are very broad ones: they pertain to open and competitive economic and political systems that maximize long-run growth. It is difficult to specify how long the test of such conditions needs to run: quite a long time, in my estimation, that is to say many decades. Over shorter periods other systems, such as centralized or centrally-planned ones, may do better and certainly may *seem* to be doing better. Let us remember the GDP figures that supposedly showed Khrushchev was right and the USSR really was 'burying' the West. Even the CIA claimed the economy of the Soviet Union was performing well almost to the moment at which Gorbachev closed the whole enterprise down! (We should remember that the CIA budget was more likely to be increased if the USSR was accepted as a serious economic challenger as well as a military threat.)

Comparing economic systems definitely needs a historical perspective. Nothing looks deader today than the rows of unhistorical books on economic systems that appeared during the Cold War, many of which, though they contrasted Soviet Communism unfavourably with American capitalism, spoke admiringly of systems like those of Maoist China and Marshall Tito's Yugoslavia! This kind of assessment reflected the political prejudices of the writers, showed that they were taken in by Communist propaganda, or in some cases indicated that they liked privileged visits behind the Iron Curtain rather than the poverty in which scholars without patrons have to live.

I am pleased that I wrote my book in 1979, well before the weaknesses of these centralized, collectivist systems had been widely recognised, and while many academics in the West were only too ready to prophesy the downfall of Western capitalism. My intuitions were right, though I intended no overtly political statement. The material used came from secondary sources, it was a sort of gloss on the academic literature that tried to draw out the economic implications of what was known in the 1970s about early modern European and Asian history. There is no intentional or coherent political or policy programme: the book arose from the raw materials.

The message of *The European Miracle*, then, is that open and competitive systems flourished best in the long run. The 'relevance' of this is that history is not over! These are the best conditions for progress and liberty today and apply equally to ways of organizing or governing advanced economies and appropriate means for developing poor economies. On the other hand, at the level of more specific comparisons, history does not work. For historical analogies to succeed the context must have remained remarkably, and improbably, stable, or else the message must be very general. The message of my book is indeed very general, an unintentional by-product of pure research in economic history whose details no longer matter. But its very generality means that the case for open and competitive economic systems is no less significant today.

Any less-developed country aspiring to economic growth would do well to adopt the formula that Europe happened across in its history. First, it should put the law above politics. Capital accumulation and technological innovation will occur when individuals can rely on keeping the proceeds of their efforts. Technology seems to offer 'free lunches' but its spectacular gains are really secondary; they are attainable by any society that invests in institutions to encourage invention and enterprise. Second, the less-developed country should free its information markets. An open contest of ideas will be uncomfortably noisy, but this is the best way to achieve self-correction, that is constantly to expose rent-seekers and bring better ways of doing things to the attention of the whole public. In poor countries where markets have been small or distorted, access to cheaper information should make a greater proportionate difference than in economies that are already developed. The message of *The European Miracle* is a very simple one about the benefits of competitive markets within contract societies.

NOTES

1. E.L. Jones, *The European Miracle: Environments, Economies, and Geopolitics in the History of Europe and Asia* (Cambridge: Cambridge University Press, 1981, 1987).
2. E.L. Jones, *Growth Recurring: Economic Change in World History* (Oxford: Clarendon Press, 1988, 1993; Ann Arbor: University of Michigan Press, 2000).
3. J. Goudsblom, E. Jones and S. Mennell, *The Course of Human History: Economic Growth,*

Social Process, and Civilization (Armonk, New York: M.E. Sharpe, 1996).

4. David S. Landes, *The Wealth and Poverty of Nations* (New York: W.W. Norton, 1998).
5. F.A. Hayek, *The Constitution of Liberty* (London: Routledge & Kegan Paul, 1960).
6. University of Nagoya Press, 2000.
7. Angus Maddison, in Ian Castles (ed.), *Facts and Fancies of Human Development* (Canberra: Academy of the Social Sciences in Australia, Occasional Paper 1/2000), p. 1.
8. Paul Krugman, 'A Country is not a Company', *Harvard Business Review* (January–February 1996), 40–44, 48–51.
9. Wolfgang Kasper, *Institutional Innovation to Enhance International Attractiveness*, Australian Defence Force Academy Economics and Management Discussion Paper 1/1993.
10. Wolfgang Kasper, 'The Open Economy and the National Interest', *Policy* (Winter 1998), 22.
11. Charles Kindleberger, *The World Economy and National Finance in Historical Perspective* (Ann Arbor: University of Michigan Press, 1995).
12. *The Australian*, 27 June 2000.
13. Kenneth Pomeranz, *The Great Divergence: China, Europe, and the Making of the Modern World Economy* (Princeton: Princeton University Press, 2000). For a critique of Pomeranz's thesis, see E.L. Jones, 'Time and Chance in the Old World Economies', *Journal of Economic History* **60** (3), 2000, 856–9.

4. World agriculture in the very long term

INTRODUCTION

World agricultural history is so vast a topic that a discussion of it could be organized in innumerable ways. Compressing even the barest outlines of the story into a single chapter requires a very tight structure. Given the present purposes of linking back to earlier chapters on long-term economic change and forwards to the section on Protectionism, the arrangement of this chapter will take the form of three pairs of contrasts: demand and supply explanations of the long-run growth of output; the contrasting histories and eventual divergence of irrigation and rain-fed agricultures; and the shift in developed countries from merely an adequate supply of foodstuffs to a harmful over-supply.

The first of these sections considers the alternatives of demand- and supply-based explanations of rising output, devoting most space to the implications for the world economy between 1500–1800 of the positive shock imparted by the 'Columbian Exchange' of plants and animals. The second section notes that in terms of physical productivity and technical elaboration the oriental river valleys eclipsed all other agricultural systems and supported the most advanced civilizations throughout most of history, but this began to change (notably from the seventeenth century) with the emergence of solutions to the problems of soil fertility in temperate Europe. The responsiveness of Japanese agriculture was also noteworthy at that time and there were parallels with European 'improvement' that would repay closer comparative examination. The third section considers the perverse response of developed countries to rising food supplies at home and abroad from the nineteenth century: agricultural protection, which is an attempt to halt the clock of structural change on behalf of producer interests. The continued intensification of production behind defensive tariff barriers and other forms of support makes the modern situation anomalous, indeed scandalous. The assumption here is that opening markets in the developed countries to food exports from less-developed ones would improve the latter's economic condition. The emergence of BSE and other disease problems may now oblige Western countries to reduce the intensity of their farming systems but it is unfortunately not clear if this will benefit consumers.

EXPLANATIONS OF THE LONG-TERM GROWTH OF AGRICULTURAL OUTPUT

Demand-side Growth

Agriculture was usually much the largest sector of most economies in the past. Britain and The Netherlands were quite exceptional in seeing the share of their workforces in farming fall to 60 per cent as early as the late seventeenth century. Furthermore, total world agricultural output has almost always tended to increase and the trend of world population, which has been rising for millennia, is in itself some measure of this.[1]

Total consumption would seem to have been in approximate equilibrium with total production for most of history. The options were limited. In societies with few other uses for additional food, for example as industrial raw materials, and with limited possibilities of bulk carriage, extra food would have to be consumed more or less on the spot. Peasants who produced a little more than their immediate household needs or than they were able to trade locally may have converted the increment into larger families, via better nutrition and reduced mortality. They could perhaps feed more animals and produce more meat or dairy products. Beyond that, they could convert grain into alcohol – and if they brewed or distilled more than they could drink, liquor at least had the advantage of being smaller in bulk and more easily transportable than unprocessed grain. Beyond that again, they could always cut back on their effort and make no attempt to maximize production. Output would therefore track population, give or take the share consumed as rent-cum-taxes by ruling elites whose diet was more varied than the average.

The main constraints on rising output were not inadequate methods of farming, an incompetent use of the factors of production (as many works on peasant rationality have shown), nor even (broadly speaking) a lack of land to be taken into cultivation. What most checked the growth of output may have been something external to farming – the scarcity of non-farm goods. Only as rural industrialization increased and more particularly after the start of factory industry would there have been a profusion of goods for farmers to buy, persuading them to grow more in order to sell it for cash. The increase of population growth seemed unable by itself to break history out of a condition of 'static expansion' or expansion without growth.

Admittedly there were important exceptions to the stereotypical peasant economy envisaged above, even in ancient times. Grain was sometimes traded over long distances, as between Egypt and Greece. During the early modern period the growth of 'millionaire' cities like Constantinople (Istanbul), Edo (Tokyo) and London drew food supplies from some way off. Literate societies in Western Europe became able to diffuse new techniques among the farm community but over most of the world technical developments were limited and slow before the modern evolution of denser networks of communication. Peasant societies found it difficult to improve technologies too weak to ward off bad weather, insect depredations, and the like. As a result we may indeed be persuaded that output was largely governed by basic needs and that most societies did conform approximately to a pattern whereby the supply of food did not run far ahead of them. For obvious reasons population could not run far ahead of the supply of food. The expansion of output and the growth of population thus marched side by side.

In sum, the possibility that the demand for food more or less created its own supply seems acceptable as a broad proposition. Ester Boserup long ago generalized her African observations to suggest – contrary to Malthusian expectations – that the pressure of more people did not mean starvation. It meant that they shortened their crop rotations and intensified production in other ways.[2] The most important of the other ways refers to irrigation works, since additional people meant labour was cheaper for tasks like constructing and maintaining dykes and ditches. But something beyond an intensification of field work and farming methods was needed in order to increase production sufficiently to satisfy the densest populations. The additional something was the spread of settlement onto fresh land and the cultivation of additional acres. Many large frontier movements took place after the early years of the Christian era. They included the southward expansion of the Han Chinese (who also cleared rich forest land) and the spread through southern Africa of the iron-age technology of the Bantu peoples. Internal frontier movements also played a part, such as the clearing of Europe's forests and the more energetic eighteenth-century phase of removing boulders from the fields that enabled farming to spread through eighteenth-century Scandinavia and New England. These movements were not smooth continuations of earlier agricultural change: they were discontinuities.

Supply-side Growth

There would thus be no point in pretending that demand and supply made a perfect match. Had they been, the economic history of the world would be very bland; in reality it is given its interest by disequilibria and distortions. A clue that something more active was taking place than an almost automatic tendency for supply to meet increasing demand is readily found outside agriculture. There were major discontinuities in the size of political units, notably about 2800 BC with the emergence of cities, about 600 BC with the delegation of power, and about AD 1600 with improvements in the speed of communications.[3] These discontinuities resulted from technological or institutional changes. Nor was world population growth itself as smooth as at first appears. The figures reveal great primary, medieval and modernization cycles, after each of which growth rates slowed.[4]

The occurrence of these cycles implies that population growth was not the product of some manifest destiny in which the human biomass increased relentlessly. There were distinct waves of economic advance, each of which seems to have permitted surges of population growth that later ran into diminishing returns. These supply-side forces included intercontinental transfers of crop and animal species, new methods of farming, trade flows, and institutional innovations that permitted larger societies to be organized and spread best-practice techniques. From time to time the growth of numbers was checked by disease shocks, only to grow again vigorously once adjustment to the particular disease organism had taken place.[5]

Among the waves of change propelling population upwards, several major diffusions may be found that increased food production. One was the introduction into Africa from Asia of crops such as yams, taro and bananas. This began about the start of the Christian era, though some of the crops did not cross into West Africa until about AD 500.[6] In the eighth century AD crops were brought into the Middle East, North Africa and Southern Europe from as far east as India, in the 'Arab Agricultural Revolution'.[7] Another highly influential transfer was the introduction of early-ripening rice from Vietnam into China.[8] The most sweeping diffusion of all was the 'Columbian Exchange' which distributed American crops (and the turkey) widely round the world and in return brought crops and livestock from Europe to the American grasslands.[9] Some of these diffusions were on a scale sufficient to make an enormous difference to world food output and none of them can be treated as a simple reflex to rising demand.

The major instances are worth a more detailed account in order to indicate their scope and effects. Islam's spread during the seventh and eighth centuries was followed by a flood of crops and practices originating in India and Iran. Sixteen food crops plus cotton were brought westwards. Tropical crops filled niches that were otherwise hard to exploit: the summer season and poorer soils of the Middle East and the Mediterranean basin, where they helped to eliminate fallow. Agricultural practices in general were upgraded. Manuring was improved. Greater crop variety helped to reduce the year-to-year variance of farm income.

The new crops and practices spread through the lands newly unified by Islamic rule. The upper classes throughout the Islamic region were inclined to imitate things eastern and developed a taste for imported crops; importation was followed by import substitution. The gardens of local rulers acted as centres of plant diffusion. Legal and tax systems encouraged investment in irrigation. Large estates tended to be subdivided and family holdings were formed in which the actual operators probably had a greater incentive to put forth effort. The smaller units could be irrigated using the divisible technology of animal-powered water wheels. By the end of the eleventh century farm incomes in the Islamic world are reported to have risen, as had the size of population and the proportion of it dwelling in towns.

Turning next to China, we find early-ripening rice of the Champa variety introduced to Fukien from Indo-China (probably present-day Vietnam) by officials and merchants at or before the start of the eleventh century. The partial failure of the rice crop in the drought of 1011–12 persuaded the Chinese emperor to order 30 000 bushels of Champa rice to be distributed to the affected area, accompanied by instructions for its cultivation. Champa rice ripened in 100 days, compared with 150 days for the prevailing 'keng' variety. During the eleventh and twelfth centuries, the ripening period for rice was cut to 60 days and drought-resistant varieties were developed. Once again this was an exogenous change, a supply-side shock, and not a development induced by population growth. The population began to grow fast once Champa rice had been adopted. The breeding of new varieties and extension of the cultivated area are each said to have accounted for about half of the increase in total output but such a distinction is hard to sustain because it was only the new varieties that enabled rice to be cultivated on much of the new land.

Shorter ripening periods made double crops possible, either two rice crops in succession or rice followed by another cereal. Although yields per acre were lower for early-ripening varieties than for 'keng', they needed less water, which meant cultivation could be extended up higher hill slopes fed only by rainwater or springs. By the late thirteenth century much hill land in the eastern half of China's rice region had been converted into terraced paddy fields. Improvements in rice breeding continued, with greater cold tolerance achieved by the early fourteenth century. Further reductions in ripening times were attained in some provinces, down to 30-day rice in Hupeh by 1834–35.

The most extensive and complicated crop transfer of all was the Columbian Exchange, whereby between the time of Columbus and the nineteenth century the range of species was extended in all continents. Old and New World crops and livestock complemented one another and permitted formerly under-used seasons, climates and soils – not to mention staggering extents of agriculturally unoccupied grasslands – to be better utilized. Apart from the occupation of the Americas by European farming, the most significant introductions were maize in the Mediterranean countries, white potatoes above the limit of technically feasible rice growing in upland China, and manioc (the highest yielding tropical crop) in Africa. African agriculture was greatly diversified by additional species; only some 50 of the 640 domesticated food crops recognized by the great Russian botanist Vavilov originated in that continent. A higher percentage of the African population now depends on what were originally New World crops than in any continent except the Americas themselves. In Europe, maize in the south and white potatoes in the north helped to dampen the price spikes when cereal crops failed.

The fastest adoptions were those that took place in China. Between the start of the Christian era and 1500 only three new crops had entered that country (cotton, tea and sorghum). On the other hand, four major dryland crops (sweet potatoes, peanuts, maize and tobacco) came in during the sixteenth century, and some others, including white potatoes, followed during the seventeenth century. These crops complemented each other. They supported continued population growth when the rate of growth of rice output was slackening. It cannot be maintained that the increase in supply from these sources was anything other than exogenous.

Meanwhile, Old World crops such as sugar, cotton, rice, indigo, wheat, grapes and olives were carried to the Americas, where European settlers also set about redistributing native crops. Old World livestock arrived in the New World, which lacked domesticable species of its own. Cattle occupied hitherto under-used grasslands and horses complemented them by making ranching operations possible. Neither cattle nor horses spread fast through the American tropics but their numbers positively exploded on the prairies to the north and the pampas to the south.

All told the Columbian Exchange was the biggest single positive shock to come about through a redistribution of the world's biological potential. Certainly the main impact awaited the expansion of settlement and maritime trade in the nineteenth century.[10] But the consequences were evident long before then. The view that 'the world economy was fragmented and completely de-globalized before the 19th century', which is advanced with such amusing scorn by O'Rourke and Williamson, obscures more than it reveals about the pre-modern world economy.[11] Certainly historians of the world-systems school, whom O'Rourke and Williamson are attacking, have provided no evidence of pre-nineteenth century price convergence among the continents. They have merely asserted the existence of a single 'global world economy' (sic) right from 1500, though it is rather forcing the issue to make Adam Smith appear to have said the same thing. The fact that economic change in the nineteenth century dwarfed all earlier change is however a commonplace. It would have been more appropriate to base-weight the analysis of the impact of the Discoveries in the *preceding* period. Technological change and technological exchange could take place in a 'traditional' world where commodity and factor flows were limited.

The immediate results of the Columbian Exchange took the form of technology transfer more than volume trade. Before there was any large trade *between* markets (compared with the scale to come) the means was diffused about the world whereby additional output could be grown *within* each market.

The appropriate test is less price convergence among initially separate markets than the counterfactual: what would have happened to food prices and world population growth if all that had remained available was each region's pre-1500 inventory of crop and livestock species?

Diverting the issue into a test of the Heckscher–Ohlin trade model, which has always had difficulty incorporating technology, as O'Rourke and Williamson do, masks the changes that took place before the trade expansions of the nineteenth century. O'Rourke and Williamson do not consider the rise in output and population founded in the complementary combinations of new crops and animals with those already available in the various continents. The trade view is base-weighted in later times; it directs attention to the numerator (income) and away from the denominator (population); it diverts attention from technology transfers that took place at periods when there was (relatively speaking) minimal trade.

The transfers of agricultural technology could be rapid: within a century of Columbus's voyages four major dryland crops from the Americas were being cultivated in China, some of them very early and none simply as a curiosity. Peanuts were being grown around Canton by 1516, sweet potatoes reached Yunnan in the 1560s and had become widespread by 1800, while the white potato reached Fukien before 1700. Maize entered China by two routes and spread more slowly, but in the eighteenth century all these crops spread to the formerly forested highlands of the south. According to one work they came to supply 20 per cent of total food output.[12]

For most of the world we possess no more than outline descriptions of these great colonizations. A few estimates do however exist of the increased acreage secured in Asia.[13] The periods covered by the estimates vary so much – and the population figures available do not refer to precisely the same years – that tabulation would convey a misleading impression. Nevertheless merely listing the figures indicates the very substantial increases of the arable area that took place in several major societies: Japan from 1200–1800, 200 per cent (population growth 273 per cent); China from 1400–1760/70, 151 per cent (population 184 per cent); and India from 1600–1901, 71 per cent (population 115 per cent). These are large numbers indicating large changes, yet in no case did the proportionate increase in the arable area match the increase in population. This suggests that there was also an intensification of farming systems. Although there were endogenous changes in technique, we know incorporating the new crops played a big part in raising output.

That the world economy, meaning the sum of the economies of its constituent regions, remained unaffected by external events – that is to say, by the Discoveries – is thus incorrect. That the continents remained isolated from one another in all important respects was not the case. The new crops which were so widely diffused were among the things that 'really mattered to the economic lives of the vast majority', as O'Rourke and Williamson have it. The concern of contemporaries was less how incomes in distant lands may have compared with theirs, much less with an international economy of the distant future, than whether more of them survived in each generation, whether they were better off than their forebears or at least enabled to maintain the living standards of larger communities, and whether they now possessed the means to smooth off the price peaks of famine years.

The accounts of new cropping systems and new land taken into cultivation are more descriptive than statistical but no one has denied the direction of change they indicate, nor its large extent. According to the McEvedy and Jones compilation cited above, there was an increase of 118 per cent in world population between 1500 and 1800, as against only 18 per cent between 1200–1500. Among constituent regions, the gain in Africa was 52 per cent compared with 44 per cent in the preceding period; in Europe 122 per cent compared with 40 per cent; and in China 220 per cent compared with a decline of 13 per cent in the preceding 300 years.

These figures are not 'colorful tales about rent-seeking', which is how O'Rourke and Williamson characterize the results of Europe's maritime expansion (they do not discuss other civilizations). The figures refer to economic achievement. At an absolute minimum this outcome was what I called in the first chapter, '*extensive* growth plus'. At a minimum, then, output in the three centuries after Columbus was sufficient to sustain a growth of population almost seven times greater than in the preceding three centuries. Furthermore humanity became equipped with more and sturdier capital and much more know-how. Although knowledge and the techniques for extending it were unevenly distributed across the globe, better means for their diffusion was already present. The economic expansion, industrialization, international trade and income gains of the nineteenth century did not arrive *ex nihil* but out of the achievements of the earlier period. *Extensive* growth was a better seed-bed for subsequent growth than a world of mere rent-seeking would have been. A world of colour without movement could not have given birth to the nineteenth century.

THE CHIEF DISPARITY BETWEEN PRE-MODERN AGRICULTURES

It is thus clear that intensified production in response to demand did not exhaust the history of agriculture. Major upswings occurred from time to time on the supply side. Because the greatest of these, the Columbian Exchange, included several dryland crops, it went some way towards lessening the dependence of Asian populations on irrigated agriculture. The highlands of southern China came to be occupied by a great internal migration that was eventually responsible for clearing woodland from 28 per cent of the land surface.

In pre-modern times the most productive farming systems had been chiefly in the alluvial valleys and deltas and monsoon coastlands of Asia. From prehistoric times until the last century or two, productivity per acre there was higher than in Europe. The main river valleys from the Nile eastwards were very densely settled and their irrigated agricultures had long sustained complex civilizations. Outside the riverine and estuarine areas, a satellite scanning the world for crops would have found little more than a scatter of arable 'islands' in a sea of forest. This was definitely the case in Europe, which until recent centuries was immensely wooded. Otherwise around the world there were great stretches of pastureland not yet invaded by the plough and often occupied only by hunting cultures. The main interest of farming in late pre-modern times was the part agriculture may have played in the failure of the irrigated agricultural areas to support sustained economic growth, and as a counterpoint the eventual development of Tokugawa Japan and Europe to the point where the latter could upset the old geographical distributions and transform the economies of the whole world.

Was Asian agriculture so backward that it held back the remainder of the economy? At least in China the record of population growth suggests that the physical performance of agriculture was adequate for a very long time. Output was high in the zones of irrigated rice, while the uptake of new crops shows that the system was not inflexible. The class of *literati* produced a stream of instructive books called *nong shu* that accumulated over the centuries and kept alive knowledge of advanced methods through episodes of political turmoil.[14] Although China lacked a literate population, its literate elite thereby fostered the adoption of more intensive techniques among the peasantry than in most pre-modern societies. The economic performance of Qing China, especially in the eighteenth century, is now regarded as better than was formerly thought, but it still did not lead to much urban and industrial growth. Moreover the ultimate cost of agricultural expansion was high. Cultivating the high ground in south China led to soil erosion, gullying, silting and flooding and from the 1860s population began to retreat into the valleys. Into the twentieth century nothing was developed comparable to the scientific and agricultural extension movements of Western countries that might have countered the exodus. The highlands supported fewer people than they had in the early nineteenth century.

Tokugawa Japan and early modern Europe witnessed less equivocal agricultural and economic growth. In Japan, once the new shogunate settled on Edo (Tokyo) as its capital at the start of the seventeenth century, this obscure fishing village rapidly became one of the largest cities in the world. A large market for farm products was created to which agriculture responded fluently. In return the city became a large source of commercial fertilizer, and this flow of fertility was supplemented by the trade in fish fertilizer organized by the Omi merchants. The development of Japanese agriculture at this period should not however be attributed entirely to urban demand for the changes brought about by the Tokugawa settlement were complicated ones. In any case, the growth of demand might have been cut off had supply not responded with quite exceptional vigour. New farming methods were very widely adopted. This was a genuinely literate society like the advanced parts of Western Europe, and 'how to' books were widely read, and sometimes written, in the villages.

The supply response was due partly to breaking up large holdings into small farms occupied by nuclear families. This raised incentives and led to the release of entrepreneurial energies. Individually the new techniques were unimpressive but they were cheap and suitable for adoption by small operators. Their interrelationships were exceptionally interesting and the parallel in form with England was striking. In Japan, 'innovations rarely if ever came singly, they hung together in clusters by a kind of inner logic; one innovation brought others in its train, and often could not be adopted independently of them'.[15] The innovations included row cultivation, which helped to control weeds, more and better-selected rice varieties, some new crops, and superior implements.[16] The population of Japan did not much increase over the second half of the Tokugawa period (1720–1840). Meanwhile competition among farmers squeezed some of them, and part of the labour time of others, out of agriculture into farm by-employments. The resultant rural industrialization helped prepare the way for factory-style industrialization after the Meiji Restoration of 1868.

In England, 'there was an ascending spiral of progress ... each advance, while small in itself, stimulated further advances in another sector, and the spiral was able to begin again at a higher level'.[17] Endlessly varied rotations of cereals and fodder crops were tried, including courses of clovers that fix their own nitrogen. Sowing fodder crops eliminated the need to leave part of the arable land fallow, which was the equivalent of expanding the cultivated area. Feeding off the 'new' crops with cattle or sheep in the field dunged the soil and increased yields of the following crops of cereals, besides producing more fatstock. These practices spread to mainland Europe (indeed many of them had begun there, especially in the intensive farming around the Dutch cities from the fourteenth and fifteenth centuries).[18] These developments were of immense value in a continent where the central task was to preserve or raise soil fertility, rather than the need for irrigation vital in much of Asia.

The cropping changes predated, in some respects long predated, the classic English agricultural revolution of the late eighteenth century. The seventeenth century was the most significant one for innovation, as has recently been re-confirmed.[19] The line breeding of animals, for example, started in the late seventeenth century.[20] Nevertheless it was mainly from the late 1830s that agriculture became genuinely intensive, adopting factory produced inputs including machinery and artificial fertilizers supplied by the chemical industry. Much of the understanding of how these things worked was at first empirical but the application of scientific research to agriculture gradually became systematic. Controlled experiments began to be reported before the end of the eighteenth century. Arrangements to disseminate knowledge (societies, shows and publications) became widespread.

A characteristic of agriculture everywhere is the extremely large number of independent business units. The emergence of an institutional structure capable of generating and diffusing new knowledge is therefore vital. The number of farms and the openness of their fields to the gaze of competitors meant however that it was difficult to prevent new ideas from being imitated. The initial response was to create non-pecuniary rewards – prizes at the shows that conferred local status (and meant that some monetary reward would perhaps follow, say from the sale of seed or from stud fees). This approach was later supplemented by establishing public institutions to undertake agricultural research and publish the results. The effectiveness of nineteenth-century institutions in generalizing the latest methods is particularly well seen in Australia, where from the very start British techniques were adapted to the exigencies of a less forgiving climate and much poorer soils.[21]

The occupation of the temperate grasslands of the Americas, Australia, Argentina and other 'Neo-Europes' represented a staggering accession of farmland per head for peoples of European origin. This is indicated by the steep fall in their overall settlement densities during periods when Asia was becoming ever more densely settled. Population per square mile in Western Europe plus the New World 'Great Frontier' fell from 26.7 in 1500 to 9.0 in 1800.[22] The main exploitation of this treasure house nevertheless awaited the nineteenth century, indeed the late nineteenth century. One of the reasons why there was a pause after the Repeal of the Corn Laws before cheap grain imports savagely undercut the profits of cereal growing in Britain was that until the 1870s overseas supply did not exist, or could not be shipped, on a very large scale.

Meanwhile British arable farmers were able to reduce their costs and guard against shorter-term price fluctuations by elaborating their systems of mixed farming and constantly 'tweaking' the rotations in response to short-term price movements.[23] Their successful adjustment to slowly and unevenly falling prices for cereals lasted for a generation, but after that there was no hope of competing fairly and squarely with the flood of cheap extra-European grain. During the so-called 'Pioneer Agriculture Explosion' between 1870/74–

1895/99 the export of cereals from North America, Russia and India rose by 178 per cent.[24] Clearing and burning grasslands and scrub around the world released so much carbon dioxide into the atmosphere that this episode has been described as the first truly global environmental insult.[25] It ushered in imports of foodstuffs at prices which British and European farmers could not meet. The primary division of the world was no longer between productive Asian systems and the less productive remainder; it was now between the expansionary commercial agricultures of Europe and its annexes like the United States, Canada, Australia and Argentina, and the more sluggish remainder.

OVER-SUPPLY

There now emerged the largely unprecedented phenomenon of over supply. Between the 1850s and the First World War, world food exports grew by almost 900 per cent. Production within the industrialized countries increased, so that despite the larger markets created by rising population and real income there was strong downward pressure on product prices and farm incomes. This bore first on the cereal enterprises, though fatstock enterprises were also affected once refrigeration made it possible to transport carcasses internationally. On the other hand dairying prospered in the metropolitan countries, helped by falling costs of feed grains and rising urban incomes that encouraged a shift towards higher protein foods. Market gardening also tended to prosper because its products were sheltered from competition by their perishability.

The structure of agriculture in the industrial world thus began to alter, but the movement was restrained by tariff protection. Britain, the first industrial and most urban of nations, was for a long time a rare exception in eschewing protection. The Great Debate was effectively concluded there when the Corn Laws were repealed in 1846. On the other hand most European countries protected their agricultural interests. If we take Germany as an example, the large estate owners, the *Junkers*, secured high levels of Protection: they were, as Hans Rosenberg remarked, ingenious in identifying the national interest with their own.[26] Behind tariff barriers, German production of cereals and other sources of carbohydrates soared just when the cereal sector in Free Trade Britain shrank away in the face of foreign competition. Yet German industrialists were not entirely willing to see the country insulated from sources of cheap food, since that would raise the wages they had to pay. The balance of political forces meant that the *Junkers* could modify but not prevent a shift in the direction of food imports and these actually quadrupled between 1873/77–1909/13. In the United States the McKinley Tariff of 1890 protected farmers against overseas competition. Even Britain eventually began to adopt a form of protectionism, when it established 'marketing boards' for several commodities and encouraged wheat production in the early 1930s.[27]

Engel's Law states that the share of expenditure on food decreases with rising income and this relationship contributed to the lessening relative importance of the agricultural sector in the industrialized world. Agricultural support has however been able to keep large absolute numbers of producers in farming but their competition with one another has created vast surpluses inside the tariff wall. However, neither protection nor an exodus from the land has been sufficient to keep the incomes of farmers and farm workers up to the constantly-rising levels of those in industrial and service occupations. Bellerby collected evidence of this for 28 countries as early as 1938.[28] On the other hand, political influence has nowhere drained off the land as fast as people have. The apparent paradox of influence far greater than can be explained by the voting power of agriculturists is partly explained by lobbying on the part of big machinery and fertilizer companies. They have a stake in maintaining support for the farm sector.

Although competition within agriculture works continually to rationalize farm production, some check may be coming with prohibitions on the feeding of animal tissue to herbivores and on the adoption of GM (genetically modified) crops. Interestingly enough, Sweden was 15 years ahead of the rest of Europe because its agricultural industries decided voluntarily in the 1980s to refrain from using animal products in livestock feed and antibiotics in fodder.[29] Comparable countries did not follow suit until absolutely obliged to do so; their intensification of production has continued and still continues. At the extreme a six-storey 'Agropark' is planned in the Netherlands, which is already the world's largest food exporter and where output per hectare is seven times greater than in the nearest competitor. The largest of four complexes in the Agropark will hold 300 000 pigs and one million chickens – and their manure will be reprocessed.[30] The justification for this type of development is that intensification *must* continue if the world is to be fed. But the argument seems self-serving. It does not take into account that farmers in less-developed countries would find it worthwhile to increase output if their products were not excluded from markets in the developed world. As it is they cannot acquire the foreign exchange to buy the know-how to raise their yields and their poverty remains unrelieved. The percentage of the population that was undernourished in 11 countries in Africa, Asia and Latin America rose between 1979/81– 1996/98; in eight of those countries it rose by over 40 per cent.[31]

The intensification of agricultural production has occurred in the wrong places, that is in the developed countries, especially the European Union, where the resource costs are high. And some of the methods adopted for raising output have notoriously cut corners. The worst example is the feeding of mammalian tissue to herbivores, which in the EU has led to the spread of BSE (Bovine spongiform encephalitis) and its reported communication to humans in the form of new variant Creutzfeldt-Jakob disease. The (belated) prohibition of the practice and the subsequent bans on trade in cattle, coupled with the withdrawal from supermarket shelves of meat from infected areas, and the mass slaughtering of livestock, have had powerful impacts on public opinion. Preferences for vegetarianism and 'organic' foods, together with vocal resistance to breaches of food safety apparent in swelling outbreaks of salmonella and other contaminations, were already evident among middle-class consumers. Consumption of beef fell on average by 27 per cent in the EU during the last quarter of 2000. The mishandling of the BSE issue, initially by British civil servants and politicians, has boosted demand for organic foods, despite the lack of actual scientific evidence that they are more nutritious or even safer than factory-farmed produce.

The problem is not a purely British one. It is endemic in the agricultures of the developed world, where (except in the Swedish example mentioned) farming lobbies have usually succeeded in capturing the relevant ministries and getting their own way politically. How else should we interpret a briefing note of the Department of Primary Industry in Queensland, Australia, which states that meat from horses and other equine species and from pigs are not 'mammalian material' according to the legislation, and may therefore be fed to ruminants and other livestock?[32] Given the existence of legislation seemingly prohibiting the feeding of 'mammalian material' most people would have been lulled into a false sense of security. Few would have scrutinized the definitions had there not been an international outcry over BSE. This is an instance where the misuse of the English language, a feature of modern times referred to in Chapter 10, may conceivably have put the public in danger.

Plentiful food has been bought at high cost to consumers in the developed world, as well as to producers in food-exporting countries. In January 2001, French police were actually reported to be raiding government ministries in Paris, looking for evidence of a cover-up with respect to the dangers of BSE. If the remedy is to be a retreat to less-intensive farming methods, the cost of food in the shops must rise – that is, unless free trade is extended to agriculture. The EU may hope to escape opening its markets to the whole world by acquiring food from the more traditional agricultures of the countries to the east that hope to join it ('Enlargement'). Such a move would however increase competitive pressure on farming within the EU as it stands at present. As one ambassador to the WTO concluded, 'after more than fifty years of the GATT/WTO system, the failure to integrate agriculture fully into the normal rules of the international trading system stands as a monument to the power of sectional interest groups and the continuing timidity or cynicism of political leaders'.[33]

NOTES

1. E.L. Jones, *Growth Recurring: Economic Change in World History* (Ann Arbor. Michigan: University of Michigan Press, second edition, 2000); J. Goudsblom, E. Jones and S. Mennell, *The Course of Human History: Economic Growth, Social Process, and Civilization* (Armonk, New York: M.E. Sharpe, 1996).
2. Ester Boserup, *The Conditions of Agricultural Growth* (London: Allen & Unwin, 1965).
3. Rein Taagepera, 'Size and Duration of Empires: Systematics of Size', *Social Science Research*, **7**, 1978, 108–27.
4. Colin McEvedy and Richard Jones, *Atlas of World Population History* (Harmondsworth, Middlesex: Penguin Books, 1978), table 3.
5. W.H. McNeill, *The Human Condition: An Ecological and Historical View* (Princeton: Princeton University Press, 1980).
6. John Levi and Michael Havinden, *Economics of African Agriculture* (London Longman, 1982).
7. A.M. Watson, 'The Arab Agricultural Revolution and its Diffusion, 700–1100', *Journal of Economic History*, **34**, 1974, 8–35.
8. Ping-ti Ho, 'Early-ripening Rice in Chinese History', *Economic History Review*, **9**, 1956, 200–218; Dwight Perkins, *Agricultural Development in China 1368-1968* (Edinburgh: Edinburgh University Press, 1969).
9. Alfred W. Crosby, *The Columbian Exchange: Biological and Cultural Consequences of 1492* (Westport, CT: Greenwood Press, 1972); Ping-ti Ho, loc. cit., and 'The Introduction of American Food Plants into China', *American Anthropologist*, **57**, 1955, 191–201.
10. See E.L. Jones, *The European Miracle* (Cambridge: Cambridge University Press, second edition, 1988), p. 82.
11. Kevin H. O'Rourke and Jeffrey G. Williamson, *The Heckscher–Ohlin Model between 1400 and 2000: When it Explained Factor Price Convergence, When it Did Not, and Why*, NBER Working Paper 7411 (Nov. 1999). It is unclear at which earlier period the authors think the world economy had been globalized.
12. Jones, op. cit. pp. 114–5; see also Gang Deng, *Development Versus Stagnation: Technological Continuity and Agricultural Progress in Pre-modern China* (Westport, CT: Greenwood Press, 1993), p. 180.
13. David Grigg, *The Agricultural Systems of the World: An Evolutionary Approach* (Cambridge: Cambridge University Press, 1974), p. 45, table 4; Kozo Yamamura, 'The Agricultural and Commercial Revolution in Japan, 1550-1650', *Research in Economic History*, **5**, 1980, 85–107.
14. Gang Deng, op. cit., *passim*.
15. T.C. Smith, *The Agrarian Origins of Modern Japan* (Stanford: Stanford University Press, 1959), p. 101.
16. K.I. Choi, 'Technological Diffusion in Agriculture under the Bakuhan System', *Journal of Asian Studies*, **XXX**, 1971, 748–59; Yamamura, loc. cit.
17. M.A. Havinden, 'Agricultural Progress in Openfield Oxfordshire', *Agricultural History Review*, **IX**, 1961, 83.
18. B.H. Slicher van Bath, 'The Rise of Intensive Husbandry in the Low Countries', in J.S. Bromley and E.H. Kossman (eds), *Britain and The Netherlands* (London: Chatto and Windus, 1960), pp. 130–53.
19. Robert C. Allen, 'Tracking the Agricultural Revolution in England', *Economic History Review*, **52** (2), 1999, 209–35.
20. Nicholas Russell, 'Who Improved the Eighteenth-century Longhorn Cow?', *Exeter Papers in Economic History*, **14**, 1981, 19–40.

21. Geoff Raby, *Making Rural Australia: An Economic History of Technical and Institutional Creativity, 1788-1860* (Melbourne: Oxford University Press, 1996).
22. W.P. Webb, *The Great Frontier* (Boston: Houghton Mifflin, 1952), p. 18, n. 18.
23. E.L. Jones, *The Development of English Agriculture 1815-1873* (London: Macmillan, 1968).
24. Michael Tracy, *Agriculture in Western Europe: Crisis and Adaptation since 1880* (London: Cape, 1964), p. 23.
25. A.T. Wilson, 'Pioneer Agricultural Explosion and CO_2 Levels in the Atmosphere', *Nature*, **273**, 1978, 40-41.
26. Hans Rosenberg, 'The Economic Impact of Imperial Germany', *Journal of Economic History*, Supplement 3, 1943, 101-7.
27. John Martin, *The Development of Modern Agriculture: British Farming since 1931* (New York: St. Martin's Press, 2000).
28. J.R. Bellerby, *Agriculture and Industry: Relative Income* (London: Macmillan, 1956), p. 270, table 61.
29. *Financial Times*, 29 November 2000.
30. *Japan Times*, 16 November 2000.
31. *The Economist*, 28 October 2000.
32. *The Australian*, 12 January 2001.
33. Geoff Raby, 'Reforming Agricultural Trade', in Harry Oldersma (ed.), *From Havana to Seattle and Beyond: The Quest for Free Trade and Free Markets* (The Hague: Sdu Publishers, 2000), p. 127.

PART II

Protectionism

5. Multifunctionality: the experience of English farming

INTRODUCTION

The topic at hand, 'multifunctionality', is defined as the creation of any unpriced spillover of benefits additional to agriculture's provision of food and fibre. The concept thus refers to the provision of public goods such as environmental values, rural amenities and cultural values, as well as rural employment and rural development. These purposes are now being cited in order to justify maintaining the high level of subsidy currently given to the farm sector within the European Union (EU), of which the United Kingdom is a member. The standard arguments for maintaining high levels of agricultural protection are thus in the early stages of being modified. If the new arguments are accepted, the option will be there for eventually shifting the justification from support for the physical production of conventional agricultural goods to support for supplying a range of public goods which, it is claimed, have hitherto been supplied free as a positive externality of farming.

The case examined in this chapter is that of England. Some other countries, such as Japan, Switzerland and Norway, are also involved in the effort to justify agricultural support under the creative, indeed open-ended, label of multifunctionality, but there is a reason for concentrating on one example. The logic, or illogic, of subsidizing the farm sector may be the same everywhere but the case for multifunctionality rests on specific claims about the unpriced contribution of agriculture in highly particular geographical settings. Nathan Rosenberg urged, in his *Perspectives on Technology*, that economists will have to get their hands dirty, as it were, if they are really to understand invention and innovation.[1] They will have to grasp the technical details in order to generate meaningful abstractions. I think the same applies to agricultural ecology, as indeed Rosenberg notes. The agricultural industries function where ecology and economics intersect. They differ from other industries in that for farm operators place of work and place of residence are the same (which introduces emotion into any debate) and that agriculture uses disproportionately large amounts of one factor of production, land, a resource on which modern society is making demands unprecedented in scale if not entirely novel in form.

Whatever one thinks of the case for multifunctionality, it cannot be denied that it is timely with respect to changes on both the demand and supply sides. On the demand side, high-income populations increasingly exhibit expenditure patterns that de-emphasize staple foodstuffs in favour of what were once high-status consumption items derived from using land. In short, Engel's Law operates and the proportion of rising incomes spent on food falls. There are significant changes slowing or limiting this effect, for instance the vogue for consuming expensive, so-called organic foods grown without the use of artificial fertilizers or pesticides. A leading supermarket chain in the UK recently estimated that this component of demand will increase four-fold in the next five years. It seems to make no difference that Professor John Krebs, head of the UK government's Food Agency, has been widely reported as stating that there is no evidence that organic food is healthier or more nutritious than the products of industrialized agriculture; the British public prefers to believe the assertions of the antiscience lobby. Nevertheless, although the workings of Engel's Law may be retarded by creating a demand for more costly foods, the law itself cannot be repealed. It is not primarily foodstuffs that consumers want today from the agricultural industries or at any rate from the land resource. They already have more than adequate access to food in historically amazing variety: the number of SKUs (stock-keeping units) offered by food retailers has grown by up to *100 times* over the past 50 years. The public applauds this outcome, certainly, and is highly conscious of the issue of food security. But in addition it increasingly desires goods of the less material kind denoted by multifunctionality.

The timeliness of the rise of multifunctionality as a justification for agricultural support is equally evident on the supply side. There, developed world agriculture is confronted by severe problems of over-production. Despite protection against imports, output continues to rise via a persistent intensification of domestic production that it is almost cripplingly expensive to subsidize. Attempts to curb output via schemes like 'set aside' (paying for some land to be taken out of production) tend to be nullified because capital inputs are immediately concentrated on the proportion of the acreage remaining under cultivation. In the case of the EU, over-production is compounded by the prospect of 'enlargement', which means incorporating countries in and to the east of Europe that have much larger agricultural sectors and will therefore simultaneously add to the over-supply of food and require budget-breaking increases in the subsidy bill.

The farm lobby in countries like England is therefore astute in repositioning itself to claim government payments for producing formerly unpriced goods. Like any of Mancur Olson's 'distributional coalitions' there is no limit to what it is willing to take from the common pot.[2] Multifunctionality means shifting from the old imperative of producing conventional agricultural commodities to the urgency of supplying less tangible and hitherto ignored externalities. The provision of these things is being converted into policy goals, in particular emphasizing environmental conservation, which has unexpectedly become so marked a feature of public taste in high-income countries. To understand what the implications are likely to be requires some account of the economic history of agriculture and of the actual record of farmers in supplying public goods.

It may be worth reminding ourselves of the philosophy underlying the concept of multifunctionality. The assumption is that agriculture is so much a part of culture and the environment that it deserves special support. A characteristic comment by a European Commission (EC) administrator claims that, 'farming for us is not an industry, it's a style of life. It is the right to have that lifestyle ... We have a fully cultivated landscape with very few spots kept in their original state, but cultivated by humans ... We cannot let something fall back to nature.'[3] This assertion is amplified in the preamble by the Norwegian Ministry of Agriculture to the papers presented at a conference in that country in July 2000, called the 'Conference on Non-Trade Concerns in Agriculture'.[4] The ministry states that every country has a sovereign right to strengthen the socio-economic viability and development of rural areas, food security and environmental protection, and it claims – without demonstration – that these goals cannot be achieved by market forces alone. Because they are unpriced the goals are somewhat unfamiliar ones; the statistics provided by the relevant English Ministry (MAFF, the Ministry of Agriculture, Fisheries and Food) make no reference to unconventional outputs or externalities of agricultural activity.[5] Nevertheless anything that consumes or produces resources properly lies within the purview of economics.

Representatives of 40 countries and economies attended the Norwegian conference mentioned. The EU submitted a paper on 'Agriculture's contribution to environmentally and culturally related non-trade concerns'. Among the propositions put forward were:

- Today's agricultural systems can maintain 'valued' landscapes, conserving biodiversity and protecting historical features
- Abandoning farmland would *reduce* environmental and cultural public goods
- Farmers should be directly compensated for generating non-market products, especially if this involves them in reducing the intensity of their food-producing operations

There are thus two related claims. One is that agriculture uniquely (but hitherto inadvertently) supplies a number of public goods that cannot be supplied by the market, the other is that farmers should now be paid for doing so out of the general tax revenues.

How are we to respond? None of the work by economists and agricultural economists on the costs of the distortions produced by protection has ever made much difference. Such work goes back at least to Gavin McCrone's excellent book, *The Economics of Subsidizing Agriculture*, in the early 1960s.[6] One might argue that persisting with technical work on the subject promises only a continued low rate of return and represents a misallocation of intellectual resources, because considerations of cost sway neither the decision-makers nor the overwhelmingly urban food-purchasing public of countries like the UK. As Bowers and Cheshire show in *Agriculture, the Countryside and Land Use*, the economic argument against protection is easy to win but it seems impossible to defeat the political lobby of farmers, landowners, and machinery, fertilizer and pesticide manufacturers.[7] Rather than add to the somewhat sterile literature of calculations about financial costs, the best way for an economic historian to contribute to the debate may be to examine the actual record of the farm sector with respect to the provision of the public goods that it now claims as its emergent *raison d'être*. If the decision-makers and the populace are unimpressed by evaluations of the cost of subsidies to food producers, they may be a little less willing to bear the burden once they realize that far from creating valuable public goods, the farm sector damages them.

I shall concentrate on the English case and within that on Lowland England. This does not affect the logic of the argument but gives coherence to the range of evidence on which I shall be drawing. Perhaps the geography needs a little explanation. The primary physiographic division of Britain is into Highland and Lowland Zones. The Highland Zone consists of hard rocks and higher ground in the north and west of the country; it receives the higher rainfall, experiences lower temperatures, has comparatively low population, and has never been home to extensive cereal-growing. The Lowland Zone lies to the south and east, has lower terrain, lower rainfall, higher temperatures, better soils, denser settlement and big cities like London; it is the long-standing arable region. Because the Lowland Zone is the more desirable habitat for people and the preferred region for crop growing, it is subject to the most intense competition among alternative uses of land.

THE ECONOMIC HISTORY OF AGRICULTURAL PROTECTION IN ENGLAND

At this point it is appropriate to consider the background to agricultural protection in England. A short economic history of agriculture can perform two tasks, one to explain the lingering, though now redundant, concerns of the population about food security, the other to show in a few sentences that periods of agricultural prosperity have been *inversely* correlated with times of environmental well-being.[8] It is simply not possible to make sense of the topic without paying some attention to the technical aspects of land use; too many accounts are over-generalized. The agricultural lobby relies on creating a picture of farming as a needy, environmentally beneficial and economically vital industry. Only by showing that this can be refuted in its own descriptive terms (rather than purely by economic logic) is there any hope in the public arena of undermining its arguments.

Caveats need to be entered, however, to show that I am aware of the limitations of a stylized account of these subjects. First, agriculture is not monolithic and some enterprises are actually in competition with one another, the clearest examples being cereal growing and livestock rearing. The latter uses the products of the former as inputs and therefore benefits from times when grain prices are low. In Lowland England, however, prosperity for most farmers is associated with periods of high grain prices. Secondly, the environment is not monolithic either. Some species of birds, animals and plants are adapted to arable environments and others to grassland habitats. A shifting balance of farm enterprises has no absolute effects, it merely changes the predominant ecosystems. Which system one prefers has a subjective component partly related, in my experience, to the contingency of the period when the individual expressing a particular taste happened to be young. As Tyler Cowen has argued with respect to culture, the formation of tastes is substantially complete by the age of 25.[9] Nevertheless, most naturalists agree that monocultural cereal production has been associated with net reductions of floral and faunal variety in Lowland England. There is reasonably good ecological information after about 1875.[10]

From the Repeal of the Corn Laws in 1846–49 until the Agriculture Act of 1947 Britain stood apart from most other European countries in espousing free trade in agricultural goods during peacetime. The initial impact on the domestic arable sector was however delayed, because in the mid-nineteenth century there were as yet no great sources of grain overseas that could be drawn on, and because a silent technical adjustment was achieved within British agriculture.[11] This involved producing grain and livestock from closely integrated rotations on the same land. It meant that the respective outputs of cereals and animal products could be adjusted to ordinary year-to-year variations in relative prices. But overseas sources of grain were dramatically expanding. From the late 1870s imports soared, prices fell too steeply to be coped with by ringing the changes on rotations, many arable farmers went bankrupt, and much arable land was abandoned. With cultivation at lower intensity even where it persisted (meaning that more scrubland habitats and uncultivated corners emerged), there was greater biodiversity. A more varied fauna and flora appeared.

It took the threat to food imports from German U-boats during the First World War to restore a temporary prosperity to English arable farmers. Wartime price support was nevertheless abruptly removed in 1922 and much of the arable countryside once again became poorly maintained. Wide areas actually became semi-derelict and sources of income such as sporting rights (for rough shooting) sometimes became more valuable than farm income or farm rents. Despite the economic depression of the 1930s, anyone actually in employment in Britain experienced rising living standards based on imported food that was cheaper than anything (except liquid milk) that the British farmer could produce: the imports were New Zealand butter and lamb, Australian wheat, and so forth. More and more of rising real income was spent on such luxuries as rural tourism and holidays in the countryside.

British farm operators, obviously, did not share in the quiet interwar prosperity for the consumers of food. But wildlife did. We can dispense with the details but merely note that there are plenty of accounts of the recovery of a more varied fauna and flora during this period, just as there had been in the arable depression of the late nineteenth century. Admittedly there was an ecological trade-off. Wild species adapted to an arable environment necessarily decreased – but there are fewer such species than on uncultivated land.

After what were for farmers the good years of the Second World War, some anticipated that agriculture would again become depressed. Thinking that the government would withdraw support, as it had after the First World War, they began to reduce operations. The arable acreage was at its peak as early as 1944 and was falling before the war came to its close. Probably much of the land hastily ploughed up during wartime was not easy to keep under crops with the inputs and technology available at the time, but the speed with which it was taken out of cultivation suggests lower post-war commodity prices were widely expected. This proved to be wrong. A sufficient supply of food was very dear to import from the Americas, which alone had much of a surplus. Britain was placed under enormous financial strain by its war expenditures. The resultant 'dollar crisis' prompted the passing of the Agriculture Act of 1947, whereby, in order to raise output, the government guaranteed support. Agriculture was protected in a way that did not apply to the remainder of the economy. The immediate post-war period was obviously abnormal and the apparent paradox is that agriculture continued to be protected once food supplies ceased to be scarce.

The saga so far exemplifies a number of facts. One, whatever its technical efficiency, English arable farming cannot compete with imported food at world market prices and has not been able to do so for 120 years. If it has flourished, this has been because wars have restricted international trade. Two, after the Second World War the farm lobby succeeded in obtaining enormous protection at the expense of the community and retained this support after the original justification had passed. Three, when their demand for food is satisfied, consumers do not just stay in town – they show an interest in spending their money on other 'products' of the countryside.

THE COMMON AGRICULTURAL POLICY

In Britain the arable area, arable production and investment in improved farm technology had all been moving up again from about 1950, following the Agriculture Act. Yet the dollar crisis brought *tighter* rationing than during the war itself and potatoes, a staple foodstuff that had not previously been rationed, were for a time added to the list of rationed commodities. Rationing was not finally relinquished until 1954. Although Western Europe as a whole was almost self-sufficient in foodstuffs by 1960, a siege mentality was therefore still just understandable. That year the organization which was to become the EU devised the undeniably protectionist Common Agricultural Policy (CAP). The objectives of Article 39 of the Treaty of Rome, which embodies the CAP, deal almost exclusively with food production, indeed they enjoin maximum production on the agricultural sector. Britain joined the forerunner of the EU in 1973 and hence became subject to the CAP.

From the point of view of its landed interest, joining the EU was undoubtedly profitable, if not indispensable. The cost of agricultural support was already high and the days of 'dollar crisis' scarcity over. Could the agricultural lobby, politically influential though it was, have long resisted attempts to reduce the bill for support without the backing of EU law and the power of the large peasant sectors in France and Germany? It is fruitless to engage in counterfactual speculation about what might have happened in Britain had the country not become a member of the EU. We do however know what the effects of the CAP have been. Individual producers have intensified production and increased output. In a competitive situation, this would have worsened the situation of producers as a whole by bringing prices down. The various instruments of farm support operated by the CAP however frustrate the normal workings of the market. In physical terms this has meant that so-called 'mountains' of butter, lamb, beef, sugar and especially cereals have built up, all unsaleable at official prices that are well above those of the world market. EU cereal stocks are expected to rise by a further 25 per cent by 2006.[12] These 'mountains' of commodities have been accompanied by 'lakes' of wine, milk and olive oil. With respect to the products in which it specializes, Britain has abundantly shared in creating these surpluses.

Economists have expended considerable effort on calculating the monetary costs. Most of these calculations understandably refer to the burden on EU taxpayers and consumers. Probably 40 per cent of the EU budget is spent on agriculture, though it is difficult to know precisely. There are so many fraudulent claims from farmers under the intricate system of rules that public sector data on agriculture, which should be particularly sound, are quite opaque. By the mid-1990s the complex support schemes had induced fraud equivalent to over 10 per cent of the CAP's costs and to that extent contributed to the criminalizing of society, though the farm sector has long been subject to corruption (witness, for example, frauds with respect to the potato crop in Britain after the war and those that took place when the grain harvest was nationalized in 1953).[13]

What is clear is that in the EU something of the order of twice the American and six times the Australian percentage of gross farm receipts come from the public purse. Having paid to subsidize agriculture, consumers are hit a second time by food prices that are some 50 per cent above competitive world market prices. Even more alarming are recent estimates by an Australian and a British economist that the cost to the world economy is US$75 billion per annum – and maybe 20 per cent higher still if one takes into account the indirect consequences, such as lower productivity induced by the suppression of international competition.[14] Of this cost, over one third (US$26 billion) is borne in countries outside the EU and represents a toll on the poorest agricultural-exporting countries that can least afford it.

The subsidy bill is still rising. What will presumably check this and force a change in the system are the costs of the BSE scandal and the projected 'enlargement' of the EU to the east. The first 'enlargement' country is Poland, which will join in a very few years time and has an agricultural sector employing five to ten times the proportion of existing member countries. The last country in the queue, but in the queue nevertheless, is Turkey, which is a very large country with a fast growing population. In Turkey, twice Poland's proportion of labour is in agriculture. If countries like these are admitted to the EU, the downward pressure on food and fibre prices, already intense because of growing production within existing member states, will become unsustainable. And the upward pressure on the subsidy bill will be unsupportable.

The EU has already made some moves to restrict the bill, often by placing limits on the output of given products. Farmers have responded by amending their product mix. The system has become driven by efforts directed at collecting subsidies. Some farmers have planted cannabis and claimed the subsidy for hemp. Claims have been made for flax that was planted but never actually harvested. The widespread move into growing hemp and flax has in fact mainly been to qualify for subsidies. There are plenty of other examples: with over 10 per cent of the total budget accounted for by fraudulent claims it would be astounding if there were not.

Apart from shifting the mix of their specifically agricultural enterprises, the most conspicuous response to reductions of support for production by farmers in England has been diversification into non-agricultural or quasi-agricultural activities on the farm. This includes such things as renting out holiday cottages, offering educational tours, switching to high value organic foods, and selling produce directly to visitors. The British government has lately promised special help to farms establishing horse-riding schools. These semi-separate business activities however require additional labour and investment, and the market for any one activity in any one district tends to become saturated quickly.

THE DYNAMIC CONTEXT OF MULTIFUNCTIONALITY

The timing of the campaign for multifunctionality is impeccable. In England, as in other developed countries, rising incomes, greater mobility, mass education, more leisure and a mainly urban or suburban population that lost touch with its rural origins generations ago, have all expanded the demand to use the countryside in ways that are either not dependent on the production of crops and livestock, or only indirectly dependent on them.[15] Much of this demand is for using rural areas for tourism, spare time and vacation purposes and can be serviced by the permanent inhabitants of rural areas. It means using the countryside as parks, and theme parks. In 1998, 1253 million day visits were made to the English countryside, 35 per cent of them to go walking. Two-thirds of the English made a visit. Tourists and day visitors spent a total of 11.5 billion pounds that year, supporting an estimated 340000 jobs.

Historical and natural historical interests, which were minority tastes when the Agriculture Act was passed in 1947, are now standard leisure pursuits. Both the National Trust, which is the main society concerned with the history of the countryside, and the Royal Society for the Protection of Birds, which is the main environmental organization, have memberships bigger than all political parties combined. The National Trust has 2.7 million members or approximately one in twenty of the whole population. The memberships of the National Trust and the RSPB may overlap, but these two organizations by no means exhaust the number of comparable bodies. People who belong to organizations like this tend to be white, middle class, over 50 and educated. They constitute a powerful lobby for rural leisure activities and accordingly for the types of good that multifunctional agriculture purports to supply.

This is another area where a caution against assuming homogeneity is required. Leisure demands on the countryside constitute at least four main forms that are scarcely compatible with one another. Spatial (and auditory) separation among them is not easy in a densely-settled country; conflicts and competition for land are evident. The first of these uses consists of the 'quiet' leisure activities already mentioned – the consumption, as it were, of scenery, wildlife and the historicized landscape, including sites with literary associations. The second comprises the traditional sports of the countryside, which are often blood sports much deprecated by the suburban section of the population. The third is made up of so-called 'loud' uses of land for non-traditional, obtrusive activities such as jogging, motorbike rallies and even the launching of gaudy hot-air balloons that impair the qualities of peace and remoteness for others. The fourth, which is on such a scale in England as to deserve a category to itself, is dog walking; this renders many public places noxious, resulting in *5000* telephone complaints per day to local authorities.[16]

None of these activities is trivial any longer. Each involves considerable leisure spending and wields comparable political influence. Three of the four create significant negative externalities. Even the 'quiet' uses of the landscape are now of such an order as to generate traffic congestion and cause damage to the small spaces that are the foci of popular interest. The management problems associated with leisure uses of the countryside are accordingly vexing but a point to bear in mind is that they are already bringing about some expansion of categories of trained, specialist workers in both the private and public sectors – park rangers, administrators and the like.

Added to the pressure of these growing demands is the fact that farming occupies most of the land and tends to block non-traditional leisure uses in favour of crop and animal production. In consequence the burgeoning demands on the land are constrained by land use patterns adapted to supplying food and fibre rather than services. The problems of congestion are intensified by a planning system that severely rations the supply of land released from agriculture for other uses. In these circumstances the working of the market is severely distorted. Although some farm operators are diversifying into leisure services, free access to land for the uses of one's choice is seldom available; even public land is heavily managed to reduce damage that, in my opinion, is less a consequence of unrequitable demand than of an artificially restricted supply of land for leisure purposes. In these circumstances, the proponents of multifunctionality may seem to have a case. Switching CAP support from the production of crops and livestock to paying for a less intensive agriculture would open the way for an expansion of leisure uses.

EXPLAINING THE PARADOX OF PUBLIC OPINION

Much of the situation relating to land use in England can be accounted for in terms of a gridlock of institutionalized rent-seeking. This however does not exhaust the explanations and is less interesting than the apparent perversity of consumer attitudes. Although revealed preference shows that the bulk of the population wishes to use the countryside for leisure purposes, what they *state* they prefer and how they behave politically are at odds with this. They wish to use the land for leisure but place an option value on being able to view the countryside as it is. This, combined with archaic notions about food security, explains the lack of political challenge to the protectionist farm lobby. Few urban dwellers appreciate the differences among crops and regard almost any crop as acceptable background scenery. Degrees of intensification in land use, which have now reached the pitch of virtually exterminating many formerly common species of the fauna and flora, escape their notice as they drive the roads.

Such attitudes exert considerable sway over the planning agencies, whose philosophy is to 'preserve the countryside', meaning keep it in agricultural use. If agricultural protection – explicit or covert – were abandoned, many farmers would however almost certainly quit the industry, making it easier to switch land uses to house building, industrial development, roads and leisure uses. As it is, the sluggish release of land creates windfall gains for those farmers who can get permits to sell for development. The fact that the public and the planners actually *support* retaining so much land for agriculture, despite the social costs of tiny and expensive houses, insufficient land for industrial and hypermarket development, an inadequate and dangerous road system, and congested leisure sites, combines with the farm lobby's protectionism to frustrate change.

The paradoxical or perverse attitude to development has two sources: a predominantly urban public is not trained to see the second-order consequences of a restricted supply of land and it is adapted to a condition of artificial scarcity where demand is always just ahead of supply.

ENGLISH AGRICULTURE'S SPILLOVER EFFECTS

To judge agriculture's record in providing what we may perhaps term 'multifunctions' we need an inventory of its consequences. First, consider the role of agriculture in forming the landscape. While the English landscape remains generally attractive, the details are not always pleasing. The harmony of the landscape has been disturbed. Farm buildings are exempt from planning controls and sheds and grain stores on an industrial scale are commonly erected. Historical buildings are altered or torn down, and prehistoric remains are ploughed out. Contrary to the claims of the multifunctionality lobby, agriculture is no friend to the humanized or historicized landscape. Farmers are much less sentimental than town-dwellers about the rural landscape, which as far as most of them are concerned is a set of resource inputs. This was largely disguised when change was slower, building materials and styles were distinctively regional, and farm technologies were on a smaller scale. What were once the raw innovations of the past became with age familiar, even loved, but the anonymous erections of modern times will take far longer to attract the same tourist values.

Claims that agriculture is a guardian of the landscape are thus contrary to common observation. It is naive to expect otherwise. Whatever its peculiar technical characteristics, farming is a business carried out for profit; as Prince Kropotkin long ago said, fields are roofless factories. Farmers would indeed require to be paid to desist from operating on that assumption. The same concern with profit applies with respect to the impact of their farming on the fauna and flora. One effect is via the modification of habitats. Continual land reclamation and drainage have destroyed innumerable uncultivated pockets of land that were rich in wild species. From the 1960s to the 1990s hundreds of SSSIs (sites of special scientific interest) designated by one government agency were ploughed up, drained or otherwise destroyed by farmers, sometimes with the aid of grants dispensed by another agency.[17] Pollution from the run-off of agricultural chemicals is a serious problem. Yet another effect bears directly on species. It was after all farmers who in the 1950s deliberately introduced the horrible disease of myxomatosis in order to rid themselves of the rabbits that ate their crops. But the decimation of rabbits not only destroyed other businesses that marketed rabbit meat and skins, it had deleterious effects on the predators that depended on rabbits and the flowers that survived only because close rabbit grazing maintained grassland habitats for them. Today the intensification of rotations, cropping practices and the use of chemicals are having further consequences on farmland bird life that are nothing short of devastating. Many species have slumped in population: the total number of farmland birds has dropped by 40 per cent since the 1970s.[18] To cite a particularly poignant example, the number of Skylarks, a species that plays a prominent role in English poetry, has been reduced by 75 per cent.

If we turn to the matter of animal welfare, I will merely mention three examples of agriculture's negative effects. The conditions in which farm animals are housed and transported are often scandalous and keep the officers of the Royal Society for the Prevention of Cruelty to Animals busy. Agricultural pressure to eradicate badgers (an emblematic wild mammal) on the scientifically dubious grounds that they spread bovine tuberculosis has led to many campaigns in which the animals have been gassed. And profit-hungry farmers who fed animal carcasses back to other animals were responsible for the appallingly high incidence of BSE (Bovine Spongiform Encephalitis) among cattle and the still-rising death toll from the consequent spread of vCJD (new variant Creutzfeldt-Jakob Disease) among humans who have eaten the meat of BSE-infected cattle.

If we move on to discuss rural communities, we find that agriculture does almost nothing to sustain them. In the whole country agriculture employs fewer than two per cent of the workforce; the villages are now dispersed suburbs occupied by commuters who have urban jobs and lack agricultural connections, and the market towns no longer exist to supply the needs of the farming community. The government's response to this has been to subsidize initiatives designed to support these towns, at the expense of the general tax revenues. As to the 'farming ladder' whereby new entrants can enter agriculture, it has simply been broken. No young person without very considerable inherited capital can hope to become a farmer. The industry is sealed off from the remainder of society.

I have already referred to the role of agriculture under the CAP in distorting the land market. Associated with this is the question of access to the countryside. Agriculture, particularly intensive agriculture, blocks access to much of the land surface. The 'Right to Roam' legislation proposed by the first Blair administration is contested by just those people who claim to provide services to the public by virtue of farming the land. Moreover farmers often fail in their legal duty to maintain rights of way across their land. I have myself found public footpaths ploughed up or obstructed in several English counties.[19] Hence, although this has been only the sketchiest survey, I have no hesitation in stating that farmers have often, perhaps typically, proved poor stewards of the countryside. The first assertion of the multifunctional lobby is, therefore, wrong: agriculture is a country mile away from assuring the citizens of England a satisfactory supply of public goods. Claims to the contrary are the claims of what economists will recognize as an Olsonian distributional coalition.

CONCLUSIONS

The second multifunctional assertion that farmers should now be paid as guardians of the countryside is equally doubtful. The provision of the non-material commodities or services from the land that high-income urban populations increasingly show they wish to consume is barely compatible with intensive modern systems of producing grain and livestock. While it would of course be desirable for the EU to remove crop and livestock subsidies, replacing the current system by paying farmers for deliberately creating what are claimed to be the positive externalities of commodity production would be a second-best solution. Farmers are businessmen who have shown themselves single-minded in employing the land resource for the purpose of physical production. When it has served their interests they have damaged rather than enhanced other values of the land. It would be ironic if the same operators were now to be paid to undo the harm they have done. Nor are they equipped by virtue of education and training to carry out such a task. What urban and suburban populations require from the countryside is its management as playground, park, theme park and nature reserve, with as much access as possible for all. Those functions require full-time specialist managers, environmentalists and park rangers whose education has been directed to this end.

It should be apparent that encouraging the deliberate creation of externalities, turning them into policy goals, is likely to bring some into conflict with others. This can already be seen in the contradictory policies of agencies responsible for aspects of agriculture and rural life, such as MAFF. For instance the interests of the environment are not necessarily served, and may actually be damaged, by the maintenance or increase of rural employment and development that is one of MAFF's aims.[20] It is equally obvious that non-market means of deciding which goals to promote are open to abuse by rent-seekers.

The public accepts the parameters as it finds them, while bitterly contesting individual decisions. It has long done so. When Frank Fox, wrote *Our English Land Muddle: An Australian View* in 1913 he remarked that English experts wrote about the issues sincerely but always according to 'the postulate ... that we must not walk out of the existing maze [of traditions and institutions]'.[21] This maze frustrates analysis of land use matters. The public does not question, notice or understand the social inefficiencies resulting from present land use arrangements. A massive increase in the availability of land, consequent on removing agricultural support, might change its attitudes. People would adjust to a new equilibrium and come to recognize it as superior. Without the 'shock' of such a change, upbringing and rural propaganda conspire not merely to reinforce the present allocation of land but to blind consumers to their own interests. I am reminded of a parallel in a quite different institutional context, Timur Kuran's observation that the character of public discourse under Islam prevents individuals from questioning or even noticing social inefficiencies.[22]

The nebulousness of multifunctionality and the ease with which it can be stretched to cover any side effect of agricultural activity means that the Australian Ministry of Agriculture website is correct in describing it as 'clearly a "stalking horse" [which is to say, an excuse] for protection'.[23] We can see in the English case that agriculture explicitly fails to create the positive externalities claimed by the multifunctional lobby: quite the contrary. And we can see that the existing, production-oriented farming industry is far from ideally staffed to manage the countryside as parkland, supplying those services that the modern public wishes to consume.

NOTES

1. Nathan Rosenberg, *Perspectives on Technology* (Cambridge: Cambridge University Press, 1976), especially chapter 4, 'Problems in the Economist's Conceptualization of Technological Innovation' and for a comment on agriculture, p. 78.
2. Mancur Olson, *The Rise and Decline of Nations* (New Haven: Yale University Press, 1982). For a summary see p. 74, 'Implications'.
3. *Australian Financial Review*, 27 August 1999.
4. See the website under that title.
5. See the website of MAFF. Maff was absorbed into the new Department of Environment, Food and Rural Affairs (DEFRA) after the election in 2001.
6. Gavin McCrone, *The Economics of Subsidising Agriculture* (London: Allen and Unwin, 1962).
7. John Bowers and Paul Cheshire, *Agriculture, the Countryside and Land Use: An Economic Critique* (London: Methuen, 1983).
8. The economic history of agriculture that follows may be found in any standard source.
9. Tyler Cowen, *In Praise of Commercial Culture* (Cambridge, Mass.: Harvard University Press, 1998).
10. A valuable starting point is Simon Holloway, *The Historical Atlas of Breeding Birds in Britain and Ireland: 1875-1900* (London: T. and A.D. Poyser, 1996).
11. E.L. Jones, *The Development of English Agriculture, 1815-73* (London: Macmillan, 1968).
12. Geoff Raby, 'Reforming Agricultural Trade', in Harry Oldersma (ed.), *From Havana to Seattle and Beyond: The Quest for Free Trade and Free Markets* (The Hague: Sdu Publishers, 2000), p. 132.
13. Details of frauds in the European Union are regularly reported in the British and Australian press, often drawing on data from the EU's own auditing body. As a schoolboy I had a holiday job helping with an investigation into the accounts of a grain silo for the 1953 harvest, though eventually the British government wrote off the whole of the losses.
14. *Financial Times*, 25 June 2000.
15. P.J. Dillon and E.L. Jones, 'Environmental Consumerism in the United Kingdom: Some Reflections on Managerial Responses and Educational Needs', *European Journal of Agricultural Education and Extension*, **3** (2), 1996, 107-18. See also the website of the Countryside Agency.
16. *Financial Times*, 19 August 2000.
17. Dillon and Jones, loc. cit.
18. *Financial Times*, 10 August 2000.
19. A recent book on a walk from north to south down the length of England disposes of this matter very early, concluding that, 'clearly, the depiction of a public right of way on a map was no indication that the route was either open to the public or technically a "way"'. Nicholas Crane, *Two Degrees West: An English Journey* (London: Penguin, 2000), p. 12. The fact that it is agriculture rather than walkers which is damaging the countryside is made abundantly clear on p. 278. See also the well-informed indictment of farmers and landowners in this respect in John Hillaby, *Journey Home* (London: Paladin, 1983).
20. MAFF, *England Rural Development Plan 2000-2006* and regional policy leaflets.
21. Frank Fox, *Our English Land Muddle: An Australian View* (London: Thomas Nelson, n.d. [1913]), p. 9.
22. Timur Kuran, 'Islam and Underdevelopment: An Old Puzzle Revisited', *Journal of Institutional and Theoretical Economics*, **153**, 1997, 41-71.
23. See the website of the Australian Ministry of Agriculture.

6.   The costs of language diversity

INTRODUCTION

Efforts to promote particular languages and hamper others are being made today by a number of national authorities and cultural producers. The aim of these moves is mainly to counter the influence of English, despite or rather because of the fact that people in almost every country are selecting it as the world's *lingua franca*. The grounds for resisting the spread of English include the threat that it is thought to pose to other cultures and national identities. Some of the individuals engaged in these campaigns may genuinely fear such a threat. Academic specialists in linguistics do tend to believe in a slightly outdated cultural relativism that makes all languages equal and treats the death of any single one of them as a tragedy. But much of the motive and the reason some governments take the issue seriously is Protectionist, as the extremely rhetorical nature of many pronouncements unintentionally reveals.[1]

The pronouncements sound like any others designed to protect special interests and, where they differ, do so only in the vehemence of the language used. They are inspired by the rents that accrue from choosing one language rather than another for international purposes now that the world economy is steadily integrating. This motive may not be admitted or even understood by the protagonists of minority languages, who tend to take as axiomatic the infinite value of each language and culture (they conflate the two). Media discussion of globalization has persuaded many non-economists that international economic integration is occurring faster and on a much wider scale than it really is, and this has lent urgency to their Protectionist outbursts. Much of the debate is couched in emotive, cultural terms without the least reference to the costs and benefits of preserving languages versus selecting a *lingua franca* for global use.

There is, certainly, much structural change underway in the world. One of the major consequences is an increase in the importance of the service sector relative to manufacturing. Service products are, so to speak, heavier users of language. Where this fact most impinges on the world economy is through the export trade in services, especially creative services. This brings other people's cultural products, or what is described as the global culture, to one's own doorstep and inside the house. In reality much of 'world culture' is produced by multicultural teams, notably by those working in Silicon Valley, Seattle and Hollywood, but people who feel anxious about it seldom admit the fact. They treat world culture as American, since it is the United States that is best at integrating everybody's ideas and marketing them globally. Local cultural producers feel threatened and nationalists are affronted. In the resultant disputes about cultural change, language issues loom large.

Economists have had surprisingly little to say about language protectionism, despite their professional awareness of the cost of impediments to free trade. In 1996 François Grin estimated that there were scarcely more than 100 papers on the economics of language proper.[2] Of those, a high proportion was inspired by Canadian or Quebecois issues. These issues are regional ones but do point up some common problems. The cost of the enforced use of French by Quebec's 'Commission to Protect the French Language' has been estimated at no more than 0.5 per cent of GDP.[3] Yet, since even 0.1 per cent of GDP would buy a number of schools or hospitals, the figure is not as insignificant as it may appear. The obligatory use of French also entails a loss of personal freedom and it is not clear that the cost of this has been, or even can be, properly accounted for. There are nevertheless proxies that indicate its seriousness: half-a-million inhabitants have left during the past 30 years and between 1976 and 1981, 100 head offices of English-speaking companies relocated from Quebec.

Almost none of the language economics papers surveyed by Grin touches on global matters. Some of those I have looked at present formal models and, as is usual with such an approach, reach logical conclusions that nevertheless (and necessarily) depend on various restrictive assumptions made in order to pursue an argument or facilitate calculations. They are hard to generalize. If an approach to the subject is to have any chance of being read by the actual decision-makers, we need to respond in their own terms to the less technical pronouncements of specialists in linguistics, bureaucrats, politicians and journalists. These are the people whose views matter, because they influence language policy and are responsible for spending resources on it.

This chapter presents some specific material exposing the extent of the moves to defend or expand language diversity. The underlying assumption here is that the primary purpose of language is to transmit information. I am unpersuaded by arguments from literary intellectuals that languages convey far more than this. Their assertion is often a semantic trick, redefining information about social experiences and emotional states as something else (more 'spiritual') than mere knowledge. The accompanying assertion that great literature and utterly different ways of thinking are lost if minority languages die seems little more than a debating point. If someone claims that there are untranslatable merits to some minor language, by definition the rest of us cannot know whether this is true and must count it of no practical importance.

Moreover, I am advocating only benign neglect of minority and dead languages, not a prohibition on access to them by adults. There is nothing to stop people continuing to use, alongside a common language, whatever other language or dialect they wish, just as I was taught at school the English of Shakespeare and the King James Bible, as well as the French of Racine and Molière. There is nothing wrong with diversity for cultural uses. But the absence of a common tongue simply raises the cost of communicating – it raises transaction costs. Sometimes the results are tragic, as when communications failures are implicated in air crashes or people cannot get proper medical attention.

THE COSTS OF LANGUAGE DIVERSITY

A graphic illustration of the transaction costs implicit in language diversity comes from Papua New Guinea, where 760 languages are spoken. In a 1970 court case, the defendant had to work through interpreters of seven languages to enter his plea. The judge dismissed the case rather than go to trial. Would you want a murderer to go free because it was linguistically too expensive to investigate his case?

The cost of translating technical works into the languages of somewhere like PNG could not be borne. Whereas standard languages are 'open' to new influences and ideas, minor languages are 'closed', just as dialects are. Their vocabularies of only a few thousand words are swamped when faced with incorporating the huge number of additional terms needed to run a modern economy. It is irrational to devote scarce resources to translating textbooks into every local tongue, as language diversifiers sometimes demand. Even countries where an appropriate vocabulary has been created find it easier to keep pace with the advance of knowledge by adopting English-language textbooks for graduate courses, a practice extended in Scandinavian countries to Honours and even undergraduate levels.

The greatest gain for the greatest number of people would come from settling on a common language. The practicalities mean that English most efficiently meets that purpose. It has already become the language of choice for many international exchanges and its further adoption should not be impeded. You may think that as a native English speaker I am biased but the case does not depend on the accident of my own birth. Paradoxically, native speakers of English, or rather native *writers* of English, have something to lose from such a choice. English is escaping into the world and ceasing to reflect the interests of native speakers as accurately and beautifully as once it did. World Standard English (WSE) is primarily an American English and those of us who began by using British English sometimes find it cumbersome. Yet at its best American English is livelier and more forceful than British English. WSE is not to be discouraged.

Professional linguists will disagree with this position. They are disposed to lament the current decline in the number of languages and recommend trying to reverse this trend. But it does not follow that adopting a common language necessitates the death of others: to repeat, I do not recommend forbidding the use of other languages. What I would like to see is the emergence of a single shared language and an end to the spending of resources on preserving languages that people are voluntarily choosing not to speak, let alone on reviving dead languages.

No doubt the disappearance of languages is scientifically deplorable if they vanish before they have been fully recorded. Nevertheless it is not self-evident (though linguists assert this) that the economic, social and political losses are greater than the gains. Efforts to revive dead languages, like Cornish (a regional British language), and foist them on children too young to have a choice, are misplaced. These efforts are potentially divisive, and certainly they are self-serving on the part of the cultural producers who advocate them. Account is seldom taken of who will really bear the costs.

Although it is a secondary matter which language should be shared, the case for encouraging the spread of English is strongest. Because English is already so widely spoken, the network externalities are plain. Scarce educational resources should accordingly be devoted to teaching English to the largest possible number of people. The English taught should be WSE, in order to reduce existing barriers and minimize the emergence of fresh obstacles constituted by divergent 'New Englishes'.

Similar arguments apply to dialects and accents. Like multiple languages, dialects and regional accents impede the exchange of information. Dialects and accents are, after all, debris from earlier periods when labour mobility was low. As John Honey has wisely pointed out, they are the heritage of poverty and enforced residence in small localities, yet they are strongly defended by many people who, given their own education, mobility and use of Standard English, should know better than to put cultural happenstance and whimsicality above clear communication.[4] In the real world, employing regional accents and dialects in television programmes restricts the market, just as clinging to Imperial measures in British industries attempting to export to countries that use metric has done. British television has a smaller share of the German market than Australian television since foreigners find many British regional accents hard to understand, if not incomprehensible. Australian television, made with exports in mind, deliberately casts actors who speak a 'general' or 'educated' Australian that English-speaking foreigners can better understand. On the other hand, a 1998 Scottish film had to be fully subtitled for American audiences.

The wife of a Japanese executive in Britain caused some offence when she observed that the trouble is 'the poor people don't speak English' but she was not wrong about impenetrable local accents or the failure of schools to enhance the social and geographical mobility of their pupils by teaching standard English. Linguistic tribalism is surely part of the reason why the labour market in England works so sluggishly: only 0.25 per cent of the unemployed move to another region each year in search of work (*Financial Times*, 17 Dec. 2000). Local and national idioms seem to be used, often unthinkingly, to signify membership of a sort of club. The point about clubs is that they exclude non-members. Mikie Kiyoi, an executive of the International Energy Agency, wrote in the *International Herald Tribune* (3 Nov. 1995) under the heading, 'Dear English Speakers: Please Drop the Dialects',

> We non-natives are desperately learning English ... Our English proficiency is tangible evidence of our achievement of will, not an accident of birth. Dear Anglo-Americans, please show us you are also taking pains to make yourselves understood in an international setting.

She is referring to a real problem, not one created by her own linguistic origins. But with respect to how people speak, her plea falls on deaf ears. In some English-speaking countries there are bodies concerned with improving the quality of English, but as far as I can tell their attention is concentrated on the way documents are written. Care and maintenance are of course sadly needed in that respect. Those who deride any effort to speak and write grammatically, and there are plenty of them, pour scorn on prescriptive grammarians as stick-in-the-muds who do not realize that languages are constantly changing and wish to freeze a set of arbitrary Victorian standards. But this derision is misdirected. The fact that languages are always in flux is a commonplace and prescriptivists are just the people who enjoy tracing the changes.

Their objection is to ignorant or unnecessary changes and grammatical infelicities that hamper intelligibility. The deriders miss the point: a standard can be arbitrary and still be useful, like a rule about which side of the road to drive on. Intelligibility is the goal, though this need not mean dull or depauperate writing. (As Hemingway said, it does not matter if a word is not in the reader's vocabulary at the start of a paragraph if it is by the end.) Public documents and notices do however need to be as plain as possible; if they are not, the sufferers are the disadvantaged and less literate. The matter can be urgent when it comes to safety notices and labels on medicine bottles.

In a similar fashion to written English there are losses, occasionally dangers, if spoken English is hard to understand. Mikie Kiyoi is, however, unlikely to find much sympathy in this respect. It has become politically incorrect to demand adherence to a common standard of speech, except perhaps when reading books to be taped for the blind. Regional accents have become acceptable on the BBC World Service and I have heard the news read in a Scottish accent which, even as a native speaker of English, I found so opaque that I missed part of it. (Ironically the same item was later reported on a German English-language service, read by a German, and every syllable could be followed).

The point needs to be reiterated that dialects and accents, even languages, evolved in a world of poverty, with far less labour mobility than today. They are the residue that was left by segmented markets. A modern global market is working to wash them away, though it is easy to exaggerate how successful this process really has been as yet. Even today communities unthinkingly reproduce localisms for essentially tribal reasons, imposing a cost on children, strangers and foreigners. For official agencies and educational systems to impose such costs is inexcusable. We should ask the lawyers' question, '*cui bono?*' – who benefits? The answer will turn out to be bureaucrats, politicians, and cultural producers who fear competition in a larger market. Quaintness and variety in language are amusing for native speakers but intelligibility for all trumps them every time.

LANGUAGE COMPETITION

We all tend to suffer from 'assumption drag'. Typically we assume that the world has changed less than it has. Despite the customary exaggeration of international economic integration ('globalization'), many people find it hard to recognize the significance of new sectors of the economy and the relative decline of older, more familiar sectors. It is especially hard to grasp how much the service or knowledge-based sectors of advanced economies have already grown. These sectors place a premium on linguistic skill and are at an advantage if they employ a world language, because that offers a big market.

The direct importance of language as an input is in any case growing with the expansion of what are termed the 'creative' industries like film-making, composing music or writing software. In the British case, these industries earn as much income in total as physical commodities do. More information on this matter and on the related growth of the knowledge-based industries, together with the international market for higher education, appears in Chapter 10. To anticipate, we may note here that 97 million people are expected to be enrolled in higher education worldwide in a decade's time, up from 48 million a decade ago. Higher education is already the USA's fifth largest service sector export. Britain receives a large inflow of foreign students and also specializes in teaching English to foreign students, attracting over half of the total number who travel to other countries for that purpose and earning about US$1.5 billion per annum by so doing. Japan, France and Germany are also stepping up their efforts to attract foreign students. One of the aims of each country is to spread its influence and create overseas markets for its own products, especially cultural items like books, films, tapes, cassettes and so forth. With a certain amount of hesitation, not to mention irony, each of these countries will almost certainly offer some instruction in English.

LANGUAGE PROTECTIONISM: THE EXAMPLE OF FRENCH

Industries that depend on the creative use of language by producers and on access to large numbers of international customers are thus growing in importance. Hence it is not surprising to note the intensity of the struggle for the rents that come from language choice. Many cultural producers in non-English speaking countries do work in English but others among them resist this and attempt to lock potential customers into their own language. I shall use French as the classic example of the claims and stratagems involved.

The late Mancur Olson insisted that there was no limit, none whatsoever, to how much the members of special interest groups will try to grasp of society's common output.[5] This always seemed to me too dramatic, but the claims advanced on behalf of French bear it out. These claims are often coupled with, or come in the form of attacks on, the use of English, besides defences of language variety for its own sake. The attacks go far beyond the usual chauvinism, present in many countries and notoriously expressed for Russian by Lenin, which tries to block the use of loan words from other languages. The French claims are far broader. At the Peace Conference in Paris in 1946 France declared that the proceedings should all be in French because it was *the* international language. The Prime Minister of England replied that French is the language of the menu.

The French did not give up: at a conference in Venice in 1984 their delegates replied to the suggestion of reviving Latin as the second language of Europe with the claim that French is the ideal towards which Latin had always been tending! I have even heard a representative of the Alliance Française argue that other languages are degenerations from the French structure of subject, verb, complement. And recently the President of France stated that cultural and linguistic uniformity (he obviously equates the two) would be 'a major risk for humanity'.

A similarly exaggerated claim was made by Boutros Boutros-Ghali, former Secretary-General of the United Nations and now Secretary-General of the Francophone Agency, in extolling the movement to entrench the use of French worldwide. He said, 'it should become a way of defending cultural diversity

... if everybody ... speaks the same language ... we risk having a global fascist-type regime'. It would surely be easier to argue that the language interventionists and cultural protectionists are the authoritarians. A Sorbonne Professor called Etiemble actually wrote that, 'to violate [the French language] is a crime. Persons were shot during the war for treason. They should be punished for degrading the language.'

France spends almost US$1 billion per year on spreading French civilization and language. It is doubtful whether the cultural protectionists could wield so much influence by means of their odd mixture of xenophobia and sentimental appeals to 'civilization' and national identity if they did not enlist economic interest too. A note of indignation has entered in because there is widely thought to have been a 'globalization shock' bringing an unprecedented expansion in the distribution of English-language cultural products.

Despite French government subsidies to the producers of films in French and the 'anti-capitalist' hostility of many European intellectuals to any cultural work that makes a profit, there is in continental Europe a sizeable market for Hollywood films and English-language books. Little credit is given to the positive attributes of content and style, and maybe superior marketing abilities, that account for much of Hollywood's success. That success perhaps depends less on language than may be thought. It had already acquired a big share of the world market in the days of *silent* movies.

Commercial temptation means that the French themselves violate the precepts of linguistic protectionism. One in every five pages on the Internet under the designation '.fr' and linked to a secure server is in English. That is necessary to reach the market but did not prevent two companies and an American university being taken to court in France for having websites written solely in English. The private sector is much more pragmatic than the authorities would like. Alstrom, the Anglo-French electrical engineering group, took just six months to decide that its experiment at putting all its documents in both French and English was too costly. It standardized on English as the working language, even though the company headquarters is in Paris and only a minority of employees is British. Perhaps more to the point almost one-third of its top 300 managers are neither British nor French, but come from 11 other countries. In Japan, where Renault has taken over Nissan, the CEO (a Spaniard) has made English the company's common written and spoken language of communication.

LANGUAGE PROTECTIONISM WORLDWIDE

Although there is no doubt that France is a prime source of cultural protectionism and gives vent to just the type of self-interest that Olson predicted, it is not alone in resisting the spread of English. Linguistic protectionism is a far wider phenomenon. This is easily shown. For example, Malaysian academics and intellectuals protested in March 2000 about satellite television broadcasts from Hong Kong, China and India on the grounds that these could have 'sinister' cultural effects. In Ireland, the former President, Eammon de Valera, once said, 'without a language, without a country'. But the rejoinder of R.C. McCormick, who had been obliged to learn Irish at school, was, 'what romantic and dangerous nonsense'.

The propensity of academic linguists to promote language diversity is aimed more widely than that of politicians like de Valera, who want to make everyone learn a particular 'national' language for ethnic or political reasons. Language diversity proper must mean encouragement to learn any language other than one's own, since the fashionable view is that all languages are presumed to be equal. The influential linguist, David Crystal, claims that, 'if everybody speaks English we all have a great time understanding each other but our identities go down [sic] the melting pot', and 'suffice to say we should all learn a language that isn't English out of a sense of principle'. He does not however explain what the principle is or how learning a different language could bolster anyone's sense of his or her current identity.

Culture does not depend on language. There is no reason to think that, say, the internationally-known children's writer, Hans Christian Andersen, would cease to be Danish even if the speaking of Danish were given up in favour of English, as was seriously suggested in the 1970s. The British, Americans and Australians differ culturally while speaking the same language. More native English speakers could probably understand a Kenyan speaking the English taught in schools there than they could someone from Carlisle, on the border with Scotland, but they are likely to identify with the latter for cultural reasons.

No one's culture is threatened by learning to speak English – there is an eloquent testimony to this in his autobiography by Richard Rodriguez, a member of a Spanish-speaking family growing up in California. Rodriguez resisted his family's wish to keep him speaking Spanish because he sensed that mastering English would give him access to a wider world.[6] To think that this threatened his 'culture' is to confuse form with function. I can quote the cognitive psychologist, John R. Anderson, to this effect: 'the apparent dependence of thought on language may be an illusion that derives from the fact that it is hard to obtain evidence of thought without using language'.[7] Conflict over language between ethno-linguistic groups is irrational when languages, like nations, have been handed down neither by some supernatural deity nor by biology, but are merely contingent, historical artifacts. On the other hand the conflict over language by cultural producers and the politicians who speak for them can be rational because there are large economic rents at stake.

Attempts to abolish free choice are still being made in country after country. Here are five well dispersed examples. The Mayor of Moscow campaigned to persuade Muscovites to switch back from Coca Cola and hamburgers to kvass and blinis and banned foreign, especially English, terms in shops because they displace 'authentic' Russian culture. Shades, once more, of Lenin! Vietnam forcibly removed foreign company names from buildings and billboards with the stated aim of controlling 'social evils' and preserving the Vietnamese language. The Algerian government, seeking to distance itself from the French-speaking governing class, decreed Arabic to be the official language – which upset not only French speakers but speakers of Berber as well. In South Korea, although Kim Dae Jung had praised Microsoft for offering to invest US$20 million in a Korean word processing firm, there were protests because a condition was giving up Han'gul. A public campaign succeeded in 'rescuing' the firm from either closure or Microsoft. Turning lastly to India, the Bombay government of Bal Thackeray, an open admirer of Adolf Hitler, forbade television advertisements with English accents or tones.

Efforts are being made in many places to reverse the shrinkage of minor languages, as well as to resurrect dead ones. In England, Cornish (the last speaker of which died in 1777), has been revived as a school-leaving examination subject. In South Australia, Kaurna, an aboriginal language whose last speaker died in the 1920s, is being revived as a university course. The State Department of Education wishes this language to be taught in kindergartens, primary schools, and secondary schools by aboriginal teachers, who would first have to learn it. Yet Kaurna has no literature. Cornish has only a tiny literature, mostly mystery plays, some of which turn out to be literal translations from the English. The option of resurrecting languages like these that are no longer spoken by anyone exposes the weakness of 'Green Linguistics' analogies between languages and species: languages can be revived and genuinely extinct species as yet cannot.

UNESCO and the UN support a 'Language Rights' Movement, which smacks of the cultural relativism now being challenged in leading American academic circles. There is a UNESCO Clearing House for Endangered Languages in Tokyo and the EU has an Office of Lesser-used Languages in Dublin. As McCormick commented on the obligatory teaching of Irish in schools in Southern Ireland, 'like most attempts to create a culture by imposing a language, it was a complete waste of time and money ... English is the world language and most foreigners rightly spend a lot of time and money learning it, not learning a dead language.'

IMPLICATIONS OF LANGUAGE DIVERSITY

These examples, which are not uncharacteristic of supplier-driven movements for linguistic diversity, have serious implications. I make three assumptions. One is that some languages have older, larger literatures and contain larger and more technical vocabularies than others; the next is that English is the one with the largest single vocabulary among the larger languages (three times the size of French or German) and houses the largest single stock of knowledge in the world; the last is that school children have only finite time, energy and in most cases application when it comes to learning languages. While I do not advocate forbidding any *adult* to make whatever private investment in learning languages he or she chooses, it is unreasonable to teach minority languages, let alone dead ones, to children. They are likely to be diverted from learning or improving their command of major languages that offer far more expansive views of human experience. Among the major languages, English currently reigns supreme and the network externalities that arise from this mean that its use should be encouraged.

There are some sad examples of the costs of diversity. The systems of health and disease control are close to breaking point in New York because many immigrants have little English, are no longer required or encouraged to learn it, and the system cannot afford translators for the hundreds of languages that they have imported with them. Even more horrifying is the fact that econometric studies have found linguistic diversity to be the main factor impeding the choice of satisfactory development policies in Africa.[8] It is positively correlated with the black market premium, electrical system losses, and the percentage of roads unpaved. It is negatively correlated with school attainment, financial depth and the number of telephones per worker. The mechanism responsible for this is that those who get political power in African countries favour their own language groups and do not build unified states.

Compared with health and development costs, the direct costs of translating, campaigning for and subsidizing national languages must be minor, but are still burdensome, especially in the European Union. Germany has closed Goethe institutes around the world and reopened them in Eastern Europe, where it hopes to establish a hyper-colony. In a world where most international business is conducted in English, and more scientific, technical and cultural productions are in English than in German, this can only tend to reinforce the isolation of Eastern Europe brought about by years of Nazi and Communist domination. Translating into minor languages in international or even national agencies is also a costly use of funds, though it is often insisted on for the sake of making purely political points. This is the case in the Welsh Assembly, where there is simultaneous translation of sessions into Welsh and English for all 60 members, and translation of all Assembly documents, even though everyone present speaks English. Twenty-five per cent of the staff and budget of the WTO are employed for translating: disputes where the participants stipulate 'no English' take far longer to resolve than those where English is used.

The European Union spends a fortune on translation but is having to find ways to limit the range of cross-translations because 'enlargement' will bring in new countries and hence additional languages from Eastern Europe. One thousand seven hundred staff of the EU are translators, producing over one million pages of text every year: if there was no call for this the savings would be enormous. Ironically, the translations are not always successful. A legal suit affecting billions of pounds sterling in British customs duty that came before the European Court of Justice hinged on the meaning of the word 'them' in French and English. Lawyers' fees in British courts had already cost one million pounds without the matter having been resolved.

The EU has a media desk for every member country (and two for Belgium, one of them French, the other Flemish). Between 1996–2000 it spent US$333 million to promote film production. Despite the subsidies and quotas, as well as the non-tariff protection afforded by having its own technical systems, the EU still has an audio-visual trade deficit of $6 billion per year. Europe's best writers, directors, actors and production specialists still migrate to Hollywood: over 100 worked on the film *Titanic*.

The biggest cost of all from promoting language diversity is the hampering of children and young people who might otherwise acquire fluent English, and therefore access to its incomparable store of humanity's knowledge. No one should keep them from that bounty.

BENEFITS OF A SHARED LANGUAGE

The benefits of a *lingua franca* are the converse of the costs. Transaction costs are reduced, global productivity rises, and astonishing cultural syntheses become possible. The advantages of a common standard are obvious, like the advantages of driving on the same side of the road. The issue that is fought over then becomes which the standard language should be. The market, which since no one actually owns languages is another name for free choice, has already made its decision. The choice of languages by schoolchildren in the EU is one test. Eighty-eight per cent study English as a foreign language, 32 per cent study French, and only 18 per cent study German. English is an economic, not a military language, and does not depend for its prevalence on the fact that the United States is a superpower. Academic conferences in Europe are almost invariably in English now, whereas ten years ago they were in French and German as well.

CONCLUSION

Countries that use English have an advantage, as is evident with respect to the diffusion of technology. Furthermore, the United States is said to be able to cope so well with labour shortages because English is used among skilled workers worldwide and a constant stream of the brightest of them is attracted to America. Indian IT engineers, whom leading developed countries are so eagerly trying to attract, are a case in point.

Countries that want to keep up with the pace of technological and structural change increasingly recognize the importance of English-language instruction and are avoiding what we may call the 'French way' of linguistic resistance. This is evident in East Asia. Singapore, which consistently produces the best English speakers among the many Asian students I have taught, is well aware of the competitive advantage English confers. It is trying to combat the rise of 'Singlish' (a local patois heavily influenced by Chinese) because it senses that this is a threat to its global competitiveness. In South Korea, a book was published two years ago entitled *The National Language vs. the International Language* in which the author predicted that Korean would eventually be replaced by English. There were the usual outraged protests by nationalists, yet 63 per cent of respondents to an on-line survey conducted by a leading newspaper favoured making English the official second language. In Japan a government report in January 2000 proposed a national debate about making English the official second language and meanwhile recommended that all official documents be published in English and all government websites be bilingual.

I do not know that English will be adopted officially in either Japan or South Korea but the market is already putting a high premium on it in the private sector. The spontaneous coordination involved is all to the good. Languages are codes and employing more than one code is an extra cost. This does not imply that any meaningful loss of identity need be involved in acquiring a second language. However inconvenient it may be to political nationalists, to cultural producers who wish to preserve local monopolies, or to language purists, it *is* possible to hold more than one allegiance at the same time, for instance to country, church, international organization – and language. In the modern world, educated people increasingly retain their local affinities alongside their membership of the international 'invisible colleges' that nowadays communicate chiefly in English.

What are objectionable and costly are French-style efforts to interfere with the use of English. Exclusion from learning and using English marginalizes people now that approximately one-quarter of the world's population is coming together to speak it. A Black South African writer has said that, because it widens his audience, 'English is therefore tied up with the Black man's efforts to liberate himself'.

It is very often said that a common language does not protect against conflict. The instances cited are struggles between co-linguists like those in Ireland and the Former Yugoslavia. This does not show that a common language is not *some* protection: think of all the countries with a single language that have *not* fallen into civil war. More convincingly, the existence of a common language surely helps the healing process. Both England and the United States fought bitter civil wars but both recovered and became single communities again in a way that is difficult to imagine had the contestants spoken different languages.

NOTES

1. Some of the examples and quotations in this chapter, not otherwise referenced, are drawn from Eric L. Jones, 'The Case for a Shared World Language', in Mark Casson and Andrew Godley (eds), *Cultural Factors in Economic Growth* (Berlin: Springer, 2000), pp. 210–35. Additional sources include the continual stream of reports on language issues in *The Economist, Financial Times* and *The Australian*. Many of the statements quoted in the press about language protectionism, the threat to other languages from English or the intrusion of English words and so forth are fungible and it scarcely matters which one is employed. There will be another along in a minute. The standard view among observers is that Global or World Standard English will prevail but the reality is that its reach is less extensive, and its 'victory' less assured, than most commentators suggest. For a sceptical view of the future monopoly of English in global discourse, see Barbara Wallraff, 'What Global Language?', *Atlantic Monthly*, November 2000, 52–66.
2. François Grin, 'The Economics of Language: Survey, Assessment, and Prospects', *International Journal of the Sociology of Language*, **121**, 1996, 18.
3. Detailed sources are cited in Jones, loc. cit.
4. John Honey, *Language is Power: The Story of Standard English and its Enemies* (London: Faber and Faber, 1997).
5. Mancur Olson, *The Rise and Decline of Nations* (New Haven: Yale University Press, 1982), especially p. 74, 'Implications'.
6. Richard Rodriguez, *Hunger of Memory* (Boston: David R. Godine, 1981). For a more direct rejection of cultural protectionism, see Mario Vargas Llosa, 'The Culture of Liberty', *Foreign Policy*, January–February 2001, also available at www.foreignpolicy.com
7. J.R. Anderson, *Cognitive Psychology and its Implications* (San Francisco: Freeman, 1980), p. 384.
8. W. Easterly and R. Levine, 'Africa's Growth Tragedy: Policies and Ethnic Divisions', *Quarterly Journal of Economics*, November 1997, 1203–50.

PART III

East Asian development

7. The ultimate significance of East Asian development

> I had always thought of Europe and America as being, so to speak, the only properly-furnished rooms in a house whose other sections were either ruined or unfinished. Now it was graphically demonstrated that in a different wing, at the end of a maze of dark halls, there had always been another brightly-lit room with furnishings as comfortable as ours. It was hard to have to admit that these furnishings were perhaps in a more consistent taste and had certainly been kept in good condition for a much longer time. (Graham Peck, *Through China's Wall*, 1945)

ORIGINS OF GROWTH IN EUROPE AND ASIA

The great economic event of the past generation, the rise of East Asia, directs attention to the fact that economic growth has had more than one beginning. Economic growth was for a long time thought to have had a unique origin, stylized as an abrupt industrial breakthrough in eighteenth-century Britain. This is still the dominant opinion and it remains easier to repeat it than to get sceptical views into print. Nevertheless, the uniqueness, abruptness and industrial complexion of this start to growth are no longer asserted by every authority. Mokyr even urges in a major book published in 1990 that the crucial changes in the eighteenth century did not amount to a macro-economic event at all but instead to a cluster of technological breakthroughs that turned out to be pregnant for the future.[1] Furthermore, the language now employed by some defenders of the unique industrial revolution or take-off view suggests that they are a little rattled.[2]

They should be rattled. While transforming in scale, manufacturing complexion, and the extent of the shift along the cline from Smithian to Schumpeterian growth, the industrial revolution was not history's unique start to growth.[3] The approach typically exaggerates the pace of change even in Britain, besides missing the opportunity to incorporate any general explanation of earlier and non-Western cases of growth or waves of technical change. While agreeing with Colin McEvedy that the concept of the industrial revolution has 'done a lot of practical harm', the reason is not that it demands unreasonably rapid change.[4] Rather, the notion truncates history, spurns other examples of growth, confounds growth and industrialization, and obscures the underlying process with purely British features. East Asia shows that growth has occurred at a variety of times and places, occasionally very fast indeed. Of course it was not expected in East Asia by Western observers of the nineteenth century and the first half of the twentieth, who often arrived at times of distress, were not familiar with the region's economic history, and in any case thought poorly of the values of Confucianism. Only after growth had become very apparent did the regional culture begin to be extolled as a good nursemaid for it. However the parent was always thought to be in the West: East Asian growth was passed off as a 'follower' process, taking place in a culture so distinctive that it held little by way of implication for the remainder of the world.

What is needed in order to show that this impression is misleading and too dismal is a fresh perspective rather than another detailed, technical investigation. The key issue is perception. We need to rearrange the elements of what is already known about the *very* long-term economic history of East Asia in relation to that of Europe and elsewhere in the world. We also need to recognize that cultures, however strong they may seem when viewed in cross-section and despite being transmitted in a path-dependent fashion, are human constructs. They only persist in their current forms when there is no compelling incentive for them to change. They are historical, not immutable.[5] On a re-shaking of the kaleidoscope the import of East Asian economic success will prove not to be what it seems. East Asia is not the world's most splendidly endowed cul-de-sac, devoid of promise for other regions, with a vigorous Confucianism exposing their cultures as irredeemably ineffectual.

There tends to be an asymmetry in discussions of the history of growth and development. Rather long periods of history usually receive some mention in the literature, with no surprise expressed if they seem to reveal little growth, yet limited growth or failures of growth during a mere decade or two of the immediate past are taken as evidence of a permanent inability to achieve it. This is sometimes attributed to the 'development of under-development' by a malign West, though it might be more in accord with the evidence to point to the failures of nation-building, endemic corruption, and ineffective policies, besides rank political instability and infamous domestic tyrannies in other parts of the world. Otherwise, slow progress in West Asia or Africa is attributed – in the East Asian mirror – to the lack of the necessary values and will. A twist to this is the praise bestowed by some writers on certain Third World countries precisely because they appear not to possess capitalist values like Europe or America, and nowadays East Asia too.

If, as in a thought experiment, we compare longer segments of both past and future time, as well as consider whether or not cultural values are genuinely independent and responsible for restricting growth, we may anticipate a more promising future for other parts of the world. Admittedly, growth deferred for a generation or century is not what policy-makers or those having to live through the experience would like but my remarks here are addressed to the quality of our understanding, not the yearning of our hearts. Even so there is room for guarded optimism as to the future: some economies – East Asian ones – that only a generation ago were written off as poor prospects did start to grow hard and fast. Over little longer than a decade their supposedly unpromising cultures became modified in economically relevant ways, during and as a result of the process of growth itself. This Chapter attempts to shake the developmental kaleidoscope and construct the implications of the experiment anew.

On an historical view, East Asia can be seen as having achieved growth earlier than Europe – in China by late T'ang or Song times. Japan displayed signs of growth or at any rate development indicators that may reasonably be taken as indicating this, during the early Tokugawa period if not before. All told, East Asia has a longer, though more interrupted, experience of growth (but not of industrialization) than the Western world. In addition, Taiwan, Hong Kong, Japan, South Korea, and the coastal provinces of China, plus most tellingly Chinese communities outside the Chinese polity, have outpaced Western nations in recent decades.[6]

East Asian experience is usually treated as a purely or merely imitative phenomenon rooted in a special responsiveness. Thus David Landes: 'the recent success of the East Asian countries is evidence that it can pay to be late – if one possesses the social and human requisites'.[7] This emphasis on prior social attributes misses the point about the underlying forces and the ultimate significance of the episode. Rather, there were indigenous origins, overlain though they were by the assimilation of borrowings from the industrial West – an assimilation not much brought about by colonialism, except that Taiwan and Korea were once colonies of industrializing Japan and, by a stretch of the imagination, might therefore be regarded as secondary colonies of the West.

Whether or not they cling to the idea that the impetus for economic growth was a second-hand Western one, innumerable authors imply that East Asia was uniquely fitted to emulate Western economies by virtue of its cultural background. It does not seem to be adequately recognized that, in world historical terms, formulations which emphasize the causal role of East Asian culture are in danger of adding a second ethnocentricity to the standard Western version. This region is most unlikely to have been predestined to be the only other part of the earth capable of generating growth, or even (more conservatively) the only other place able to imitate the achievement of the West. What meta-theory could possibly be directing us to such a strong conclusion?

Much the largest share of the literature deals with Japan. Authors can be found who locate the origins of Japanese growth in this or that period or decade: the Tokugawa or before, the Meiji Restoration, the Matsukata deflation of the 1880s, 1890–1905, the 1920s, the 1930s, after 1949, or after 1960. In other words, there is little agreement about the timing of the process, let alone its causes.

According to Minami, what Japan did was to take advantage of the technological backlog of previously developed countries. Although the huge gap ought to offer similar opportunities to other countries today, they lack what he regards as Japan's special, historical advantages.[8] In the tradition of one-country studies, Minami proceeds to enumerate this legacy. In so far as his account relates to Japan's ability to absorb the backlog, the approach is understandable; after all, a proper account must offer an explanation for Japan's especially rapid nineteenth- and twentieth-century industrialization. Nevertheless, the national economy approach can scarcely avoid giving the appearance of over-emphasizing Japan's individual features and under-playing the prospects of a repeat performance elsewhere.

Japan's rate of growth is no longer overwhelming and the length of time that the country took to achieve a high level of income has been beaten by other countries in East Asia. We are dealing not with a single successful country but with a cluster of rapid industrializers, the shared characteristics of which may be more interesting than the differences. Japan may have been first, as Britain was, but just as it is proper to look at the common features of European development and not simply at Britain, East Asia also calls for a regional approach.

Although Minami does quietly observe that, 'in the future there will probably be a great deal more research into comparative economic history', there is as yet less work on East Asia as a whole than on Japan.[9] Relatively speaking, there is little on the implications of recent high growth rates in nearby Southeast Asia, including Singapore, Malaysia and Thailand, not to mention industrializations outside the region, like that of Brazil.[10] The commoner approach is to take East Asian success almost for granted and contrast it with Latin American performance, often concluding that the former offers the best policy lessons for the latter. These lessons typically boil down to recommending that Latin American economies should open themselves to trade and start fostering export-oriented manufactures, as if all other requirements are already present or of no account.

Thus the rapid growth in the 'Little Dragons', and in nations which have become successful even more recently, has not led to a large integrated literature. In Western syllabuses genuflecting towards growth in the East remains directed mainly towards the altar of the Rising Sun. Accordingly the developed world continues to be portrayed as bi-polar, with the primary growth pole in Britain and the secondary one in Japan. The latent interpretation is that, deep down, Japanese or Confucian values substituted efficiently for the Protestant ethic. This view is to be detected in the Weberian-style analyses of Bellah or Morishima, which is ironical given that Weber was so sceptical about the material capacity of the eastern religions.[11]

Admittedly, there is some discrepancy in that specialist writers point out the value systems of the various East Asian countries are in reality distinct.[12] However, the concept of culture is vague enough for it be open to others to retort that they are discussing the central tendency of a shared Confucianism.

ONLY TWO GROWTH-PROMOTING CULTURES, EUROPE AND ASIA?

A key passage which may stand for both bi-polar and cultural arguments occurs in a study of Hong Kong and Singapore by Theodore and Frances Geiger, quoted here for reasons which will become apparent from David Morawetz.[13] Geiger and Geiger first state that the civilisations of India and the other Indian-influenced lands of South and Southeast Asia, the Muslim states of West Asia and North Africa, and the indigenous tribal societies of tropical Africa, were all more profoundly different from Western civilization than was that of China. Note that the measuring rod is Western civilization, assumed to have generated capitalism uniquely and spontaneously. Geiger and Geiger continue:

> Western and Chinese societies – each in its own way – were more practical and rationalistic, more oriented toward achievement in this world, more disposed to physical and mental work as the pre-eminent – and not perforce simply the predominant – human activity, more inclined to save and invest, and more conducive to social mobility. The values, motivations and institutional constraints responsible for these similarities were different ... But they were not incompatible. A Chinese – or Japanese or Korean – *given the opportunity to engage in Western-type economic activities* did not find it psychologically too difficult to do so because – unlike many other Asians or Africans – he was *already accustomed* to think and act in ways that were substantially consistent with the motivational and conceptual requirements for successfully adopting Western techniques. (Italics supplied)

Before we attempt to grapple with and disengage from sundry meanings in this passage, let us consider Morawetz's comment which immediately follows the quotation. This will enable us to establish one or two positions with respect to cultural explanation. Morawetz observes that 'some societies value spiritual matters more than material wealth'. The dead in parts of the Northern Province of Papua New Guinea are buried with all their chattels and bank savings books. 'Such value systems', he observes, 'are not likely to be conducive to success in exporting manufactured goods in competition with the most efficient countries in the world.'

This weakness may perhaps exist, at least in the short run (say a generation). Nevertheless, Morawetz seems to be introducing not merely substantivism but that mainstay of cultural determinism, cultural fixity. In its extreme form this must be false, since there was a time before any culture had created itself; the distinguishing features we see today were not recognisable in the caves. Anyone with a knowledge of history will also understand that even the most obdurate of cultures has changed, whether or not the available sources make it easy to detect those perpetual, covert fluctuations in the force of the variables to which Alfred Marshall was fond of referring (and the recognition of which gives cultures back their historicity).[14] In any case, allegedly permanent features of cultural life do not square with and are unable to account for differences in economic performance among regions within the same cultural area or from one period to the next.[15]

Returning to Geiger and Geiger, note the bi-polar message. There are two, not one, growth-motivated or growth-tolerant cultural areas in the world, the Christian and the Confucian. The former led and of all cultures in the world only the latter was able to follow; it was *inherently* capable of adopting Western techniques whereas the cultures of South and Southeast Asia, of West Asia and North Africa, and sub-Saharan Africa were incapable of so doing. 'Chinese' values are different from Western ones but they, and outside the Western world they alone, are compatible with economic growth. Undoubtedly Japan is subsumed under China in this account, which is really concerned with sinitic culture or values broadly derived from Confucianism. Geiger and Geiger certainly include Korea as their passage proceeds. The remaining cultures in the world are purportedly devoid of the necessary values and virtues. In the terms of Morawetz's comment this includes *a fortiori* places like Papua New Guinea.

The analysis does not consider growth in the East Asian past. Yet although the revisionism that detects growth in the Song (and in Tokugawa Japan) would strengthen a counter-argument, it is not indispensable. Merely recognizing the increase in the aggregate size of China's economy over recent centuries provides the clue. The huge increase in population and the replication of the pattern of economic activity to match it guarantees that innumerable acts of investment and other business decisions were constantly taking place, in increasing volume.[16] This means that it is not necessary to refer to the underlying culture in explaining East Asian receptivity to Western capitalism; the economies of the region were already very active economically, profit seeking was nothing new to them.

With respect to growth potential, Geiger and Geiger are in effect triaging the cultures of the world: Western culture active, Chinese culture latent, everything else inert. Merely to establish that Chinese values were capable (only) of following Western development the authors would need to demonstrate a radical difference between the Christian attitudes that gave birth to economic growth and the Confucian ones that merely floated the vast expansion of the Chinese economy. They do hint at this. But what Geiger and Geiger mainly show is something else, that is to say differences in matters such as record-keeping and institutional structures and functions. Yet they do not establish such a great difference in these business practices that we can believe that this by itself would have prevented independent growth in East Asia.

They throw their analysis into doubt by referring to the capacity of the Chinese (and Koreans) to engage in 'Western' economic activities *given the opportunity*. This admission gives the game away. There is an identification problem. Their interpretation fails to distinguish between *supposedly* constraining yet potentially responsive values and *observably* restricted opportunity. The proposition is that if economic growth occurred because of Western contact, then and only then the distinctive but facilitating Confucian values of East Asia would be activated, whereas other non-Western cultures would scarcely respond to the contact. This overlooks both the evidence that there had been independent growth in East Asia, say in the Song, and the already-mentioned fact that until growth was well underway in recent decades Western and some Eastern observers thought Oriental values incompatible with it. For instance, Morawetz quotes representative passages about Korea as late as Choi (1966) and Kim (1966), in which they urge that the Confucian ideal 'still overwhelmingly sways Korean social usages', is hostile to diligence and the will to work, and 'should be thoroughly eliminated to make way for the ideological bases for democratic and liberalistic modernization'.[17]

Although, in defiance of historical experience, the culturist proposition is that value systems outside Europe were and are incapable of giving rise to growth by themselves, we cannot be sure that all others are paralysed nor that they will prove incompatible with economic growth, if and when exogenous changes make it possible. They are only taken as incapable of so doing on the assumption that, because to date we detect the strongest growth in the Christian and Confucian worlds, the reason must lie in their special systems of value. The corollary is that other cultures, lacking growth, must be unable to achieve this because their value systems are inappropriate. Leaving aside the fact that *some* positive growth is in reality being achieved in most parts of the world, values and growth are being made to form an endless circle. Moreover, the teleology involved in looking on economic history as if it culminates in our own day, with no prospects remaining for latecoming cultures, is quite evident. The banes of the study of economic development are dealing too cursorily with early historical experience; treating any failure to achieve growth in a single, recent generation as evidence of permanent inability to do so; and talking as though the successful emulation of the West by East Asia is the end of history.[18]

The discussion of cultural differences becomes more problematical in the final chapter of Morawetz's book, the title of which, we can remind ourselves, is *Why the Emperor's New Clothes Are Not Made in Colombia: A Case Study in Latin American and East Asian Manufactured Exports*. Morawetz is not satisfied that he can explain the downturn of Colombian textile exports by referring to standard economic variables alone. He therefore turns with some enthusiasm to cultural explanations, specifically to values influencing quality control, punctuality and hard work, but at length senses the fragility of this approach. Eventually he comes to chide himself for not heeding Epicurus, whose recommendation to 'hoist sail, my dear boy, and steer clear of culture' he uses as the heading quote for his cultural chapter.

The reason for his change of heart is that Morawetz notices the shift in the way Confucian values have been evaluated since the 1960s, when the phenomenal success of several East Asian economies became apparent. He also discovers that those managers in his Colombian sample who delivered their export goods on time were either immigrants or Colombians who had lived in the United States or Europe for at least a year or two.[19] In other words, values conducive to economic success can be learned, and rapidly at that. As Ernest Gellner remarks, many societies have learned market behaviour with alacrity once circumstances permitted or encouraged it: 'single-end rationality may not be quite such a difficult accomplishment'.[20]

In his final footnote, Morawetz refers to the abrupt change in Korean attitudes in just over a decade from the mid-1960s and acknowledges a hypothesis quite different from the one in which culture determines action. The explanation, he says,

> may be that Korean culture was always potentially compatible with rapid capitalist development, but that it was necessary to enter a period of political and economic stability and to 'get the policies right' before this potential could be realized. If this hypothesis is credible, it is interesting to speculate on whether it might not have some application in Colombia and other parts of Latin America as well.[21]

POLITICAL CONDITIONS FOR GROWTH

The remainder of this chapter will be devoted to urging that this alternative explanation does indeed have such an application; that Geiger and Geiger's observation that 'given the opportunity to engage in Western-type economic activities [East Asians] did not find it psychologically too difficult to do so' should not be restricted to East Asians, and that the central impediments to economic growth are not culture or values, which can demonstrably remodel themselves in response to growth itself, but political incentives and disincentives.[22]

In the immediate post-war years it was not unusual to find the British industrial revolution paraded as if it was a model for what were then called backward nations. Occasionally the Japanese case was included, as the one early and successful non-Western industrialization, although at that stage its growth rates were not spectacular. But no sooner had the 'backward' economies been sanitised as 'less-developed' than there was likewise a reaction against such remote comparisons. History was swept aside in favour of algebraic growth models. These in turn have begun to fade; they abstract from too much. Role models, though decreasingly over time the socialist command economies, have come back into fashion.

Since East Asia has performed so superbly during the last 30 years, the East Asian model has become what is recommended. Beyond the region's supposed cultural advantages the attraction is the belief that its success can be attributed without too much of a blush to government planning. In other words there appears to be a prospect of contriving something similar, and along the non-market lines which seem to appeal to the political classes of the Third World and those Western individuals most interested in its fate. Plenty of examples could be cited. For Southeast Asia, for instance, one result has been the 'Look East' policy. Otherwise the proposals tend to be targeted at Latin America, where a case can certainly be made that autarkic policies have done a great deal of harm.[23] In the Caribbean, Jamaica is said to be consciously emulating Taiwan.[24] For many writers there seems little point in wasting words on the African countries or others that seem much further behind, though some do proclaim the export of manufactures to be a universal panacea, often adding the rider: provided the economies are steered in that direction by their governments. One implication of this strand of the literature is thus that policy changes on supposedly East Asian lines are more than desirable, they are necessary. Electing governments responsive to capitalist interests is *sine qua non*, as history is said to tell us: 'neoclassical theory to the contrary, comparable resource endowments and export opportunities in no way assured similar patterns and speeds of economic growth'.[25]

CULTURES ELSEWHERE

Strong cultural as well as policy meanings may be wrung out of bi-polar interpretations of the type advanced by Geiger and Geiger. More than one are chosen but no more than two. Only European and East Asian societies were pre-adapted for growth. The remainder of the world does not possess suitable cultures, appropriate values. Cultures are not malleable. In this litany, the

Western world and East Asia are tied together by Weberian-style arguments about permanent cultural differences, which are unsatisfactory for the following reasons.

Firstly, despite claims in some quarters that the Third World fosters values neglected by the capitalist West, such as altruism, a lack of greed, or tenderness towards the environment, it is possible to identify growth-promoting attitudes in many such societies. Comparable attitudes or plausible substitutes have certainly been identified as being held by a number of religious groups in various countries.

Second, to repeat a point made more than once, it has not been shown that cultural attitudes are responsible for growth at all, or alternatively that culture is not itself to a substantial degree an artefact of prevailing economic structures and activities. A lagged result it may well have been, outlasting, especially in its forms, the precise economic circumstances that gave birth to it, and acting as a drag on subsequent economic change, rather than as an absolute barrier. Thus cultural phenomena may be the *product* of economic activity, my favourite example being the construction for purposes of trading and slaving of pidgins, which by definition have no native speakers. Indeed, Olson suggests that significant cultural attitudes may be a function of the extent of the division of labour. Most poor countries lack large organizations and hence do not generate the organization man and his values.[26] A theorem follows: the growth potential of culture is limited by the division of labour.

Interestingly, Dwight H. Perkins's informed commentary on the development of China urges that, once one compares China not with Europe but with other less-developed countries, several principal features of its society can be taken to be 'a vital positive force', summed up in his words as '*a prior accumulation of experience with complex organizations or institutions*'.[27] Even more significant, however, is Perkins's rider: the positive force became vital 'once other real barriers to economic development were removed'. This returns us from culture to the importance of political change, the removal of structures which restrict the market, produce oppression or widespread instability, and do not supply adequate law and order or public goods.

An extreme argument that Christianity and Confucianism as such were responsible for growth could not be correct. They existed for hundreds or thousands of years through occasional episodes of growth and others of decline, as well as during vastly longer spells of expansion without growth. Were we to pursue cultural explanation we would need to convince ourselves that value systems were not only powerful but autonomous, as well as becoming immensely more subtle about the changing content behind the labels of particular value systems and more explicit about the variable economic histories they are required to explain.

The message that only the Western world and East Asia possessed appropriate cultural values chimes with another fashionable, and equally incorrect, opinion, which holds that development is unusual. While no one doubts the immense technical difficulties of growth and development, it is unreasonable to base such an opinion on the experience of a few decades alone. Part of what is actually being observed are the relative income positions of the First and Third Worlds, which may give the impression that the latter as a whole is standing still. The statistics do not bear this out, despite the regression of certain sub-Saharan African economies.[28] In some versions the opinion that development is rare serves a polemical purpose, associated with dependency theory or the extreme position that the West is responsible for 'under-developing' the Third World.

The astonishing policy prescription, still espoused by some, is to establish a command economy – along the lines of the pricked balloons east of the Iron Curtain – facilitated, in a further irony, by additional massive aid from the West. The final irony comes when these demands are coupled with a purported justification for nationalization in South Africa, which is that uncompensated nationalization is desirable because this is what was done in the Taiwanese land reform. But that reform amounted to an uncompensated reallocation of the land, not its nationalization. The purposes to which the East Asian model may be put have thus come full circle, at precisely the moment when the parliament of Czechoslovakia has voted to return nationalized property to its original owners, the first country in the former Communist bloc to do so.[29]

The model has indeed been construed in several ways. One group of writers finds that Confucianism Mark 1 was superior to the Protestant Ethic, apparently because it was *not* likely to generate capitalism or industrialism. A variant of this is the suggestion that it was a Buddhist component that dominated, meaning (to the uninformed) an absence of the drive for the Faustian Mastery whereby the West and the West alone supposedly damaged its environment. The reality of pre-modern environmental damage in the Orient was rather stark.[30] Another group finds Confucianism Mark II attractive because on the contrary it has been re-evaluated as the source of Asian capitalism or industrialism. The ambiguity of cultural explanation becomes ever more apparent.

Since it is not evident that its culture was responsible for East Asia's economic success, we have no need to take a bi-polar view of the world. Why should purported cultural defects, no more convincingly expressed than were earlier Western dismissals of Confucianism, be what impedes growth in the remainder of the world? There seems no reason, especially when we accept not only the evidence of widespread modern growth but allow ourselves to recognize the signs of occasional ancient growth in a number of societies outside both Christendom and the Confucian realm, such as the Abassid caliphate.[31]

Economic change, when it comes, can be rapid. Cultural attitudes can adjust rapidly too – in little longer than 10 years in South Korea, Morawetz tells us. Political revolutions can change the public culture even faster than that. But features which are in reality adapting to growth can seem to be pre-adapted, part of the 'prerequisites for growth', because even in the modern period adaptations in institutional functioning may be hard to detect if they take place within relatively stable institutional forms.

As Alexander Gerschenkron commented, 'the line between what is a precondition of, and what is a response to industrial development seems to be a rather flexible one'. Furthermore, 'what can be reasonably regarded as a prerequisite in some historical cases can be much more naturally seen as a product of industrialization in others'.[32] As he concludes, 'there is no *a priori* reason to suppose that the underdeveloped countries which today stand on the threshold of their industrial revolutions will show less creative adaptation in compensating for the absence of factors which in more fortunate countries may be said to have "preconditioned" the initial spurts of industrial growth'.[33] Yet another irony: Gerschenkron was writing in 1952 when South Korea and the rest of East Asia were still poor. As a proponent of economic malleability, he would have been unsurprised that the culture of East Asia subsequently failed to prevent the region's rise.

In a similarly optimistic vein, we may forecast that there will be further cases of super-successful growth, probably in Southeast Asia, possibly in Brazil, perhaps elsewhere. The management of industry is increasingly taught and increasingly shown to be transferable.[34] We may anticipate that as a country succeeds, so its success will be rationalized. The historiography of the entire field suggests that part of the rationalization will be culturist. The values of successive happy lands, those that achieve very high rates of growth for a decade or so, will cease to be passed off as obstacles and instead will be described as positively virtuous, just as happened to Confucianism or Japanese culture or the culture of Korea.

Pre-adaptation will once more be mooted, as it actually was for India in 1947 – an economy considered at that date far more likely to achieve growth than was war-torn Japan. After all, India had a British-style civil service, then regarded as a plus, with other elements of infrastructural provision, parliamentary government and apparently stable institutions. Instead, India chose central planning and moved along only at the 'Hindu rate of growth'. But if India recovers vigorously from her present downturn, her institutional and cultural features will once more be lauded, if only for their adaptability. Likewise, the neo-European aspect of Latin America will be emphasized, not its Third World features. The Iberian element in its culture may come in for praise instead of censure: after all, Spain's recent performance in Europe could be taken as legitimizing a change of opinion. It may even be within the bounds of possibility that parallels will be drawn between the consensus politics of the Arab 'nation', or tribes in some revitalised part of Africa, and Japanese methods of running business by consensus.[35]

CONCLUSIONS

The ultimate significance of East Asian development is four-fold. Firstly, the East Asian experience presents us with the opportunity of replacing models of the command economies of the USSR, Yugoslavia and China, so popular in the Third World. Just how disastrous these models were can be gauged from the finding by Justin Yifu Lin of Beijing University that the agricultural crisis caused by forced collectivization in China between 1958–61 resulted in about 30 million excess deaths and about 33 million lost or postponed births. This he calls 'the worst catastrophe in human history'.[36] As Lin points out, and as is well known, the Chinese communes were widely touted at the time, by Joan Robinson and others, as a proper model of agricultural development in under-developed, densely-populated economies. The demographic qualification was presumably needed to rescue the model by distinguishing China's condition from that of the USSR, where the drive for collectivization had already caused many millions of deaths. Although it is to be feared that even now the East Asian case may be represented to suit any purpose, candid observers will perceive that at bottom its instances of spectacular growth were free-market successes reinforced but not replaced by the contribution of the public sector. The fact that the region is non-Western, despite some absurd labelling of Japan as Western, should make it a more palatable role model for less-developed countries.

Secondly, properly construed, the example will also help to demote cultural explanation as a whole by showing the inadequacy of a unique Western cultural explanation for economic growth or industrialization, either in terms of Christianity or more narrowly of the Protestant Ethic. Attempts to patch up this style of explanation by defining Japanese religion as providing a substitute for the Protestant Ethic are implausible, even ignoring the difficulties involved in proceeding to the next step and making religious values responsible for economic growth. As countries with cultures different from those of either the West or Japan succeed in achieving high rates of growth, the stretching of 'Protestant Ethic' arguments to cover each of them will become more and more strained – even disregarding the failure of such cultural 'theories' to predict which economy will be the next to succeed.

Notwithstanding the objections raised here to treating culture as primary, it may still be thought that the world's major cultures are arranged as if on a cost-ladder. The attainment of growth by some will probably be expected to turn out distinctly more expensive than others, in psychic, social and political respects. This may be so – the world is not a cultural *tabula rasa*. Nevertheless, to assign great importance to the fact is to be too much impressed by the visibility of cultural phenomena, as well as their large element of historical continuity, without accepting that such features need not deny malleability in general, including modification which takes place in response to economic change itself

In any case, evaluations of the cultural costs of growth are fraught with difficulty and easily become entangled in prejudice. Very precise and dispassionate analyses along international affairs lines would be vital. The argument here is that other sources of cost are likely to predominate: environmental and locational circumstances (though their importance may be reduced by modern opportunities to substitute for resources by transport and trade, as well as eroded by medical and agricultural improvements); political and institutional arrangements; economic policies; and contingent factors.

East Asia may have been fortunate in its political circumstances after the war, with decolonization, the Korean war dividend and American forward defence expenditures, the transfer of American technology and institutions, and governments not getting wrong too many targetings of growth industries.[37] Notwithstanding any special circumstances, the scale and pace of the achievement have been stellar. It is important not to let this lead us back into the bi-polar trap. The achievement was a historical one.

Thirdly, then, the example will help us to deprovincialize economic history through providing a control on those explanations of economic growth which, by drawing on the West alone, risk taking Western particularities for general causes.[38] This will carry us part of the way: from models of growth as unique to models of growth as bi-polar.

We can go the whole way and shun the bi-polar trap on a fourth count, which is that the inconsistencies of cultural explanation make it improbable, unhelpful and damaging to treat East Asian growth as something attained not merely by the second but by the *last* of two preordained cultures. For the sake of the remainder of the world, let us hope that East Asian development has no such abiding significance and that after all growth will prove to be multi-polar.

NOTES

1. Joel Mokyr, *The Lever of Riches* (New York: Oxford University Press, 1990), p. 82.
2. For example, David Landes, 'Why Are We So Rich and They So Poor?', *American Economic Review*, Papers and Proceedings, **80**, 1990, 1–13.
3. E.L. Jones, 'Patterns of Growth in History', in John A. James and Mark Thomas (eds), *Capitalism in Context* (Chicago: University of Chicago Press, 1994), p. 25.
4. Cf. Colin McEvedy, *The Penguin Atlas of Modern History* (Penguin Books: no place or date given), pp. 5–6.

5. I have discussed this issue in E.L. Jones, 'The European Background', in S.L. Engerman and R.E. Gallman (eds), *The Cambridge Economic History of the United States*, I (Cambridge: Cambridge University Press, 1996), pp. 95-133, and in 'Culture, Environment and the Historical Lag in East Asia's Industrialization' in J. Melling and J. Barry (eds), *Culture and History* (Exeter: University of Exeter Press, 1992), pp. 75-91.

6. On the remarkable example of the overseas Chinese, see S.G. Redding, *The Spirit of Chinese Capitalism* (Berlin: Walter de Gruyter, 1990); on earlier East Asian economic history see E.L. Jones, *Growth Recurring* (Oxford: Oxford University Press), 1988.

7. David Landes, 'Rethinking Development', *Dialogue*, **21**, 1991, 70.

8. Ryoshin Minami, *The Economic Development of Japan: A Quantitative Story* (Basingstoke: Macmillan, 1986), pp. 423-4.

9. Ibid., p. 423.

10. Admittedly, one problem in Third World countries that has not unsettled the Western democracies of late is political succession by means of coups. However countries such as Thailand have sustained high rates of growth despite successive military coups. Palace coups, though a great nuisance, seem not to amount to a fundamental economic problem unless they reverse policy settings.

11. Robert N. Bellah, *Tokugawa Religion* (New York: The Free Press, 1957), Michio Morishima, *Why Has Japan 'Succeeded'? Western Technology and the Japanese Ethos* (Cambridge: Cambridge University Press, 1982).

12. E.G. Bruce Cummings, 'The Origins and Development of the Northeast Asian Political Economy: Industrial Sectors, Product Cycles, and Political Consequences', *International Organization*, **38**, 1984, 1-40.

13. In David Morawetz, *Why the Emperor's New Clothes Are Not Made in Colombia: A Case Study in Latin American and East Asian Manufactured Exports* (New York: Oxford University Press, 1981), pp. 136-7.

14. Early anthropologists took an ahistorical view of the tribal and island societies they studied, representing oral testimony to mean that the same practices had continued throughout time. But as P.L. Sack points out, the specific aim of oral history is 'to maintain the illusion of stability in the face of change'. ('The Triumph of Colonialism', in P.L. Sack (ed.), *Problem of Choice: Land in Papua New Guinea's Future* (Canberra: ANU, 1974), p. 201).

15. Mark Elvin, 'Why China Failed to Create an Endogenous Industrial Capitalism', *Theory and Society*, 1984, 379-91; Jones, *Growth Recurring*, op. cit., *passim*.

16. See E.L. Jones, 'The Real Question about China: Why was the Song Economic Achievement not Repeated?', *Australian Economic History Review*, **XXX**, 1990, 5-22.

17. Quoted by Morawetz, op. cit., p. 141.

18. For a view of the dismal prospects for much of the world, see Landes, loc. cit., 1991.

19. Morawetz, op. cit., p. 140.

20. Ernest Gellner, *Plough, Sword or Book: The Structure of Human History* (London: Collins Harvill, 1988), p. 175.

21. Morawetz, op. cit., p. 142 n. 15.

22. This is a theme of Jones, *Growth Recurring*, op. cit.

23. For discussions see e.g. S. Chan, 'Comparative Performance of East Asian and Latin American NICs', *Pacific Focus*, **2**, 1987, 35-56; and J. Macomber, 'East Asia's Lessons for Latin American Resurgence', *The World Economy*, **10**, 1989, 469-82.

24. Peter Berger, 'Can the Caribbean Learn from East Asia?', *Caribbean Review*, **XIII**, 1984, 7-9, 40-41.

25. Cynthia Taft Morris and Irma Adelman, *Comparative Patterns of Economic Development 1850-1914* (Baltimore: The Johns Hopkins University Press, 1988), p. 221.

26. Mancur Olson, 'Diseconomies of Scale and Development', *Cato Journal*, **7**, 1987, 77-97.

27. Dwight H. Perkins, 'The Persistence of the Past', in Dwight H. Perkins (ed.), *China's Modern Economy in Historical Perspective* (Stanford: Stanford University Press, 1975), p. 3.

28. World Bank, *World Development Report 1980* (Washington, DC: The World Bank, 1980).

29. *The Guardian Weekly*, 3 March 1991.

30. Georg Borgstrom, *The Hungry Planet* (New York: Collier Books, 2nd rev. edn., 1972),

p. 106.

31. See for example E.L. Jones, *Growth Recurring*, op. cit., and Geoffrey Barraclough, *An Introduction to Contemporary History* (Harmondsworth, Middlesex: Penguin Books, 1967), p. 197 n. 1.

32. Alexander Gerschenkron, *Economic Backwardness in Historical Perspective* (Cambridge, Mass.: The Belknap Press, 1962), p. 33.

33. Ibid., p. 51.

34. Peter Drucker, 'Japan's Choices', *Foreign Affairs*, **65**, 1987, 923–41.

35. On the consensual style of African decision-making, see George B.N. Ayittey, 'The Political Economy of Reform in Africa', *Journal of Economic Growth*, **3**, 1989, 4–17. In some of the Third World consensus may act as a weak means of curbing venal authorities who are not constrained by representative government or independent law.

36. Justin Yifu Lin, 'Collectivization and China's Agricultural Crisis in 1958–1961', *Journal of Political Economy*, **90**, 1990, 1229.

37. Although it is the successes that are discussed most in the West, both Japan and South Korea did make mistakes by emphasizing inappropriate industries. See e.g. Michael E. Porter, *The Competitive Advantage of Nations* (New York: The Free Press, 1990), pp. 4, 474.

38. The continuing need for theories of history which adequately encompass non-Western experience is stressed by K.C. Chang, *Art, Myth, and Ritual: The Paths to Political Authority in Ancient China* (Cambridge, Mass.: Harvard University Press, 1983), pp. 128–9.

8.   The East Asian crisis in context

INTRODUCTION

The world economy has long been dominated by the West and the arrival alongside it of East Asia as a second massive, economically successful region was bound to have profound implications. A suitable metaphor would be the launching of a big ship into the water. The creation of a second rich area in the world ought in the long run to offer the West great opportunities for trade but some early displacement was unavoidable. The West would have to change the structure of its economy, though before the 'Asian crisis' of 1997-98 it was unclear whether serious disturbance would be involved. With believable luck the displacement might have been gentle.

Speaking in terms of aggregates like 'the West' raises difficulties because the term has more than one definition. One meaning refers to the material realm of geography: the location of the Western world taken as the OECD countries except for Japan, which obviously needs to be included in 'East Asia'. The other meaning of 'the West' refers to the realm of institutions and ideas, and is taken as referring to the politico-economic organization of the established Western democracies, with their decentralized powers, independent courts, and free press. In the space of a chapter it seems reasonable to imply both by the same term and ask the reader to sense when one meaning may be implied more than the other.

The currency crisis has added two problems to the initial displacement effect of 'Asia rising': one is the shrinkage of the region's imports and the threatened abnormal surge of exports to the West, and the other is the likelihood that many of the enormous loans and investments by Western banks will not be fully repaid, if they are ever repaid at all. The great disequilibrium of the crisis has plunged into question former, complacent interpretations of miraculous growth.

Part of this chapter draws on a wide range of contemporary sources in English, among the chief being *The Economist*, *The Financial Times*, the *Australian Financial Review*, *The Australian* and *The International Herald Tribune*. During a crisis, sources like these help to shape behaviour as well as record it. They may be more influential than the slower-moving technical literature of economics, although, as we shall see, their dogmatism and extreme variety of opinion point several ways at once and do not necessarily instil confidence in the reader. To counter that, economists could and should have done more: as Krugman observes, the proportion of economists writing 'carefully constructed, well-targeted articles, based on serious economic analysis, for a wider audience . . . in the United States can be counted on the fingers of one hand'.[1] There is no reason to suppose that the number is larger outside the United States; given the lack of widely-read journals of opinion in the other English-speaking countries it is probably fewer.

Although some of the economies of East Asia have shrunk distressingly, they still account for a considerable share of global trade and investment. The region's polities also interact strongly with those of the West. The management tasks created for Western countries are innumerable. This chapter concentrates on three highly-interrelated topics: why so few forecasters anticipated the Asian crisis, as well as why those few were almost never heeded; the relationship of the currency crisis to underlying institutional problems; and the likely resurfacing of these problems if the financial and banking problems are tackled without more comprehensive reform.

First, and predominantly, the chapter tries to disentangle the recent political economy of East Asian growth. The thrust will be that the currency crisis was essentially a 'premature crisis'. Narrowly conceived, the downturn resulted from an excessive misallocation of investment encouraged by specific rigidities in policy (notably the pegging of currencies to the US dollar). But the suggestion here is that pressure for restructuring and reform already existed. Tensions built up like those along a geological fault, until they precipitated an earthquake in the form of the financial crisis. Unfortunately the crisis pre-empted responses that would have been provoked, perhaps sooner rather than later, by the accumulating stresses.

THE INVESTMENT CONTEXT

Policies tended to reinforce prior patterns. The worst-afflicted economies had not moved round the Product Cycle speedily enough to escape intense export competition from new entrants, notably China. The crisis when it came was only on the surface the textbook financial or even macro-economic crisis that many are claiming today. It was also less a market failure than a non-market failure in the sense that, by pegging their currencies to the US dollar, the politicized economies of the region had tampered with the thermostat. Institutions remained inadequate, for instance in failing to superintend or regulate banking. Corporate governance was opaque. All this led to the misdirection of a large part of the capital inflows received during 1996 and the first half of 1997. Once the confidence of foreign investors started to ebb and then turn to panic, the nature of the asset bubbles, the extent of the bad loans, and the number of unbankable projects, became evident.

Western institutions, too, were shown to be less than satisfactory in their management of risk: they failed to discourage a flood of unwise investment. In 1996 Western commercial bank lending to the region was about two-and-a-half times what it had been in 1994. In the earlier year profitable opportunities had doubtless been available, though that may be a rosy reading of the situation since investment was already running at 30 per cent, in some countries as much as 40 per cent, of GDP. Blood ran hot and the 'animal spirits' of which Keynes wrote were in full play. The contrast between East Asian and Western, or at any rate English-speaking countries, where the proportion was 15 or 20 per cent, invited criticism to the effect that 'we' were under-investing whereas 'they' had got it right. The question of how much of the investment in East Asia was likely to pay off was not coolly appraised.

High rates of GDP growth were somewhat naively taken as signals that individual Western companies might expect to make high rates of profit in the region, more or less in any industry or country, whatever the difficulties they might face in establishing themselves in unfamiliar markets. This is the 'macro-economic fallacy' in which the profits of individual corporations are assumed to reflect the movement of national incomes. The attitude was taken that firms had to 'be in it for the long haul' and form joint ventures with local companies, liaisons with local go-betweens, or with members of the families of local politicians. Investors and the shareholders of banks may almost as well have been serenaded by Judy Garland singing 'Somewhere Over the Rainbow'.

Partly as a result of the direct and indirect preferences of governments within the region, too much investment was entering industries with global excess capacity, such as steel, automobiles and semi-conductors. The investment built compulsively on past successes. This is a recurrent type of human behaviour and reminds one of the problem that hunting populations face when game is scarce. They are drawn to seek prey in areas where they have previously found it but where, often as a result, game has been hunted out. Human beings are not reliable randomizing agents. In the case under review, the destinations of investment beyond the older manufacturing industries tended to be real estate and infrastructural projects. Property investment became a 'bubble' and, while there are undoubted deficiencies in the infrastructure of the mega-cities of Asia, projects to remedy this are necessarily 'lumpy'. Only a few need be misplaced to reduce expected returns sharply. In any case their gestation periods tend to be measured in years, sometimes decades.

On the face of it, the crisis may seem to be the kind of nose-dive recurrently associated with emerging markets. Yet, although some Western commentators have reverted to talking about 'developing Asia' whereas yesterday they spoke of 'miracle economies', this cannot disguise the fact that several of the affected countries were well above the GDP per capita threshold of $7790 for emerging markets defined by the World Bank. Moreover, after all the crises in world history, not to mention the advent of modern data collecting and processing techniques, one might have hoped that gross errors in forecasting and its tendency to spurious arithmetical precision would have been fading away.

WEAKNESSES IN FORECASTING

As it is, precise-seeming forecasts of East Asian GDP continue to pour forth, only to be amended after every quarter. The data on which they are based are reworked months after the fact. The accuracy, or rather inaccuracy, of investment data is particularly disturbing. A study of investment flows between 1950–89 found that in one quarter of the cases measurement errors were over 10 per cent.[2] During autumn 1997 some fund managers grew disbelieving of official data on the foreign investment supposedly entering Southeast Asia. They added up the dollar figures claimed in 'tombstones' (indirect advertisements boasting of the deals that firms had done). Given that no company is obliged to publish a 'tombstone', this is a source that must understate the true totals; even so the investment recorded was far higher than available official figures.

Problems of poor data affecting economic evaluations are not of course confined to this region. The authors of an analysis of the reliability of quarterly national accounts in seven major countries find revisions of initial estimates of output growth to be large, sometimes greater than the average growth rate. They call the results 'disappointing' given their importance for policy-making and are alarmed that the estimates, especially those for the financial sector, are often published near the outer time limit of their usefulness.[3]

A further problem stems from the tendency of evaluators working for international agencies to find themselves 'captured' by national governments. Most data are provided by the ministries of host governments. Even when these bodies are not dissembling (and the Thais and South Koreans were accused of this at the start of the crisis), they are prone to insist that interpretations put the best face on things. Economic forecasting is not as scientific as its econometric methodology might suggest. Embassies, for example, have been known to argue the point of view of host governments to their own government evaluators; in other words, departments of foreign affairs can be made captive by the states with which they are dealing.

As someone unkindly quipped, economic forecasters are worse off than meteorologists. They at least know what the weather is today. It is anomalous that forecasts resting on such weak foundations should be acted on simply because they are quantitative - exaggeratedly so in that some are stated to a decimal place of a percentage point - whereas appraisals of the institutional and political situation are disregarded as 'soft'. It is noteworthy that the Head of the Australian Treasury now wishes to sidestep the whole issue, proclaiming that 'the heavy concentration on forecasts, by both governments and markets, may have been one of the most unhealthy developments of recent decades'.[4] He advises running policies that assume shocks will occur and thereby seeking to minimize financial vulnerability. Such an approach would be too conservative for many people during what seem to be good times.

If the crisis were a textbook crisis, it should have been anticipated. Consider the trade data for six East Asian 'Tiger' economies, Hong Kong, South Korea, Taiwan, Thailand, Malaysia and Singapore in 1996. The total value of exports increased only 3 per cent, despite having risen 23 per cent in 1994, while imports also rose only 3 per cent after having risen 26 per cent in 1995. Whatever the deficiencies of the figures, that degree of contraction was surely indicative.

Occasionally, it is true, the problems were foreseen. As early as April 1997, a few Western economists, bankers and consultants were sounding the alarm about East Asian financial and banking difficulties. Some of their clients may have become wary as a result but the general investment rush was not perceptibly slowed. Those who warned that deeper institutional problems must eventually surface like a drowned body had their work passed over as academic speculation. The mood was revealed in a 1996 paper which presciently noted that 'foreign investors have clamoured into Asia in the 1990s hoping to tap into the spectacular economic growth, but have often done so without awareness of existing or likely future political and social conditions which could affect their investments and business operations'.[5] The paper continued by pointing out that although political risk insurance was available it was not consistently sought. Finally, the paper's reworking of forecasts by The Economist and Business Environment Risk Intelligence, Inc., urged that they 'clearly indicate future trouble for investors'.

The forecasting issue is not solely a question of method and data but of how best to offset the emotional or evaluative cycle affecting decision-making; that is, how to ensure that a bearish forecast receives a proper hearing in bullish times. A failure to allow for contrary evidence during the Asian crisis was evident in both West and East. Medieval kings did better when they kept jesters to whisper in their ears the truths that courtiers dare not voice. Churchill did better when he accepted General Sir Alan Brooke's rebuke: 'I don't hate him. I love him. But the first time I tell him that I agree with him when I don't will be the time to get rid of me, for then I can be no more use to him.'[6]

A major problem may have been the self-censorship that Western governments, economists, and ratings agencies, as well as international agencies, now claim to have practised. In other words, they imply that they really did recognize the upcoming problems but felt obliged to play them down. The defence offered by the International Monetary Fund is that the Thai government refused for 18 months to act on advice that might have averted the crisis and furthermore the Fund had no option but to press its case behind closed doors. 'For the IMF fire brigade to arrive with lights flashing and sirens wailing before a crisis occurs risks provoking a crisis that might not otherwise happen', urges a senior official.[7] Maybe this was true but the chances were that the eventual problems would be permitted to become much worse than they need have done. Even had Thailand succeeded in skating across the thin ice of its banking system, the problems of corruption and cronyism would have surfaced in the end. They are intrinsic to politicized economies. Had international agencies been candid about the rickety institutional underpinnings of the East Asian miracle, they would certainly have become embroiled in disputes with governments but less imprudent investment may have taken place. Growth may have slowed but it would have been surer and the wrenching readjustment now needed may have been reduced.

Despite their inevitable resentment of foreign criticism, some East Asian countries may even have embraced earlier reform. There were certainly individuals in the region who deprecated the authoritarianism of their own societies. I have space for only two examples. In South Korea, Kim Dae-Jung said that, 'the underlying cause of the crisis, in my view, lies in the collusive relations between government and business, an economy dictated by bureaucrats, corruptions and malpractice on the part of the chaebols . . .'[8] He was quickly followed by the Indonesian economist, Sumitro Djojohadikusumo, who stated that the problem was not just an economic crisis but 'a series of institutional diseases in almost our entire body politic . . . We only need to take an aspirin to cure the monetary upheaval. But we should take antibiotics to cure the institutional diseases.'[9]

CURRENT PREOCCUPATIONS

As the middle of 1998 approached, opinion darkened. After a lull in the bad news reaching foreign investors, a new pessimism gathered strength, with talk about 'false dawns', 'Meltdown II', a 'dead cat bounce', and even a mordant 'dead Tiger bounce'. A second wave of selling of Asian stocks took place in the April–June quarter when the scale of the crisis was at length recognized – which throws into relief the insouciance of earlier forecasts. More commentators turned despondent. Surveying Thailand, Martin Wolf, a penetrating observer, remarked that 'this crisis has not even reached the end of its beginning'.[10] Other writers, though fewer than before, continued to sound optimistic. Assertions in the media and a wide range of academic and commercial surveys ranged from promising an end to the crisis within six months to insisting that it would last as long as ten years. Small wonder that another notably judicious commentator noted in May that 'assessments by different observers are conspicuously, even ludicrously, at odds with one another'.[11]

Many of the assessments are undeniably based on incomplete evidence and others, though by no means all, are devoted to justifying whatever their author's previous interpretation happens to have been. Some are little more than market rumours. Those who are expected to act on them have a hard task sorting the wheat from the chaff. Few commentators take a long enough view, or pay enough attention to institutional economics, to determine whether the growth rates of the 'miracle' years would have been sustainable even in the absence of the currency crisis. The usual implicit assumption, encouraged by the 'Asian Values' school of thought, is that high growth rates represented a long-run equilibrium intrinsic to the region because it possessed qualities lacking in the Western world. This is a misleading benchmark that takes little account of the likely dynamics.

THE MARKET FOR INSTITUTIONAL CHANGE

The very inconclusiveness of the debate over what special qualities East Asia possesses, or possessed, ought to warn us that basing an argument on them is unsafe. Why should we have believed that the region has a means of defying economic gravity in the presence of such uncertainty about what the magic carpet may be, let alone since the crisis has revealed there is no genuine means of levitation after all? An exceptionalist view of East Asia fosters the almost tautological belief that the crisis is soluble by whatever policies can restore the previous rates of growth. The question becomes all too simply how soon debt can be purged and a return made to the *status quo ante*. In other words – and it is a point worth labouring – few observers dwell enough on the long-run dynamics of East Asian development to question whether a recovery to previous levels was ever on the cards. This is curious given the attention paid over the past three or four years to Paul Krugman's article on 'The Myth of Asia's Miracle', the most famous of all the thousands of papers published on East Asian growth.[12] Krugman disavows having predicted the currency crisis but it is inherent in his analysis that high growth-rates were destined not to last.

The industrialization of East Asia took place in a single hectic generation, concentrating the associated stresses into a far shorter period than Western society had been obliged to accommodate. Extraordinary adjustments were required on all sides and it is hardly surprising that some aspects of economic, political and social life responded faster than others. East Asia lacks the West's long genesis of pluralist politics and therefore of channels through which any major interest may hope to influence policy. An important point to add is that pluralism is not merely a production good but a consumption good too, hence the desire for it among middle classes everywhere, whether or not their wishes are concealed.

The indications are that restructuring and political change were pressing needs that remained largely unacknowledged. Institutional change lagged relative to the maturing of the leading regional economies. It may have come about by means of political reform (perhaps at the hands of new cohorts of younger leaders), as a Schumpeterian gale of creative destruction, or as a breakdown, with dissatisfied citizens rebelling against authoritarian governments. The social changes brought by economic growth virtually ensured that, one way or other, unprecedented political demands were in the offing. During the miracle years, this was seldom recognized. Cronyism was virtually elevated to the 'Asian way'. The miracle created its own constituency among businessmen, bureaucrats and politicians. Governments in effect purchased their support for existing ways of managing macro economies and doing business. Among the wider community, subservience to the will of those in authority was counted as part of 'Asian values'. The rationalization was that these reflected a distinctive willingness to subordinate the self to the common good. The 'mandate of heaven' traditionally conferred on rulers could nevertheless be withdrawn if they failed to sustain the prosperity, the 'positive freedoms', which they themselves held to justify their authoritarianism. That the acquiescence of the miracle years was merely conditional is now revealed by the extent of riots and protests in several countries, of which Indonesia is the most striking.

THE WEST'S RESPONSE

The West faces problems relating as much to putting its own house in order as to what has happened in East Asia. The resilience of the West in the face of external shocks is at stake. The immediate need is to retain the openness of Western economies in the face of a real, or feared, increase in imports from the crisis-ridden countries. This relates to the management of public opinion rather than to policy choices, since appropriate trade policies are well understood. Economists are not noted for their endorsement of Trade Protection.

Of more fundamental concern is the essence of the Western system. Political capital is always under threat from within as well as without, constantly being eroded by the rent-seeking of interest groups along lines made famous by the late Mancur Olson.[13] Western ability to resist this erosion, to respond to shocks and recover from them, resides just where East Asia is unreformed: in the self-correction supplied by pluralist politics, an independent legal system willing to enforce lawful contracts, and a press free enough to protest against political and economic abuses.

Self-correction is the leitmotiv of decentralized societies in the Western world. Internal debate and constant shifts in political representation weave an unsteady but nevertheless flexible course. In the eyes of the tidy-minded, such expedients look inferior to the straight-line policy solutions that might be imposed by elites such as those in East Asian countries. But Western governance is more open to dissenting ideas and correspondingly more likely to reverse its errors than is that of authoritarian systems. The limited degree of self-correction in East Asia is its ultimate weakness.

EAST ASIAN EXCEPTIONALISM

The achievement of rapid economic growth was extremely praiseworthy, taking millions out of poverty, but apologists for authoritarianism within the region and among 'fellow travellers' outside (such as the 'New China Lobby' of Westerners bargaining for favourable market entry) are unpersuasive. They contend that the 'positive freedoms' of material prosperity justify a failure to provide 'negative freedoms' (civil freedoms). They also seem to believe that the region will be able to make the transition to a service economy as readily as its leading economies formerly shifted from one core manufacturing industry to the next – and without altering its political systems. This is the sticking point.

Paul Krugman made an enormous impact on opinion with his claim that the 'miracle' had derived from cheap factor inputs rather than higher productivity. Given that the most developed of the region's economies had exhausted their supplies of cheap labour and had little prospect of raising their already high savings rates, adjustment of some kind was unavoidable. Countries offering cheaper labour and lower wages were starting to compete with them. Productivity would have to be raised and, as developments in the world economy and regional tastes both implied, an unprecedented shift to the service sector was indicated.

A range of problems was created by divergences in the rates at which different elements in the region's economic, political and social systems responded to modernization. Some components did change smoothly enough.

The pace at which fertility rates fell was an outstanding example. This was unexpected, above all by the doomsaying commentators who make a profession of anticipating dire effects from population growth. Other features, especially political institutions, proved less responsive.

Western economists often seem to assume that East Asian economies operate with the flexibility of their own market democracies; perhaps they are dazzled by the striking economic performance into embracing 'economism', that is into thinking that growth must automatically lead to the replication of the other features of high-income Western countries. Political scientists and area specialists are more pessimistic, more prone to accept 'cultural fixity' and East Asian exceptionalism, and thus to think that East Asians will not adopt the individualistic politics of the West. Because they tend to favour cultural relativism they seldom recognize what a dismal prediction that is.

MODES OF INTERPRETATION

This exposes a gulf between streams of interpretation, each of which creates different expectations for the future of the region. Analysis is bedevilled by what is called the 'Humpty-Dumpty problem' – the intellectual fragmentation of the social sciences. Humpty-Dumpty was an egg-like character in a nursery rhyme common to northern European countries; he fell off a wall and 'all the King's horses and all the King's men, couldn't put Humpty together again'. The particular split in his shell that concerns us is the one between the universalism of market economics and the 'each country is unique' exceptionalism of area studies and much of political science. Disagreement over whether the East Asian miracle can be explained without reference to its institutions and cultural values has never flagged. No social science has delivered a knock-out blow to the others.

The decisive superiority of one type of analysis over the other would be signalled, in Kuhnian terms, by a brain-drain of young scholars from other fields.[14] Adherents of the inferior approach would dwindle in number. In so far as there is such a drift, the direction in English-speaking countries is not being kind to economics. Somewhat earlier, political science was invaded by rational choice models, but no general capitulation by other social scientists to the methods of economics has followed. There is now a growing aversion to economics, at least among the rising generation of students. Economists who are strongly of the opinion that they are in the right would not *ipso facto* convince an observer from another planet. Conclusions in all social sciences too often seem to derive from the assumptions of the particular disciplinary culture. Economics is no exception.

My own belief is nevertheless that the universalism of economics offers the best single vantage point. Of all the social sciences, economics offers the greatest internal consistency. By definition it also offers generality, though it tends to vitiate this by providing little detail on social and political phenomena and thus remaining open to the charge of lack of realism commonly levelled against it. The subfield of economic systems analysis, which necessarily incorporates political factors, brought itself into disrepute by focusing throughout the Cold War on the relative merits of capitalist and communist systems yet failing to predict the approaching demise of the Soviet system. Although that sub-field has been somewhat revitalized by work on the economics of Transition from Communism in Eastern Europe, its integration of social and political factors still relies on casual theorizing.[15] Not surprisingly, therefore, economic systems analysis again failed miserably by overlooking the signs of the East Asian crisis. Clearly we need a better way of handling the feedbacks between economic and political change.

THE CHALLENGE OF THE SERVICE SECTOR

To return to East Asian specifics, what was significant towards the end of the miracle years was the approach of the leading economies to thresholds where they would have to restructure or suffer falling growth rates, perhaps so steep as to be accompanied by political disturbance. Competition from cheaper and sometimes better-educated labour in the follower economies, notably in China after its 30 per cent devaluation in January 1994, was threatening to drive down returns in established manufacturing industries. The more developed economies would need to shift round the Product Cycle into unfamiliar territory, supplying financial and legal services, entertainment and software.

Service industries typically create non-material and short-lived products, young and fast-changing firms tend to do well in them, and competitive success depends on an almost artistically-minded workforce. They are hard to routinize and do not fit the Fordist, or Stalinist, model of large-scale factory labour that marks the earlier stages of industrialization. As international economic integration confronts producers with lower-cost foreign competitors in manufacturing, it exerts pressure to move into the services, with all the attendant changes in attitude that this portends.

This is not however the whole reason for the shift, which is only partly attributable to external competition. Changes in domestic demand point the same way. The US Labor Department's index of wages in newly-industrializing Asia showed that they rose from 8 per cent of the US level in 1975 to 32 per cent in 1995.[16]

When workers are better paid they become accustomed to material possessions and start to assume their demands for them can be met. They want something more, that is to say services. Providing services necessitates a free-wheeling class of labour which is likely to express its own individual tastes in other spheres, including in politics. The authoritarian regimes of the Tiger economies were entering a trap where failing to maintain growth would undoubtedly lead to political discontent – a progressive withdrawal of the 'Mandate of Heaven' – yet sustaining growth by transforming themselves into service economies also threatened new political demands.

The service sector puts a premium on creativity, which depends on intellectual freedom. In large measure freedom is isomorphic, likely to spill over from one realm to others, including – as mentioned – to political life. Can governments avoid the implication? Just possibly they might succeed in directing creative energies into a mixture of work pursuits and anodyne pastimes. Singapore is certainly trying to raise creativity by reducing rote learning in schools, inviting young foreigners to bring their ideas, and through Lew Kuan Yew's exhortation to his countrymen to gossip more over lunch. There has not been time to assess the outcome.

If the shift to intellectual adventurousness does succeed without roiling the political waters, it may do so for an ironic reason. If intellectual guest-workers are relied on, they may afford some insulation from the political demands that might follow from the rising confidence of a domestic middle class. Expatriates will watch their manners, especially under repressive regimes. They form part of the world's 'floating elite' for whom, in Albert Hirschman's terms, 'exit' (removal to another jurisdiction) rather than 'voice' (political action) is the natural response to discontent. If they do have political interests, which will be rather seldom among technicians, these may well be directed at the tax regime of their home country or wherever they expect to retire. By employing mercenaries, so to speak, Singapore may conceivably elude the political consequences of its economic success: it may be able to import creativity and make it self-limiting. But Singapore is a confined island of only three million people, well schooled, and much easier to oversee than larger populations. Elsewhere there is little sign that creativity is being greatly raised despite concern over educational rigidities in Japan and South Korea, and for the moment there is resistance to any widespread hiring of expatriates.[17] Raising the quality of work and shifting its focus will be even harder in countries with far weaker educational records, such as Thailand.

THE UNDERLYING DYNAMICS

To the extent that my view of development in the region coincided (and coincides) with the 'economistic' interpretation, I had in mind a model of more discontinuity than most economists seemed to anticipate and more change than political scientists expected: a sort of 'cohort theory' in which prosperous young people became impatient with and at some point rather rapidly threw off the restrictions their parents' generation thought inescapable or actually desirable. I saw in young East Asians, including some of my own students, an eagerness to acquire non-material items like cleaner environments and participatory politics, and to think of these things as consumer goods. After all, their generation is accustomed to a high level of purely material consumption. I also envisaged that demand would create supply in the sense of inducing a new generation of politicians to meet the demand for more refined public goods. Taiwan and South Korea have made a start at democratizing. Nevertheless, while some countries might transform themselves faster than political scientists and area specialists anticipated, via the sudden, unheralded social changes called 'Quebec Effects', the process seemed likely to bring more upsets than expected by economists. In Indonesia it has already done so.

The outcome depends on details such as the age of rulers and their willingness to step aside – in systems that lack orderly procedures for dealing with succession and where the military often remain a political force. Conflicts are always possible, maybe probable. The region was running into diminishing returns to its institutional capital even during the miracle years, despite the economic success with which authoritarian rule had been associated for 30 years. The next transition would be more difficult than the initial industrialization had been and might destabilize some countries, maybe the entire region.

This version of the underlying dynamics was intended to set the East Asian 'miracle' in historical context. And the purpose of that was to project what might happen into the future and suggest the problems that might come. The analysis has not been invalidated by the currency crisis. According to Krugman, the literature reads like a Greek Tragedy, everybody's position has been adopted in advance, and everybody claims that events justify his or her pre-crisis interpretation. That is an over-generalization: some high-profile commentators such as Clyde Prestowitz and Jeffrey Garten have come forward to admit that they grossly exaggerated the strength of Asian economies.[18]

Robert Kagan remarked in March 1998, that 'the model is dead, long live the model'.[19] He claimed that whereas East Asian regimes had formerly been praised for achieving higher growth rates than the Western democracies, the fashion had shifted almost overnight: their approach was now decried as having been flawed from the start. There is something in this; during the miracle, a majority of observers did lavish praise on the East Asian model of the 'developmental state' and a not inconsiderable number went so far as to imply, or even to recommend, that the governments of Western countries should rely on their example to intervene much more in economic life. Many who held these views now appear to have taken cover.

The statist model in East Asia was nevertheless flawed, or maybe totally empty, as current research into Japanese industry policy and the active economic policies of the Japanese government increasingly shows. According to the *Australian Financial Review* (18 July 1998), despite thousands of books and academic papers and hundreds of conferences to the contrary, Japanese economic policy was astoundingly passive. We find Professor Yoshiaki Miwa (Economics, University of Tokyo) declaring that, despite the seminal work by Chalmers Johnson on MITI (the Ministry of International Trade and Industry) and Krugman's insistence on the influential role of MITI and the Ministry of Finance, 'it was all just an illusion'.

Admittedly the financial crisis is not certain evidence of general and deep-seated institutional deficiencies within the Japanese state and economy, other perhaps than in the banking sector. Nor would a portrayal of institutional sclerosis in East Asia as a whole have enabled one to predict the currency devaluations. Had countries managed to cross what I term 'Krugman's Bridge', that is, raised their productivity once cheap inputs started to become scarce, reasonable growth rates might have been maintained, with little disturbance in the meantime. By embracing enough reform to establish pluralist politics, a free press, and an independent judiciary, each country might have transformed itself into what the Japanese politician, Ichiro Ozawa, calls a 'normal country'. In that case the urgency of the East Asian problems and the implications for Western countries, indeed the whole world, might have subsided.

Such an outcome seems most improbable. The politics and institutions of the region seem unlikely to have responded fast enough. 'If Japan could make difficult decisions quickly', proclaimed an official of the Ministry of Finance in Tokyo, 'we would have won World War II'.[20] If Prussia was an army with a state, post-war Japan has been something like a bureaucracy with a state. Undoubtedly, therefore, Japan is a special, or at any rate a particular case, though it cannot be unique in the sense of being exempt from the workings of economics. Despite the newly-fashionable opinion that its governmental activism was 'all just an illusion', the battle is by no means over between market economists and those students of Japan labelled 'revisionists' who emphasize culture and the steering role of ministries. Maybe it will turn out that the interventions and corruptions of the Japanese state distorted income distribution more than they determined decisions about production. Maybe institutions affect consumption more than production. Even so, non-institutionalists will find it hard to maintain that particular distributions of income have no feed-back effects on modes and levels of production.

But if Japan is an exception, so is every country. The strength of economics is that it looks for common structural features and avoids tracking round in the wilderness of special cases created by the area studies' approach. Let us therefore return to the East Asian region as a whole. What we may say is that the crisis was premature in so far as without it East Asia was reaching the point where major adjustments had become essential. There has been little comment on this point; it appears to have been overtaken by events, yet a narrow recovery brought about, say, by recapitalizing the banks, will run the risk of leaving untouched until the next crisis all the other defects of politicized economic life. The point has been well put by Fukuyama.[21] He observes that the region's microeconomic institutions and policies, amounting all told to industry policy,

> will account for declining long-term rates of growth in the states that maintain them. But they were not heavily implicated in the currency crisis of 1997–98, which is what allows people like Chalmers Johnson and many Asian officials to continue to assert that there is nothing fundamentally wrong with interventionist economic policies in the region.

Whether economic contraction will lead to leadership turmoil or decisive political change remains indeterminate. The indeterminacy may be attributed to the Humpty-Dumpty problem; political responses to economic change, like economic responses to political change, fill the media and the history books without eliciting enough usable theory about how either works from economists or, come to that, from political scientists. A parallel to the Asian situation was the earlier failure of economists to anticipate the negative political reactions to structural change in post-Soviet Russia. With respect to East Asia one did find, here and there, an astute contrarian such as Kasper who prophesied a dysfunctional, rent-seeking response by authoritarian systems.[22] But it was customary to encounter silence about the deficiencies of such systems, perhaps along the lines of the half-remembered Biblical injunction, 'sufficient unto the day is the evil thereof'. Nevertheless official forecasters have since been obliged to downgrade their predictions of rates of GDP growth and regional exchange rates time and time again in the wake of sliding currencies. They had started out unconscionably bullish.

CONCLUSIONS

The financial crisis exposed the rigidity of authoritarian systems and their tendency to misallocate resources. This institutional failure is the explanation of the crisis presented here. It is consistent with the first of four explanations drawn from the recent literature by Martin Wolf.[23] The three other explanations to which Wolf alludes refer to proximate matters of financial excess: the belief of international investors that international lenders would always bail them out; the unsustainably pegged exchange rates; and the panicky retreat of investors from their earlier exuberance. Policy conclusions differ according to which of these explanations one accepts: ending rescue packages to avoid moral hazard in future; refraining from fixing exchange rates in order to allow currencies to indicate truer values; and establishing a credible lender of last resort or controlling (that is, restricting) short-term capital flows to emerging markets, perhaps by a Tobin tax.

One or other of these three diagnoses may be correct and the matching remedy may succeed in curbing the excesses of international lending. But they are not likely all to be right. The first two are compatible with one another in attempting to make markets work better, but are less compatible with the third, which is interventionist. None of the three addresses the inherent tendency of politicized economies to misallocate resources and stifle expression of contrary opinions that could draw attention to this. We may therefore conclude that a central flaw of authoritarian systems is the way they suppress information markets, which means they weaken their chances of self-correction.[24] This is to concur with Alan Greenspan, chairman of the Federal Reserve, who stated (in Wolf's words) 'that the afflicted countries should move as fast as possible towards US standards of liberalisation, transparency and financial regulation'.[25]

Lecturing East Asian leaders publicly in this way may however be counter-productive. 'Face' is important in Asian societies and causing someone to lose face is unacceptable. Given that the efforts of Thailand and the Philippines have failed to persuade ASEAN (the Association of South East Asian Nations) to abandon its practice of non-interference in one another's affairs and start to exchange critical, warning comment, the West faces an intractable problem. Western countries, especially the United States, are seen as outsiders with too much to gain. The insurance that economic systems can buy through decentralization and bounded dissent is not well understood in East Asia. Even in the West, for all its decentralization, the role of the contrarian or whistle-blower is unenviable and reliance on spontaneous coordination is constantly questioned.

The problem throughout the world is how to institutionalize independent critical thought without permitting its expression to become destructive. Natural science perhaps offers a more comforting analogy than politics: it has found ways to accommodate the tension between caution and inspiration. Contests between scientific theories are messy – Kuhn's Scientific Revolutions – and as such are distasteful to the conservative mind. Yet a not dissimilar species of open, non-destructive conflict will eventually have to be domesticated in Asian political and economic systems. The behavioural, institutional and political changes required will be extensive enough to constitute a second miracle.

NOTES

1. Paul Krugman (n.d.), 'Two Cheers for Formalism', formal.html at web.mit.edu.
2. Peter A.G.Van Bergeijk and Nico W. Mensink, 'Measuring Globalization', *Journal of World Trade*, **31** (3), 1997, 161.
3. Robert York and Paul Atkinson, *The Reliability of Quarterly National Accounts in Seven Major Countries: A User's Perspective* (Paris: OECD, Economics Department Working Papers, no. 171, 1997), pp. 11–12.
4. *The Australian*, 10 March 1998.
5. Llewellyn D. Howell and Donald Xie, 'Asia at Risk: The Impact of Methodology in Forecasting', *Management Decision*, **34** (9), 1996, 6.
6. Noel Annan, *Changing Enemies: The Defeat and Regeneration of Germany* (London: Harper Collins, 1996), p. 49.
7. *The Australian*, 23 July 1998.
8. *The Australian*, 9 January 1998.
9. *The Australian*, 13 January 1998.
10. *Financial Times*, 2 June 1998.
11. David Henderson, 'Industrial Policies Revisited: Lessons Old and New from East Asia and Elsewhere', *The Pelham Papers*, 3 (Melbourne: Centre for the Practice of International Trade, 1998).
12. Paul Krugman, 'The Myth of Asia's Miracle', *Foreign Affairs*, **73** (6), November–December 1994, 62–78.
13. Mancur Olson, *The Rise and Decline of Nations* (New Haven: Yale University Press, 1982).
14. Thomas S. Kuhn, *The Structure of Scientific Revolutions* (Chicago: University of Chicago Press, 1962).
15. Thrainn Eggertsson, 'The Old Theory of Economic Policy and the New Institutionalism, *Lectiones Jenenses*, **12**, 1997, 28, n. 5.
16. Krugman,'Two Cheers', loc. cit.
17. Ivan P. Hall, *Cartels of the Mind: Japan's Intellectual Closed Shop* (New York: W.W. Norton, 1997).
18. *Australian Financial Review*, 9 May 1998.
19. Kagan, Robert, 'What Korea Teaches', *The New Republic*, 9 March 1998, 39.
20. *The Australian*, l9 June 1998.
21. Francis Fukuyama, 'Response to Sebastian Mallaby on "America in Asia's Mirror"', *The National Interest*, **52**, 1998, 25.
22. Wolfgang Kasper, 'The Stillborn Tiger Cub', *The Independent Monthly*, November 1994, 70–71, and 'The East Asian Challenge', in Helen Hughes et al., *Australia's Asian Challenge* (Sydney: Centre for Independent Studies, 1994), pp. 22–33.
23. *Financial Times*, 16 June 1998.
24. Christopher Lingle, *The Rise and Decline of the Asian Century: False Starts on the Path to the Global Millennium* (Barcelona: Sirocco, 1997); Eric Jones, 'East Asia's Achilles Heel', *Agenda*, **5** (1), 1998, 119–21.
25. *Financial Times*, 16 June 1998.

9. 'Asian Values' and cultural explanations of economic change

INTRODUCTION: THE REVIVAL OF CULTURAL EXPLANATION

After many years during which cultural relativism has prevailed, there are moves afoot to return to explaining levels of economic development in terms of cultural differences.[1] Perhaps 'moves' is too strong. Most of what has appeared so far amounts to little more than claims that cultural differences do indeed matter, accompanied by requests for other scholars to investigate the topic. The new trend involves a willing and unhistorical suspension of disbelief about the ambiguities of cultural explanation. The reasons for this seem to be two-fold: one set of authors is, understandably enough, dissatisfied with standard explanations of economic development by way of either the ordinary categories of economics or Marxist-style 'theories' of dependency, while a different set is determined to find an explanation for the 'East Asian Miracle' in intrinsic *and therefore permanent* features of regional society.[2] This second group uses cultural explanation for political ends, just as the cultural relativists do, but in its case not urging the equivalence of all cultures but the actual superiority of Asian ones. Western scholars have often been nervous about arguing against either position. As the Indian-born economist, Amartya Sen, observes 'Western discussion of non-Western societies is often too respectful of authority'.[3]

Both types of author dismiss cultural relativism, explicitly or implicitly. I have no quarrel with that. It was always an irritating feature of intellectual conformity to find that any reference to cultural differences had become taboo and that all cultures must be presumed equal. But dissatisfaction with existing explanations does not license any particular alternative. I shall hope to show that, although culture is not to be dismissed in quite the *a priori* terms that most economists use when they mention it at all, it nevertheless has too little substance to account for the phenomena it is now being asked to explain: economic development, under-development in general, the so-called 'European Miracle', and the recent 'East Asian Miracle'.

There are four main objections to relying on culture to explain economic change, at least in the way that the current literature is trying to do. The first, and dominating, problem is that there seems to be no agreed, consistent and operational definition of culture. Explanations in cultural terms often slide from one aspect and one meaning to the next in the course of the argument.

The second objection is that values and institutions are often taken to be one and the same thing. This is not helpful. Values are intangible and communicated largely in informal ways. It is hard, though not impossible, to alter culture in this sense by direct acts of political will. Institutions on the other hand are usually creations that reflect conscious choices. They can be changed by deliberate policy, although the changes may be concealed because the same old names are likely to remain attached to institutions whose functions are quietly altering. In other words there are labelling errors, which can be compounded in translation. Translators often equate an institution with some similar institution in their own country, even though it may have quite different functions.

The third problem is that there are excessively wide variations in underlying assumptions about how fixed or malleable culture is. Some authors, mostly non-economists, are inclined to treat culture as fixed and not to recognize how much it changes over time. Others, especially economists, tend to imply that culture is plastic and remodels itself automatically in response to economic incentives. Neither extreme is acceptable. Cultures can be shown to have changed historically, whether or not the old names and labels have been retained. Yet cultures do also display 'stickiness'. We are conditioned from childhood to behave in certain ways. Most people are content to adopt the behaviours prevailing in the societies in which they grew up. This stickiness leads to lags in adjustment, which means that economists cannot dismiss cultural influences as automatic reflexes to economic incentives. Admittedly, some features, like regional dialects and even whole languages, probably survive for reasons connected with the economy, in this case when labour markets are not fully integrated. As markets do become more integrated there is some degree of cultural homogenization involving, for instance, a reduction in language variety. In *Language is Power*, John Honey goes so far as to suggest that the French language may one day disappear.[4] On the other hand, there is a propensity for humans to recreate regional differences. Thus neither complete cultural fixity nor complete malleability are reasonable assumptions.

The fourth problem relating to culture is, as mentioned, that differences have come to be used for overtly political ends – to try to manipulate values in some parts of East Asia and present a hostile account of value changes in the Western world in order to predict a relative, maybe even absolute, Decline of the West. This is what the 'Asian Values' debate is about – though it must be emphasized that the values are those of only a subset of Asians. The literature of this debate is 'Occidentalist', that is to say it involves a false reading of the prospects for the West in the distorted mirror of one phase in the development of the East. Since it relies on an incorrect description and faulty understanding of the essentials of Western civilization, I shall attempt to refute it in this chapter.

The West has plenty of critics of its own but the claims of 'Asian Values' writers have given them additional ammunition. Some business people wish their own companies (but presumably not those of their competitors) could receive the sort of government support they think East Asian businesses receive, together with a workforce guaranteed to be passive. Other critics of the West belong to the 'New China Lobby' of ex-bureaucrats and former politicians who are capitalizing on the contacts they made when in the public service to push private business ventures. They seek to excuse their dealings with dictators by showing that (some) Asian authoritarian systems work better than the liberal ones of the West.

The apparent ease with which authoritarian figures outside the West deal with opposition appeals to Westerners who feel they are not appreciated in their home countries. It is not only Asia they misread; they seem not to grasp the essentials of the decentralized Western economic, political and social system itself. The most pertinent point about Western individualism, political pluralism, independent law and free press is the self-correcting nature of these things taken together. They add up to a noisy, untidy system, which, in spite or perhaps because of this, has always managed to correct major failings and must be presumed capable of doing so in the future. Authoritarian systems may perform well in the short run, because they can, in the famous phrase used of Mussolini's Italy, 'make the trains run on time', but over longer periods their centralism leads to unopposed and therefore uncorrected error.

CULTURE AND THE DIVERGENCE OF CIVILIZATIONS

(i) Lal's *Unintended Consequences*

In this chapter I shall criticize two types of approach to differences between the West and East Asia that rely on culture for the main part of their explanation. I want first to consider the views of Deepak Lal, an economist at UCLA, on the comparative long-run economic performance of the Western world and East Asia, as presented in his 1998 book, *Unintended Consequences.*[5] This is a subtle and impressive work, or I would not pay it so much attention, but I think it is wrong in portraying changes in the West as heralding Decline and in claiming that 'Asian Values' will shield East Asia from similar changes. Lal offers a synthesis of several factors but, if we strip his work down to the barest bones, his position on the 'big picture' issues of world economic history does fall into the cultural category. He locates the East–West divergence primarily in cosmology, with the West's shift from belief in what anthropologists refer to as a 'sky god' to man-centered values being in his view the ultimate cause of its decline.

One of the problems that has to be solved before any economy can function well is how to curb the destructive opportunism of individuals. Lal's thesis is that Western civilization inherited vital constraints on opportunism from early Christian periods, only to begin to abandon them once the Scientific Revolution, followed by the work of Charles Darwin, metaphorically ejected God from His throne. East Asian Confucianism took another course. Once East Asia had adopted law from the West, the mixture with Confucianism proved not merely compatible with but actually inspired rapid growth. Lal thinks this growth can continue or at any rate will resume after the Asian Crisis of the late 1990s. The West, already on a descending path, will go on declining because of a fatal deviation from its founding values.

Hence Lal contends that the West has eroded the 'social cement' that preserved it from destructive individualism and faces a future of decay and disorder. In East Asia, on the contrary, Confucian cosmology still suppresses the destructive tendencies of individuals. A double cultural immunity, consisting of the borrowed law of contract and its own indigenous value-system, thus protects the future of East Asia, or at least those parts with which Lal concerns himself, which seem to be mainly those occupied by the Overseas Chinese. Lal is too knowledgeable to try, as a number of others have tried, to pass off the East Asian Miracle as a simple bonus for Confucian values. He argues against this. In passing we may note that the emergence of 'neo-Confucianism', from which the conservatism and veneration of the elderly characteristic of Confucianism proper have been dropped, is witness after all to the mutability of East Asian values, and so is the fact that Western-style commercial law has been adopted.

Where culture appears in Lal's scheme, it comes in as a sort of perpetual insurance policy: family values hold families and family businesses together and guard prosperous Asian societies against dissolving into licentiousness. Family members discipline one another and look after one another. There is no need for East Asian states to expend an ever-increasing share of revenue on welfare with the unintended consequence of a downward spiral because the Welfare State offers such incentives for free-riding.

Things are supposedly different in the West. There, for a very long time in history, opportunism had been checked by the culture of guilt invented by the Roman Catholic church and accepted, even intensified, under Protestantism. This form of moral control was effective and cheap, because it was self-policing. Fatal blows were however struck against it when the Scientific Revolution and Darwinism undermined religious certainties. Into the consequent spiritual void poured Marxism, Freudianism and most recently Eco-fundamentalism. The assault was reinforced by economic growth, which presumably reduced human fears and discounted the solace of Christianity. Later came overkill, when the Welfare State generalized claims on the public purse hitherto reserved for the truly destitute. The social decay and demoralization that Lal finds so visible in the United States will be followed in other Western countries as they too abandon the manners and deference associated with old hierarchies.

In this negative version of Western history the key innovations combined to create a Christian cosmology in which personal behaviour came to be governed by a terrifying form of *internalized* thought control, whereas in East Asia opportunistic behaviour was checked *externally* by the threat of public shaming. Lal thinks that economic growth was generated first by cultural and institutional changes that liberated Western markets from the constraints of custom and command, rather than by technological innovations or other materialistic causes. This interpretation follows from the detailed account he gives of religious developments in very early centuries.

Equally clearly, the key changes initiating Western decline came from abandoning belief in the cosmology that had supported the guilt culture. Lal's evidence that the West is entering a bleak, amoral future (surely rather a long time after Charles Darwin?) is little more than graphs of rising crime and illegitimate births in the USA between 1950–80. Yet crime rates have fallen since then and what happened before 1980 is doubtfully relevant. Whether illegitimacy is really an indicator of decay we will consider in a moment.

Is it indeed plausible that social changes in the West, whatever they are, really derive from some deep ideological shift – some unwise abandonment of the guilt culture? There are surely explanations of more material kinds, such as higher, independent incomes for women, to which an economist might have been expected to turn first. Lal does not accept materialist explanations. Nor does he entertain the possibility that the West may reach a new social equilibrium through the voluntary choices of individuals. He does not really think that markets can be trusted nor accept that the decentralized societies of the Western world are set up in such a way that, despite successive problems and through all the heat of debate (indeed because of heated debate), self-correction is likely to emerge, just as it has in the past.

Thus Lal, to my mind, falls into a trap that observers have fallen into before, of taking Western societies at face value and being over-influenced by the social dangers of the moment. Yet the decentralized polities, economies and societies of the West do work, in the sense that millions of people move their jobs and home from one city or even country to the next, raise their children, and join or rejoin all kinds of institutions, including churches. Lal goes out of his way to assert that the fact that 60 per cent of Americans belong to a church is simply hypocritical, given the violation of many Christian injunctions by American society. To say the least, this misunderstands the roles of repentance and forgiveness in Christianity. It also fails to accommodate the fact that church membership in the United States is far higher than in most other Western countries. The Western world as a whole is surely not uniform enough to be explained by a single set of religious developments. A failing of contemporary Western writing on social issues is that they often wander between discussing the United States and the rest of the West, sometimes speaking as though America is the whole of the West or at least entirely representative of it. Occasionally this is unavoidable because of the nature of the sources but it needs to be taken into account.

The pessimistic air with which Lal discusses the West and the optimistic one he reserves for the non-Western world are hard to justify given actual social behaviours in these two giant, diverse regions. The book's concluding injunction to the West is, 'physician heal thyself'. This hostile remark seems to suggest that the social ills of the West and East are no different. But that is the fallacy of moral equivalence. It is not in the West, after all, where Amartya Sen finds that 100 million fewer women are alive today than would be expected on ordinary assumptions about birth and death rates.[6] It is not in the West that we find beggars and illiteracy on India's scale. We do not find in the West political prisoners, a trade in the organs of executed criminals (the buyers mainly Overseas Chinese), or kidnappings of children (with buyers protected because society accepts their 'traditional right' to have a son), on the scale of China. One response to this might be to note that the West and Asia are not at the same level of economic development; neither is of course uniform even in its *internal* level of development and we can speak only of modal tendencies. Each great region may be expected to display different social problems at any given date, at least unless and until secure high incomes have made it possible to accept international standards of conduct. The West practised plenty of barbarities in its day. Quite so, the stage of development is different – but if the differences are explicable on that basis, the effect of cultural values disappears.

Let us look more closely at the evidence and prediction of unending decay in the West. Is the forecast right? To answer shortly, it isn't. Consider the question of illegitimacy. A monotonic removal of constraints on extra-marital conceptions beginning as far back as Darwin's demotion of God, and even further back, from the Scientific Revolution, simply cannot account for fluctuations in the rate of illegitimacy. The common Western European pattern was of *declining* illegitimacy from 1870 to 1930. This decline preceded the decline in marital fertility. Illegitimacy rose after 1930. It is neither easy to square a full 60 years of Darwinian rationalist onslaught with a *fall* in illegitimacy nor to blame the Welfare State for a *rise* that began 15 or more years before it was established.

Illegitimacy need not in any case reflect social dysfunction. All 'illegitimate' births are scarcely of the same type. They do not, or do not invariably, demonstrate the debauching of women. They increasingly denote choices made by individuals who, given the ready availability of the birth-control pill, could have chosen otherwise. There is no reason to pick out single women as preternaturally responsive to economic inducements, in this case to income and child support payments. Today they may be supporting children courtesy of the taxpayer but to be indignant about this is to accept too readily the present distribution of income and employment opportunities, as if these things are permanently and justly fixed. In some not inconceivable future, when economies succeed in generating sufficient paid employment, single young women may be able to support their children out of their own income. We have no guarantee that they will then return to a conventional matrimony on which so many of them have already turned their backs.

Labour markets that will provide them with jobs and induce them to return to them are about to emerge. Most developed countries are soon going to run short of labour. Without (even) more immigration, the annual rate of growth of the United States labour force will fall to 0.2 per cent from 2010 to 2030, whereas the economic growth of the 1990s was underpinned by a rate five times higher.[7] Unless there are wholly unprecedented rises in productivity, the United States and other countries will be able to maintain economic growth only with much larger and politically unpopular flows of immigration or by drawing unemployed and under-employed people back into work.

It is not clear in any case that there are very large numbers of supposedly 'immoral' single mothers, since total US fertility and even more so fertility in several European countries is below replacement. Only the fertility of immigrant women keeps the American rate as close as it is to replacement. As Francis Fukuyama has pointed out, a 're-norming' was under way in the West throughout the 1990s, with falling rates of crime, divorce and births to single mothers.[8] Even as Lal wrote, his sour view of his adopted country was becoming out of date.

Perhaps, then, young American women will return to matrimony. A sizeable fraction of single mothers do marry the father of their child shortly after the birth, which reduces the impact of the purportedly shocking figures of illegitimacy. As for cohabitating (living together without marrying), it was illegal in all American states until about 1970 but now precedes more than half of all first marriages. There is little evidence that it weakens matrimony. A study of ten European countries shows that people who lived with one partner whom they subsequently married were no more likely to divorce than those who married in the conventional way.[9]

The approach that Lal takes is what I have labelled elsewhere 'cultural fixity', in which culture helps to shape economic change but the feedback is not powerful enough to reshape culture. More precisely, his case rests on one culture, the East Asian, surviving intact enough to resist damaging social changes whereas another, the Western, has stripped away its own moral defences. Traditional family life protects one but not the other. As an exception to the rule of decay in the West, Lal urges that America's Jews are protected by their tight family values, inherited from their life during past centuries in European ghettoes. This places heavy weight on past experience and on path-dependence. It overlooks actual changes in Jewish behaviour – the soaring level of out-marriages to people of other religious faiths and the high divorce rates affecting Jews and non-Jews alike. I find it difficult to think these everyday social changes are comparable with the horrendous problems of Asia, such as Amartya Sen's finding, already mentioned, that 100 million fewer women are alive today than one would expect.

How stable non-Western families really are, or will continue to be, when confronted with the fruits of economic success and the fresh choices that high incomes bring is also debatable. There is an element of stereotyping in speaking of East and West in these ways. Overseas Chinese families, seemingly so coherent and disciplined, are known for the bitterness of their disputes over business assets once the dominant patriarch and founder of the family firm has died.[10] There is plenty of testimony that East Asian family ties were already fraying while the Economic Miracle was taking place (as people got more choices) and continued to come untied during the Crisis (when they were subject to greater stresses).[11]

In Thailand, rising unemployment has led to many more children dropping out of school and an increase in mental illnesses and crime. According to the Thai Prime Minister, speaking of the Crisis, 'all these problems have negatively impacted on our traditional strong family institutions'. In China children are said to be rebelling against convention and, according to a Professor of Sociology at Shanghai University, 'the influence of the family is declining'. *The Far Eastern Economic Review* reports that a growing number of young Chinese are 'experimenting with everything from sex and rock-and-roll to living away from home and cohabiting with their mates before marriage'. The Chinese government has admitted that sexually-transmitted diseases, which were reported to be almost non-existent in the late 1970s, now account for one-third of all contagious diseases. Even in Japan, social discipline has been dissolving, as witness the rise in schoolyard violence. With respect to the whole continent, an East-West Center study suggests that 'patterns of family formation and dissolution in Asia are converging with those in the U.S. in many respects'.

These examples, which could be multiplied, are sufficient to undermine any assumption of a cosmological difference between West and East so great as to dictate the former's decline and to insulate the latter from the effects of economic change. Similar causes (rapid and extensive economic growth for instance) are likely to have broadly similar effects on any society experiencing them. The past is not the sole influence on the present. Reality lies where current forces intersect with historical ones, that is where current pressures react together with the menu of choices given by history. This tends to damage any thesis that relies on the lasting influence of some ancient cultural trait.

How would we know that continuing social behaviour has been produced by such a trait? Maybe cultural traits do not have the force claimed for them, but survive until, and only until, there is reason to abandon them. They can perhaps appear to have survived, but have less and less of their original function. For example, it has been suggested that 'Chinese conservatism is not a symptom of rigidity but rather the result of adaptation to conditions which remained unchanged for thousands of years'.[12] We do not have to take this as literal history (many things have changed in China) to see the challenge it poses: cultural beliefs may be the outcome of other forces, or testimony to the absence of strong contrary forces, without necessarily exerting a controlling influence themselves. Consider how very rapidly Chinese culture – in the sense of the values admired and practised – responded when Deng Xiao-ping reversed the prohibitions and ambitions of Maoist times.

On the other hand, we need not doubt that material trends such as changes in levels of income, fertility and urbanization do modify behaviour. There seems no reason to accept that East Asian societies and cultures have been, or can remain, unaffected by developments of these kinds. The results are already plain; the shrinking size of families alone has brought enormous strains. As for Western society, there seems little reason to think that rather ambiguous indicators of supposed current dysfunction must mean terminal decline, and certainly not to claim that the Decline of the West is under way just because the influence of the churches has been reduced. As Tyler Cowen has shown in an article entitled 'Is Our Culture in Decline?' there is a good case for being optimistic about Western, or at any rate American, culture.[13] Although he is speaking primarily of the Arts, his work does indicate that, contrary to fashionable opinion, Western culture is very buoyant.

Cowen remarks that the opposite viewpoint suffers from cognitive bias in that it tends to focus on the decline of familiar traits, while neglecting, or even deprecating, the rise of new ones. People tend to form their tastes between the ages of about 15 and 25 years. They tend to judge innovations against that benchmark and, more broadly, to judge the present against the best of all past 'high' culture. This will inevitably make the present seem less impressive than it is. The accumulated achievements of earlier times are far greater in total than the achievements of any single moment, such as the present. As time advances, cultures are judged against a higher and higher mountain of accumulated achievement and, in scorning some new practitioners of the Arts, it is forgotten how the work of many past 'greats' was itself scorned and resisted in its day.

I have tried here to refute Deepak Lal's thesis. Other people hold similar views to his, but none has expressed them so cogently at book length and devised an all-embracing model of Eastern and Western history to back them up. My attempt at refutation is a tribute to the importance of Lal's book.

(ii) The 'Singapore School' and 'Asian Values'

Of less intellectual but greater political significance is the campaign by the so-called 'Singapore School' to praise 'Asian Values' and explain the economic success of East Asia in their terms.[14] 'Asian Values' have been celebrated in a number of widely-read publications by Lee Kwan Yew and members of the Singaporean foreign service. Politicians in other countries, notably Prime Minister Mahathir of Malaysia, have made statements along similar lines. The high tide of the movement came during the mid-1990s; less has been heard of it since the Asian Crisis. The central idea is that a particular set of values, adding up to neo-Confucianism, was responsible for economic growth in East Asia. These values include hard work, high savings, desire for education, concern for family and willingness to put society before self.

Coupled with a cultural interpretation of Asian economic performance were statements gloating that the West was not only experiencing terrible social decay but was destined to be replaced by a morally and therefore competitively superior East. This 'Occidentalism' is a variant of arguments that became fashionable during the 1980s and early 1990s, when it was widely feared by Americans that the United States was doomed to surrender its place as leading economy in the world. 'Declinist' views centred on the hypothesis that the United States is an empire (which by any reasonable definition it is not) in a condition of 'over-stretch', meaning that it would become unable to afford its foreign policy commitments. It is not surprising that less has been heard of this during the American economic boom, though there are disgruntled people who gleefully anticipate the collapse of the New York stock market (and who will take that as evidence of a 'permanent' collapse of the real economy in the United States).

The Asian values argument was and probably still is influential because of the prominence of the people who published their opinions in highly visible international publications. Not all Asian intellectuals accepted arguments of these sorts. It depends who one reads, almost 'which Lee' one reads. Lee Kwan Yew and the Singaporeans take this line but Lee Teng-hui in Taiwan and Martin Lee in Hong Kong do not, indeed Lee Teng-hui has observed that there are no such things as *Asian* values, only values, and added that the cultural argument is based on a misreading of Chinese history. Declinist and Occidentalist types of theory are as insecurely based as they are antagonistic. They depend on thinking in cultural or nationalistic terms, and worse, they imply that the process of change in world economic geography is necessarily zero-sum. None of the protagonists of an Asian Values case seems willing to admit that new social, political and economic systems may simply grow up alongside existing ones, to their mutual benefit through voluntary trade.

The cultural argument was congenial to Asian authoritarians who wanted to maintain social control and also had, so far as one can judge from their rhetorical style, personal reasons for being offensive towards Western society in which as individuals they had often been educated. It is not that there are not plenty of critics of the West actually living in the West. Sometimes these resemble the prominent figure described by Timothy Mo as follows: 'Like many ethnic intellectuals who have taken up residence in the advanced West he takes the enlightened decencies of the host country for granted, while he cheers on the benighted from a safe distance.'[15]

It makes little sense to contrast two broad and heterogeneous systems as if each is fixed at this particular moment of history. Asia and the West are at different economic stages, though we can already see some of the most developed Asian societies starting to exhibit the modern and sometimes damaging behaviours of rich, urban, Western societies. The Singapore School started to gloat too soon, as some Singaporean politicians now seem implicitly to be admitting.

A better way of thinking about culture is to visualize it as a resource, as a menu of possible behaviours from which people make choices. This has the advantage of directing our attention to the way choices change. Culture is *contingent*, a statement that requires us to say what it is contingent upon. The answer is the stage of economic growth, including in this economic structure, that is, the composition of industry, as well as the level of per capita real income.

As economic growth proceeds, modal cultural behaviour and beliefs adapt to it. They adapt generationally, which is to say that there may be no smoothly continuous progression but a series of 'Quebec effects' or cascades of change when new age cohorts, conditioned by new life experiences, reach positions of influence. Certainly some elements of culture may be quite sticky. Any culture reflects adaptations to past risks and past relative prices, and these adaptations become built in, as it were, to the preferences of successive generations. But what has been selected in the past can be deselected in the future, when incentives and disincentives change.

Political figures may seek to legitimize certain cultural attributes, introduce new behaviours and eradicate old practices. Their attempts at social engineering will be well publicized if they have control of organs of public opinion (they will certainly have special access to the media). We should probably look on the Asian Values campaign in this light. But the task is a hard one. Economic growth will be silently working to bring about other changes that are not likely to suit authoritarian ends. Prosperity tends to erode older values

The Singaporeans were apparently becoming aware of the dynamics of cultural change when they tried to promote 'Asian Values'. The very fact that they were picking and choosing among the components, producing a *neo*-Confucianism, shows that values are not immutable. The existence of a hard-working, high saving, politically docile population is obviously an advantage to those in authority. The government of Singapore has explicitly referred to the threat to these values brought about by rising prosperity. Young people are catching the social disease of 'Affluenza'. Cohorts that have grown up in comfortable material circumstances are disinclined to work and save as hard as their parents, who climbed out of poverty and carried society up with them. Ironically, Singapore has also become concerned that the docility of its workforce means too little creativity to compete on rapidly-changing world markets for services. It has required the school system to replace rote learning by debating and to permit pupils to criticize their teachers.

'Affluenza' is a modern American term for an old phenomenon. The eighteenth-century English preacher, John Wesley, who founded a nonconformist Protestant sect, feared that, once the hard-working Wesleyans prospered, they would neglect the values that had made them prosperous. The early twentieth-century economist, Joseph Schumpeter, was afraid that capitalism would undermine itself because prosperity would destroy the work ethic. There is nothing new about a strong economic effect on culture and no special reason to assume that 'Asian Values' will succeed in protecting East Asia from changes like those that occurred in the West.

Singapore, to cite only one example, has found it can no longer rely on the Confucian family to provide old-age care and cut the welfare bill; it has passed a law requiring children to support their parents in their old age. I agree with Lee Teng-hui, that while it may be helpful in some circumstances to talk about cultural values, it is seldom helpful to speak of distinctly 'Asian Values'. The values of East Asia during its years of rapid growth were not significantly different from the 'Protestant Ethic' of the West during its industrialization. Nor is the future experience of cultural change in a rich East Asia likely to be fundamentally different from what happened somewhat earlier in the West.

NOTES

1. See especially L. Harrison and S. Huntingdon (eds), *Culture Matters: How Values Shape Human Progress* (New York: Basic Books, 2000).
2. Singaporean writers and various Asian politicians tried hard in the early 1990s to account for the 'East Asian Miracle' in terms of culture; their views are discussed below. See also Eric Jones, 'Asia's Fate: A Response to the Singapore School', *The National Interest*, **35**, Spring 1994, 18–28.
3. Amartya Sen in *Atlantic Monthly*, December 1999.
4. John Honey, *Language is Power: The Story of Standard English and its Enemies* (London: Faber and Faber, 1997).
5. Deepak Lal, *Unintended Consequences: The Impact of Factor Endowments, Culture, and Politics on Long-Run Economic Performance* (Cambridge, Mass.: The MIT Press, 1998).
6. Amartya Sen, 'More Than 100 Million Women are Missing', *New York Review of Books*, 20 December 1990. For other ills in present-day Asia see for example *Japan Times*, 14 December 2000, and *The Economist*, 23 December 2000, and compare n. 11 below.
7. Robert Dunn, in *Financial Times*, 31 July 2000.
8. Francis Fukuyama, *The Great Disruption* (New York: Free Press, 1999).
9. *The Economist*, 6 February 1999.
10. R.A. Brown, *Capital and Entrepreneurship in South-East Asia* (New York: St. Martin's Press, 1994).
11. News reports and surveys of unfavourable changes in family behaviour in East and Southeast Asia have become frequent; the following examples are drawn from a single rather short period: *Far Eastern Economic Review*, 17 September 1998; *East-West Center Observer*, Fall 1998; *The Australian*, 12 and 22 January 1999; and *Australian Financial Review*, 1 February 1999.
12. R. Wilhelm, *Chinese Economic Psychology* (New York: Garland, 1982).
13. Tyler Cowen, 'Is Our Culture in Decline?', *Policy*, Summer 1998–1999, 31–4
14. See Jones, 'Asia's Fate', loc. cit.
15. Timothy Mo in *The Spectator*, 18 December 1999.

PART IV

Adjusting to global change

10. Making business competitive: the Australian experience

INTRODUCTION

Very few commentators predicted the onset of the Asian Crisis and those who did so were not heeded. This lapse led to much soul-searching, not to say hand-wringing, on the part of forecasters. It made even more embarrassing their subsequent failure to anticipate that the Australian economy would be able to shrug off many of the effects of the Crisis. Yet, by the second quarter of 1999, loud notes of self-congratulation were being sounded about Australia's performance. For the first time since the Second World War the country was at the top of the OECD league for productivity growth with a rate twice that which it had achieved during the 1980s. The economics' editor of *The Australian*, Alan Wood, greeted this as no less than 'a remarkable break with [Australia's] economic past' (1 June 1999).

The productivity achievement seems attributable less to strong business leadership in the major corporations than to a combination of input-saving technologies and changes in policy reforms that have obliged firms to respond. Much of the gain seems to have originated outside the individual firm – in the form of reduced assistance to manufacturers, especially tariff reduction, the deregulation of financial markets, privatisations, and the opportunity to secure more flexible labour contracts. Smaller firms have tended to perform better than large ones, and certainly the current level of productivity seems pleasing when contrasted with the earlier lacklustre performance and with sluggishness overseas. Therefore it might be churlish to quibble about the accompanying weakness of the currency, the size of the foreign account deficit, the low household savings rate, and the degree to which productivity growth in the services has been secured by shifting onto the consumer tasks that once were supplied, to make the point rather literally, across the bank counter. Nevertheless, whether or not we believe that all is well, awkward questions remain about what is to come.

This chapter originated as a response to questions posed at the Australian Business Foundation in Sydney about Australian business's ability to cope with a purported 'threat of globalization'. The 'threat' is commonly exaggerated but the invitation to discuss it did set me thinking about the social and educational environment in which Australian businesses operate, the quality of their governance and management, and the implications for staff recruitment of the double shift that is taking place – towards an expanding role for the creative service industries and towards trading and operating overseas.

The invitation was a licence to present my own impressions, which are all that one can offer when commenting on the aggregate behaviour of hundreds of thousands of business people and tens of thousands of firms. Likewise, when dealing with the contributions of Australian culture and government policy to the business environment, it is possible to comment only on the more prominent tendencies. In view of the criticisms which I voice below, this should be understood.

Despite these criticisms and other concerns about the robustness of the macro-economy, it would be unfair to pretend that the pot of Australian business is not half-full as well as half-empty. Change is taking place faster than before and in some respects, though unfortunately not all, the situation is hard to capture before it has flowed into something new. An unexpected robustness in the face of the Asian Crisis and a substantial growth in productivity represent considerable achievements; in the very middle of the 1990s there had already been improvements in the running of certain corporations, not unconnected with the need to recover from clumsy ventures into various Emerging Markets. These amendments were no doubt helpful in meeting the Crisis that was soon to follow in the Asian region. But if the goal is to secure the progress made, in order to cope with what promises to be a marked change in world economic structure, the half-empty part of the pot will need to be filled. Let me emphasise the point by a jarring change of metaphor: this is no time to be resting on one's laurels.

STRUCTURAL CHANGE IN THE WORLD ECONOMY

The prices of commodities have been subsiding slowly for two centuries and, whatever short-term cycles there are to come, we cannot expect a return to a long-run upward trend. The Australian economy has an opportunity to wean itself off dependence on resources and the commodity dollar – not by shifting into manufacturing, the share of which is also contracting in advanced economies, but by continuing with the move into services. It is the services sector that is advancing worldwide. Even in the poorest countries services now account for about one-third of GDP.

The world economy as a whole is entering a distinctive phase of the shift towards services and the knowledge industries. This phase promises to be qualitatively as well as quantitatively different from anything that has occurred before. International economic integration has advanced furthest and will continue to advance with respect to financial and, more significantly for present purposes, information markets.

In all countries the services sector is extremely heterogeneous, comprising routine and elementary functions and the most complex and creative activities. Productivity is notoriously hard to measure in these spheres. One cause of imprecision is that in many statistical series the joint products of goods-with-services sold by some firms are assigned rather arbitrarily to one category or the other, the rule-of-thumb being to allot them to the sector in which a given firm is bigger. Nevertheless the movement away from manufacturing during the past generation is plain, as data from both Australia (Table 10.1) and the United States (Table 10.2) show.

Table 10.1   Australian manufacturing

	Output volume	Share of total output	Employment
1966	100 units	26 per cent	1.2 million
1996	200 units	14 per cent	1.1 million

Source: Industry Commission, *Annual Report 1996-97*.

Table 10.2   United States manufacturing (percentages)

	GDP	Corporate profits	Jobs
1960	27	47	31
1998	17	26	15

Source: *The Economist*, 29 May 1999.

The Australian figures show a doubling in manufacturing output accompanied by a 9 per cent drop in employment – whereas employment in other sectors, almost all of them services, doubled from 3.6 million to 7.2 million over the same period. The shift from manufacturing to services was evident throughout the OECD countries between 1980-94; there was a similar trend in South Korea, Taiwan and especially Hong Kong.

Over the period 1980-94, knowledge-based industries accounted for one-quarter of GDP in the Group of Seven and contributed still higher fractions to productivity growth: in the United States almost one-half (*Financial Times*, 14 December 1998). As to world trade, almost 20 per cent is already in services (*The Economist*, 8 May 1999). The United States is by far the biggest exporter of services with 18 per cent of the world total. Britain is next with nearly 8 per cent, whereas it has only a 5 per cent share in the export of goods and is in fifth place.

In Britain the sum of revenues from fashion, films, popular music, advertising and the like was £60 billion in 1997 and growing at 5 per cent per annum, twice the rate of growth of the economy as a whole. Britain earns more from rock music exports than from steel (*Financial Times*, 6 November 1998; 10 July 1999). British music, design, software, publishing, fashion, architecture, art and antique marketing, film and television employ approximately one million people and their exports account for 16 per cent of the global market in creative goods and services. The policy implications had become sufficient by 1998 to warrant a government enquiry.

The findings of the enquiry are that the creative enterprises, which had not previously been considered together, are generating 50 000 new jobs annually in Britain, offsetting the decline in manufacturing employment. New activities such as feature-film effects and computer games have repeatedly sprung up, countering downturns in more mature areas. The metabolism is exceedingly rapid in industries like these. The fastest-growing British company is Eidos, the computer games maker. The computer games industry earns £1.6 billion per annum and of all commercially successful games worldwide Britons create approximately 40 per cent.

It is wise to abandon *Materialismus*, the notion that making *things* is inherently more productive and maybe morally sounder than 'shuffling bits of paper', which is what the service sector is disparagingly described as doing. Efforts to shore up shrinking manufacturing industries can only be at the cost of increasing the burden of tax on higher-growth activities and thus reducing their competitiveness. Similarly, the attempts that are now being made in many countries to exclude foreign competitors from service industries – notwithstanding the 1994 General Agreement on Trade in Services – can only generate distorting effects of the types always associated with Protection: reducing consumer choice and lowering the quality of the home product by permitting local producers to shelter behind tariffs, quotas or other artificial impediments.

In future, the leading edge activities will be services producing rather insubstantial, fast-changing items in every sphere from computer software to television scripts, from new financial instruments to consultancy advice about international law, and so on in almost unclassifiable profusion. The demand for creative services is income-elastic. Notwithstanding temporary set-backs like the Asian Crisis or the prophecies of the end of capitalism to be met with daily in the media, large overseas populations are getting richer and are likely to continue doing so. They will want more by way of services. This offers splendid prospects for a type of trading economy that will be a far cry from the one characterized by Australia's resource exports, traditional industries and large corporations.

For some preliminary indications of the way competition is intensifying we can turn to the so-called 'new economy' of the United States, where 70 per cent of net new jobs created between 1993–96 were in 'gazelles' – firms that have achieved 20 per cent growth in profits for four straight years. There are 355 000 such firms, most of them small.[1] American companies have greatly increased their collaborative relationships with suppliers, customers, universities, federal laboratories and so forth, far more than have firms elsewhere. Product Cycle development times have speeded up: 77 per cent of Hewlett Packard's revenues are from products less than two years old, while IBM had incorporated over 30 per cent of its 1995 patents into products by the following year.

Even in Asia there is evidence that the biggest economy, Japan, is not uniformly moribund in the way so often depicted in the West. Rather, an almost dual economy has emerged in which the services sector is the fastest-growing part (*The Australian*, 17 July 1999). The bankers, bureaucrats and politicians who until recently dominated the Japanese economy have been discredited. In the stream of once-unthinkable occurrences, Moody's has downgraded Mitsubishi's debt. The banks show little sign of changing, permitting finance companies to move into the business of lending to consumers. A whole fresh set of Internet-literate industries led by a new group of entrepreneurs has arisen and seems set to continue expanding. Infinitely more Japanese households are expected to be using the Internet within a few years. Other highly-profitable businesses are engaged in retailing, fast-foods, telecoms, tourism and acting as agencies for temporary workers. These are not the industries of 'Japan, Inc.' but rather those which a middle-class consumer society demands and they are likely therefore to go on growing. McDonald's Japan, for instance, which already has 2500 outlets, now plans to establish a chain of 1000 McCafes.

THE AUSTRALIAN RESPONSE AND ITS LIMITATIONS

How does the shift towards services in Australia compare with that in other developed countries? Australia is up with the world leaders in a general sense, with a services' share of GDP and employment in 1996 of 74.5 per cent (70.5 per cent in 1987) and 72.4 per cent (67.6 per cent in 1987) respectively.[2] However, with respect to exported services, Australia has only 1.2 per cent of the world total, less than Singapore, Hong Kong, Taiwan or South Korea and considerably less than most European countries. When we restrict the focus to creative services, the picture is not entirely rosy though DFAT (Department of

Foreign Affairs and Trade) tables do not permit all of the categories to be separated. (However Australia does have about 1.7 per cent of the global market for recorded music.)

The Australian Service Sector Review (1998) provides data on the output of 'all bodies mainly engaged in providing cultural and recreational facilities and services (including motion picture, radio and television services; libraries, museums and the arts; sport and recreation; and gambling'. (p. 108) These are extremely miscellaneous activities, some of which produce tradeables and some of which do not. The *Review* also shows that the cultural and recreational sector has grown significantly during the 1990s, outpacing the remainder of the service sector, let alone the economy as a whole, but it is nevertheless only the fifteenth largest 'industry' in the economy. Its output was valued at $12 220 000 in 1996-97.

The composition of the sector is by no means strictly comparable with the creative service category distinguished by the British government enquiry but one comparison that is not utterly unfair is that whereas the creative sector in Britain is growing at 5 per cent per annum, cultural and recreational services in Australia are growing by only 3.4 per cent per annum. Indeed Australia is a heavy net importer of cultural, recreational and personal services (Australian Bureau of Statistics trade data do not distinguish between these categories). During the period 1991-96, imports outweighed exports by three-to-one and although the balance became more favourable between 1996-98, opportunities for export and import-substitution are surely being overlooked.

The question is what can best be done in Australia if the move into the services, especially the creative ones, is to be continued? Alan Wood added to his comment on the new level of productivity growth the perceptive remark that the country, 'needs to make an equivalent cultural break and stop confusing mediocrity with equality'. This chapter will urge that Australia really does need to change. The country must cease tolerating mediocrity and vigorously expand creative and knowledge-based activities that are not yet completely recognized as major industries of the future.

The alteration in economic structure, though laudable in itself, is not and cannot be a once-over process. The changing character of consumer demand and of competition from foreign companies, in Australia and overseas markets, means that the shift will need to be continual. The long string of questions that arises pertains to how free the Australian economy will be to continue its structural shift; whether enough major companies will restructure towards service production; whether enough start-up firms will arise in the service sector (and stay in Australia); whether the educational and cultural resources of Australia can generate the additional qualified labour that the creative services industries will need; whether enough career openings for skilled and creative workers will present themselves; whether more relaxed managerial practices conducive to creativity will emerge in individual firms; and finally whether Protectionism can be prevented from stifling healthy competition within Australia's cultural markets.

MANAGING A CREATIVE WORKFORCE

Skilled and creative labour needs to be attracted and it needs to be retained. There is little need to dwell on Australia's non-pecuniary attractions to labour: climate and space. Yet these are perhaps of more appeal to people with families than to young adults looking for inspiration and excitement. They are somewhat offset by a taxation system that includes a hefty capital gains tax and tax rates on earnings that are unattractive to young professionals. The Economist Intelligence Unit has recently ranked the business environment of 60 countries on such features as tax and labour market policies, market potential, infrastructure skills and the political background, placing Australia overall thirteenth for the years 1994–98 and anticipating that it will merely maintain this rank during 1999–2003 (*The Economist*, 21 November 1998).

Potentially the response of Australian businesses to the new market situation could be strong. The country possesses some important advantages. A parliamentary democracy with independent law and a free press should be well equipped to respond to structural change. It has been making an adjustment ever since the dollar was floated in the early 1980s. Perhaps these features are what Prime Minister Goh Chok Tong was referring to when he contrasted Australia favourably with many Asian countries: 'we were concentrating on fast growth, quick infrastructure, but forgetting the fundamentals' (*The Economist*, 15 May 1999). Singapore has also paid the compliment of explicitly trying to persuade young Australians to move there and share their ideas. Yet it remains doubtful that Australia's report card warrants more than 'has made an effort; could do better', coupled with an admonition that the big wide world, so to speak, is going to be a lot harder than school.

Changes in the world market will in future confront Australian businesses with unprecedented competition from firms in other countries for a not-very-elastic, but increasingly mobile, supply of skilled and creative labour. There is said to be a shortage of IT skills in Australia amounting to 30 000 vacancies; the deficiency is exacerbated by the relatively low participation rate of women (*The Australian*, 27 July 1999). According to a section labelled 'Competition for an Educated Workforce' in *The Australian Service Sector Review*, 1998, Australian professional service firms in general are experiencing a shortage of skilled staff.[3] The *Review* accounts for this by asserting that Australian business schools do not produce graduates as good as the best in the USA or Europe; that pay is too low to attract enough of those high-calibre professionals from the northern hemisphere who were formerly relied on (it is candidly admitted) to transfer new skills to their Australian colleagues; and that the best professionals in their mid-twenties now seek careers in the USA and Europe.

Managers will need to acknowledge the enlarged role that labour of this calibre, especially creative workers, will be able to command as scarcity becomes apparent. Will businesses in Australia adjust well to such a development? The sternest recent test of their adaptability was the drive to 'go global' and in that respect the performance of many CEOs, boards and managers in the larger Australian corporations was less than dazzling. Several of the biggest firms have now curtailed overseas operations the risks of which they had brushed aside.

There are disquieting signs that Australia is already proving inhospitable to relevant classes of enterprise. Although exports of services have been rising faster than merchandise exports, and a positive trade balance for services was achieved for the first time in 1996–97, the country's share of the value of commercial services exported by economies in the Asian region fell from 7.4 per cent in 1990 to 6.7 per cent in 1997.[4] The ten largest law firms in the Asia-Pacific region are Australian but only four have won licences to practice foreign law in China (*Australian Financial Review*, 23 July 1999). Too many entrepreneurs in fields that did not exist 20 years ago, in knowledge-intensive software, biotechnology, semi-conductors, communications and Internet servicing, are restructuring their corporations and registering them in the USA, building them afresh by means of public share offers on the NASDAQ.[5] Sometimes firms leave staff, especially R&D staff, behind because local rates of pay are lower than competitors overseas might offer them. But other companies are quitting entirely and re-forming with American offices, shareholders and employees.

'Tell me the barrier and Australia will put it there', says the CEO of ANDSoftware, which moved from Perth to San Adagio. The investment community in Australia has 'absolutely no understanding of technology', adds the CEO of Arsenide, which has also moved to San Adagio. Certainly the Information Policy Advisory Council reported that Australia has been a 'bystander to international trade' in the information industry, securing only 0.3 per cent of the global market compared with 6.9 per cent for Singapore and 5.5 per cent for Malaysia (*The Australian*, 28 August 1997). The report continued, 'many of Australia's indigenous companies appear to lack a strong international outlook' and 'too much of Australian innovation is under-capitalised and undermanaged'.

Part of the problem no doubt derives from the lag as an older generation of business people only gradually alters its habit of dealing primarily with people from its own background, in what have now become slow-growing industries. The entrepreneurs involved in a migration of high-tech firms sizeable enough to be termed an 'exodus' complain that Australian business and government are happiest dealing with large firms in mining and property, and with the financial giants. They point to negative attitudes towards young entrepreneurs and to disincentives in the tax regime. The opportunities and excitement of the vast American market cannot be duplicated in a small country, but an effort should surely be made to dismantle specific barriers to growth. Given all that cannot be done, the things that can be done acquire a greater urgency.

The limitations of Australian managers have been exposed before, most notably in the Karpin Report of 1995. Surveying the opinions of 500 Asian executives, Karpin disclosed that they ranked Australia fifth or sixth on each of eight management qualities (*The Australian*, 11 April 1995). Australian management skills were rated overall the worst of those in six countries including the UK, the USA and Germany. Similar findings – that the Australian business community is 'naive and low in self-esteem' – were arrived at from a DFAT survey also made public in 1995. The then Minister of Trade claimed that 'out-of-date' perceptions of Australia were as much a barrier to trade as any tariff or quota (*The Australian*, 10 April 1995). All the more reason, one might think, to adopt policies that would change the reality; perceptions would surely follow. The Minister instead launched a $10 million advertising campaign to combat the negative opinions held in Asia about Australia's technological incapacity, work ethic, industrial relations and immigration policy. One cannot help wondering what that sum of taxpayers' money actually bought.

The resilience of the Australian economy in the face of the Asian Crisis may suggest that Karpin was wrong but I think that would be mistaken. Explanations of the success are unclear but it has been suggested that an important element was that business ignored the strident pro-Asian advice of the Keating administration and held off from investing in the region, as opposed to trading with it.[6] Only 6 per cent of Australian direct foreign investment was placed in East Asia. The National Australia Bank was a strikingly successful hold-out against the drive into the region. Business as a whole refrained from adopting the consensus-building approach recommended by the 'Asian Values' lobby as a superior mode of commercial practice to contracts backed by Western law. Whether this was because businessmen were sluggish and fearful of the foreign, or alternatively made a shrewd appreciation of the insecurity of Asian markets, can now be only matters of opinion. Probably it was some of all these things.

The troubles of businesses in neighbouring countries cannot make Australian firms more efficient either in absolute terms or relative to firms from competing Western countries. There are no grounds for complacency about the ability of Australian companies in general to perform overseas, or at least in non-Western countries, as is shown by the findings that, whereas expatriate Japanese managers remain in foreign posts four years on average and fewer than 5 per cent of them fail, Australians stay less than two years on average and 30 per cent of them fail (*The Australian*, 14 May 1996). With respect to entering the Chinese market, a report commissioned by the Australian Chamber of Commerce and Industry found that only 28 per cent of companies provided workers with any pre-departure training (as opposed to 91 per cent of European and 63 per cent of American companies) (*The Australian*, 31 March 1995). Only 3 per cent of over 300 Australian expatriate executives in China could speak any Chinese. Eight per cent of companies had executives who failed their assignment because they 'could not cope with China'. This suggests a chronic cultural under-preparation, which is disturbing to anyone concerned with international business or foreign trade.

The danger is that the Asian Crisis may now make the deficiencies seem unimportant and thus have unfortunate effects similar to those that follow every surge in commodity prices: a slowing of structural adjustment, a breeding of complacency about the need to seek fresh markets or undertake linguistic and cultural preparation, and a turning of some firms away altogether from 'difficult' foreign markets.

In a knowledge-intensive world corporations will need to be able to find staff who are self-starters. Firms will be obliged to offer much greater encouragement than now to individuals who possess creative talent. They will have to afford such people autonomy in the workplace to an extent that may be distasteful to managers who gained their own authority in earlier circumstances. A recent survey showed that 60 per cent of all workers would like to work at home at least part of the time and the proportion is certain to be greater among the individually creative (ABC radio, 20 June 1999). Middle managers are inclined to resist telecommuting because they see their positions depending on the number of people they supervise in their offices – the so-called 'red braces' syndrome. Radical changes in workplace practices will have to be initiated from the top, from the level of boards and CEOs.

EDUCATING A CREATIVE WORKFORCE

Meanwhile government has removed some barriers and distortions but has not always undertaken domestic reforms that might provoke objections. Consider education: raising educational standards by means of selective schools, rigorous external examinations, the independent evaluation of teachers, and steep pay differentials, has been neglected. No one seems to be discussing whether Australian university degrees ought to cease being examined piecemeal, course by course and term by term, instead of after three or four years with genuine finals' examinations and external examiners. Presumably this is because unions and, in the case of schools, parental lobbies could be relied on to mount noisy political resistance. It was much easier for the former ALP governments to spout slogans about the 'Clever Country' and for the Coalition government to mark time during its first term than for either actually to lift education towards overseas' best practice. To any scholar these issues matter for their own sakes but they matter commercially too, because they relate to equipping the workforce better.

CULTURAL ASSETS

Consider Australia's cultural standing: second only to the USA for use of the Internet, fourth from the top of the league for number of hosts of Internet sites, and tenth for the output of scientific articles per billion US dollars of GDP (*The Australian*, 30 June 1999). Australia's membership of the English-speaking world is a major asset which in principle affords ready cultural access to high-income markets. Belonging to English-language culture means that if literary, film and other products created by Australians are of sufficient quality they can be exported fairly readily to the larger markets. The use of English as the native language is therefore an asset and, more surprisingly, so is the Australian accent. The point is not that the accent is intrinsically advantageous but rather that, except at the Broad extreme, it does not suffer from the disadvantages that attend some of the English spoken in Britain. General and Educated Australian are closer to World Standard English than are many British regional accents.

Some Britons cling to their regional accents for almost tribal reasons. Others find in regionalism an opportunity for rent-seeking and are prepared to defend such historically-contingent markers of 'identity' as dialect or accent to the death, or at any rate to the last redistributed tax dollar. Market considerations seem irrelevant to the linguistic Balkanizers.

Since that part of British humour which does not harp on the class system plays heavily on regional differences, the export of British television programmes tends to be restricted (letter in *The Economist*, 9 January 1999). One distributor who was offered BBC Scottish television programmes dismissed them in ten minutes as 'incomprehensible'. The result is to open space in the market for other English-language producers, including Australian studios which already provide 10 per cent of light entertainment on German television (*The Economist*, 12 December 1998). That is *eight times* as much as British studios. Globally intelligible English is thus of direct commercial value, as well as being an aspect of the 'soft power' which will be the locus of much future international economic and political competition.

DOMESTIC EDUCATIONAL PERFORMANCE AND THE SUPPLY OF SKILLS

Given the importance of English to the business of education, as well as to the education of business, it is unfortunate that the standard of usage in Australia has been permitted to deteriorate. Once that process starts, Gresham's Law operates. On various indicators of educational performance, Australia's world rank is only middling for a developed economy (Table 10.3).

Table 10.3   Australian education, international rankings, 1992

12-17 year olds enrolled in secondary school: 11th (83%)
25-64 year old men with completed secondary schooling: 11th (63%)
25-64 year old women with completed secondary schooling: 14th (48.3%)
25-64 year old men with completed higher education: 10th (12.3%)
25-64 year old women with completed higher education: 9th (8%)

Source: *Gale Country & World Rankings Reporter*, 1995, 79.

The relationship of formal education to imaginative thought is complicated and not invariably positive. I take the view, however, that in the main it *is* positive and will become more so. Some tertiary education is nowadays almost indispensable even to make a start at creating advanced cultural products. In addition, given that there is shrinking demand for blue-collar workers, educating the whole population to a higher level is more important than ever. This is reflected in the qualifications for which employers ask and which the market rewards. It does not do so as generously in Australia as in the USA, where the gulf between the earnings of high school graduates and college graduates, and to a lesser extent between college graduates and the holders of postgraduate degrees, began widening significantly almost a generation ago.

High among the skills that formal education imparts is literacy. This is of prime significance in itself and can also be looked on as a proxy for all the other aspects of education that need attention if the economy is to operate at full capacity. Basic literacy is important even for repetitive jobs, since nowadays they are almost certain to involve the reading of instructions and safety notices. For skilled, and *a fortiori* creative, workers a high degree of literacy is needed. In my experience, literacy in English is the best single indicator of student performance in Australia; now that grammar is not taught and little attention is given to style or vocabulary, an ability to command these things and decipher the rules on one's own denotes considerable native wit. Some employers complain that many of the people they hire no longer possess adequate ability in reading and writing and have to pay for them to be taught privately; it is rumoured that in certain companies this extends to the remedial teaching of college graduates, a matter so embarrassing to all concerned that the relevant information is virtually a commercial secret.

Comparative international statistics on literacy are far from reliable. The available series vary widely and many of them claim that literacy rates in developed countries are as high as 98, 99 or 100 per cent. This is thoroughly implausible, not to say ironic given the amount of public money spent on adult literacy programmes. Clearly difficulties are encountered in collecting data and greater ones still in trying to standardize the definition of literacy. It is often uncertain whether literacy is being measured as the ability to sign one's name, read or write (or read and write) a simple sentence, or read and write more advanced material.

Thus the *Gale Country and World Rankings Reporter* cites a source which asserts that in 1980 the literacy rate in Australia was 100 per cent, meaning that every individual of 15 years and older would have been able to read and write.[7] More credibly, a survey ten years later showed that 7.6 per cent of the adult population - one million individuals - were incapable of reading or writing in English well enough to fill in a job application, read a bank statement or legal document, or take down a telephone message. Approximately 330 000 of these individuals were native speakers, a higher proportion of illiterates than was reported at the census of 1911![8]

Whatever the definition adopted, it is not clear just what the Australian level of literacy is. In 1993 five dissenters to the report on literacy by the House of Representatives Standing Committee on Employment, Education and Training - they included the Deputy Chairman - announced that State, Territory and Commonwealth educational authorities had been unable to tell the committee the extent of illiteracy among primary schoolchildren.[9] The proportion may have been as high as 25 per cent and in some educational districts may have included an actual majority of pupils. Most schools did not systematically test basic skills. Moreover many teachers had not been instructed in the teaching of decoding skills, spelling or grammar, and in some cases such instruction was '*actively discouraged*' (emphasis supplied).

Gone, then, are the 1960s, when Clive James could boast that in England, 'Australian supply teachers were in good repute, especially if they taught English, because among the natives the ability to spell and parse their own language was already becoming scarce.'[10] My own information, gathered by questioning many hundreds of Australian university students at various levels, is that none is nowadays taught English grammar at school. The term parsing is unknown to them and they cannot perform the operation, let alone teach it to anyone else. Furthermore, after teaching regularly at two universities in Australia and two in England during the past dozen years, my firm belief is that, if the standard of literacy did begin to fall later in Australia than in

England, which is what Clive James's remark may imply, it has since fallen (even) more steeply. Comparing the 'quality' newspapers and magazines of the two countries conveys a similar impression and putting the ABC and BBC side by side reinforces it. Interestingly, American print media come off better than the Australian and British press, which have abandoned sub-editing.

Linguistic standards need to be improved since the base of skills is narrowing precisely when the opportunities for employing it are on the rise. Reintroducing the formal teaching of English would be valuable as a means of encouraging attention to linguistic precision and dexterity. It would help to reduce the costs of communication. One good sign is the turning away from the 'whole word' method of teaching reading and the call for a return to phonics, which for several decades has been denounced by fashionable educationists.[11] As to prescriptive grammar, those who argue against it on the grounds that it is the arbitrary creation of Victorian males seem not to grasp that a rule system, arbitrary or not, reduces transaction costs: whether we drive on the left or right of the road is arbitrary too but an agreed decision about the matter is rather useful. Nor do the objectors admit that they must still be using vestigial rules of grammar themselves or they would be incomprehensible. It is interesting that Art is still taught in Australia with reference to rules that may be relaxed only when one has grasped the common techniques of visual communication.

Educational establishments are defensive about this topic. Fortunately for them, 'post-modernism', a fashionable device to permit the simultaneous holding of contradictory opinions, enables them to reply that grammatical accuracy is meaningless *and* is not declining.[12] The matter is too important to be left as the plaything of ideologues.

CAPITALIZING ON THE INTERNATIONAL MARKET FOR EDUCATION

Worldwide, 97 million people are expected to be enrolled in higher education in a decade's time, up from 48 million a decade ago (*The Australian*, 28 April 1999). Higher education is already the USA's fifth largest service sector export. With respect to Australian education, however, the Industry Commission is pointing to major variations in cost and effectiveness, and how much remains to be done by way of reform, at the precise moment when competition for international students is approaching a new pitch and Japan, France and Germany are stepping up their efforts.[13] Japan is trying to attract 100 000 foreign students. Some of its teaching will undoubtedly be in English; parallel engineering courses at the University of Tokyo are already taught in

English. Edufrance wishes to surpass the British intake and reach the American level within four years, competing not by raising the quality of France's educational offerings but by lowering their price, that is, by not charging fees. Edufrance is ambivalent with respect to the language of instruction, commenting enigmatically that 'English is no longer a foreign language here'.

Germany likewise wishes to re-enter the world market for students, according to its Federal Education Ministry. It, too, will waive fees. The aim is to produce a cohort of foreign graduates who will favour trading with Germany and the plan is to teach those who desire it in English. German educationists attribute their poor past record of attracting foreign students to the language problem. Although they do not want to give up German – to 'McDonaldize our system' – they accept that English is the *lingua franca* of science and education. Although most Rektors of German universities at first opposed teaching in English, applied science courses are often now so taught.

Countries where English is either at home or widely understood thus possess a head start in several respects. As *Business Week* (31 August 1998) commented about impediments to the spread of advanced technologies in Europe, 'language and cultural differences are part of the problem ... change tends to happen first in Britain and in countries where English dominates, such as [in] Scandinavia'. There is no inherent barrier in Australia to the quick assimilation of the relevant information, and with respect to consumer technologies, at least, uptake is fast.

Australia currently has 8 per cent of the international student market and its positive trade balance in educational services has been growing throughout the 1990s. Higher education visas issued to American students, for example, rose from 570 in 1992–93 to 4035 in 1997–98 (*The Australian*, 9 June 1999). However part of the attraction for Americans is that at current exchange rates Australia is cheap. The attraction for non-native speakers from poorer countries is partly, and deplorably, the lax entry requirements in English. This means that some find difficulty in coping once they arrive. The educational system adjusts to this but standards suffer in the process. Australia seldom attracts the best students from its main trading partners and cannot guarantee retaining even its present share of foreign student intake in the face of stepped-up competition. For example, the country lacks the network of university alumni among members of the Japanese Diet that the United States can exploit. (There are Harvard and Georgetown clubs in Tokyo but not Melbourne or Sydney ones.)

Import substitution in the Asia-Pacific region will increase competition as successive countries develop their own teaching establishments and seek to reduce the outflow of foreign exchange. Malaysia, a prime source of students for Australian colleges, is energetically pursuing such policies, aiming to become a regional centre for higher education in Southeast Asia (*Far Eastern Economic Review*, 27 May 1999). Private colleges there, which enrol as many students as the government-run universities, teach in English. They represent a growth industry. In these circumstances Australian suppliers need every advantage they can command.

RECRUITMENT AND CREATIVITY

Let us turn to the related issue of recruitment into business. The challenges are to improve the supply of skilled and creative workers, and to hire the most open-minded executives possible. Lessons are surely to be learned by noting the attributes of people currently seeking to enter business after various levels of business education; those who are actually being hired; and established executives. Nevertheless I do not propose to distinguish systematically among these three categories since cultures tend to reproduce themselves: apart from the deficiencies of some in the oldest group with respect to the use of computers, and although the cohort of young people entering business nowadays hails from somewhat more diverse backgrounds than before, there has been no fundamental alteration in the culture. Recruitment procedures are still narrow and suffer from a lack of imagination, even an anti-intellectual bias. It was not in Australia that Merrill Lynch launched its programme to hire doctoral candidates from seemingly recondite fields and capitalize on their research (*The Australian*, 17 June 1998).

When someone rises to the level of CEO it is often after working as a technical specialist in one branch of a corporation. But when he or she has reached the summit, the daily round turns into a scanning of the horizon for threats and opportunities that cannot be defined or pigeon-holed in advance. The tasks become those of the generalist. Wider goals for the company are not necessarily best promoted by former technicians: visionary strategic thinking is unlikely to be their forte. When this is compounded by a purely technical education, or when a majority of business leaders have much the same educational, personal and geographical origins, we have a recipe for restricted thought that does not bode well for the taking of businesses into foreign markets.

'Vision' is perhaps a personal quality but is usually aided by a broad educational background. In my observation, the general knowledge of Australian executives in the larger firms is seldom remarkable, even at the topmost level.[14] This may go some way towards explaining the mixed record of their enterprises in Asian markets, as well as the emergence of consultancies that specialize in correcting the howlers of firms dealing with foreign cultures. Perhaps there is no reason to suppose that the weakness is greater on average than in the UK or USA (though I am sure that the Germans and Japanese are more knowledgeable). The UK and USA however possess larger absolute supplies of talent. In the smaller Australian market individual performance matters more and talent needs to be carefully nurtured. By and large there is simply too little knowledge in the Australian business community about the political economy of Emerging Markets, too little understanding of the risks of corruption, and too little effort has been expended (the need may not be fully recognized) on due diligence. Someone with a first-class honours degree in engineering told me that he had not realised China has a different legal system from Australia. He was bright enough to know he had to catch up but one wonders about the less able.

In business, behavioural conformity and faddism reach their heights. The over-emphasis in training programmes on team work as opposed to intensive personal study displays the mind-set. Learning to work together has its uses but tends to reinforce the herd instinct that is so risky an influence on decision-making.

Very few business people in Australia contribute significantly to public debate about the broad problems of society, economy or polity: the volume that George Soros wrote may have shown, in the words of a reviewer, that it is possible to have a brain like a teenager's bedroom and still make billions of dollars, but at least Soros takes intellectual life seriously and made the time and took the trouble to write an ambitious book (*Australian Financial Review*, 13 March 1999). The interests of leading business people are revealed by the hobbies they report in *Who's Who in Australia*: many mentions of games but little by way of personal intellectual or creative endeavour, as opposed to occasional memberships of cultural bodies. It has been suggested to me that the entries are not always candid, because Australian culture absolutely requires males to parade an interest in sport. If that is even half-true, I rest my case about conformity.

The point can scarcely be laboured too much. Once one moves beyond economics or econometrics (which appeal to people with quantitative backgrounds by virtue of their air of precision) to incorporate political risk factors, the need for contextual knowledge becomes evident. Some executives appear to believe that they can obtain the requisite knowledge quickly and painlessly by hiring consultants. But if people at executive level do not know enough to start with, the firm will be unable to sort the wheat from the chaff among the advice it buys. Consultants are not perfect substitutes for managerial knowledge. The purpose of consultants has been said cynically to be a means of generating some policy, any policy, or to supply external scapegoats for unpleasant actions that management proposes to undertake anyhow. If that is so, so be it. On the other hand, if consultants are hired for serious purposes, the procedure too often falls short of acceptable standards. Consultants' reports are neither externally refereed nor reviewed, in Australia or elsewhere, as though nothing has been learned about safe procedures from long practice in the world of scholarship.[15] A lack of insistence on these standard procedures is disturbing given the resources with which shareholders entrust companies.

Among entrants to business education the range of interests is becoming more varied but still runs excessively to sport and collecting wine. I have come across almost no one who paints, composes music or writes poetry and no one who has tried to write a novel. Few play a musical instrument. The disciplinary backgrounds of entrants are widening but are still overweight with engineering and accountancy. As practised these are not invariably the most creative of subjects. I note that engineers have been told that they are not the ones who will build the next generation of consumer electronics equipment.[16] Such equipment is at present abnormally complicated and late adopters will not accept it, meaning that in future the 'softer' skills of psychologists and social scientists will have to be involved in design.

Corporations understandably hire from the pool of people who make themselves available for jobs in business. But at present, and more so in the past, such people are self-selected and come from a limited range of backgrounds. Disciplines that are conspicuously underweight among entrants are the biological sciences and the humanities, despite the growth of opportunities for management in the health and environmental sciences and the difficulties people from Arts subjects have in finding well-paid jobs. Is it the business culture that deters them?

A LOOMING BRAIN-DRAIN?

Business at all levels needs, in my opinion, to make a vastly greater effort at recruiting individuals of varied personal and academic backgrounds, of independent minds and unusual interests, and then giving them their heads. Without this, and if Australian firms do not expand creative work more actively, the prospect is of an increasing brain-drain. Such an outflow will not have to be large to siphon off a high proportion of the tiny absolute number of outstanding individuals. The best candidates have the most options and already a large number of excellent Australians work overseas, especially in educational and creative fields. Sometime in the 1960s my Oxford supervisor, a graduate of the Universities of New England and Sydney, pointed out in a letter to *The Times* that every single college in Oxford and Cambridge had by then an Australian or New Zealand Fellow. How many ever returned? What changes might induce the most talented to do so?

In Australia there was a 30 per cent rise (to 33 580) in temporary business visas issued in 1997–98 compared with 1996–97, but disquiet may still be felt about the quality of those who are being attracted given the lower pay here than in the USA, the short stays allowed and the unfavourable tax treatment (*The Australian*, 22 January 1999). The nationalism and protectionism evident in bureaucratic and academic circles seems out of touch with the needs of the international market for skilled labour, perhaps because these circles are largely made up of older individuals whose views were formed in other days. A spokeswoman for the Department of Immigration said that the government was still sensitive about 'safeguarding' Australian jobs, apparently not comprehending the potential of expatriate employees to generate jobs for the host population.[17]

Certainly Australia is an immigrant country and in principle can hire from overseas. I happen to think that the rate of immigration should be increased but not that this will necessarily improve the quality of the workforce in the short run, though it may spur entrepreneurship. First-generation immigrants, like the native-born who stay, are not always as well-educated as the best Australians who leave. It is the children of immigrants, wherever they come from, who outperform the host population, at least so American studies show (*The Australian*, 10 February 1997). There is a one-generation gain until their children in turn regress to the local educational mean. Immigration is also the best long-term bet for breaking up the (predominantly male) old school networks that have for too long dominated Australian society and the larger Australian corporations. Since socially-mobile immigrant children tend to norm on the behaviour and status symbols of the host population, the immigrant stream must constantly be renewed if society is to maintain the highest level of effort and originality.

In future, residence in Australia will not guarantee that workers are contributing directly to local output. There is potentially a hidden outflow. The Internet means that people can live in one country and transmit what they produce direct to a company somewhere else. Foreign firms may appropriate part of the value generated. Again, the number of individuals involved is less pertinent than their quality. Some highly-talented people may well choose to live in the Australian environment but sell their wares overseas. Even if they are fully taxed in Australia, which will prove a difficult exercise, overseas interests may be the first to capitalize on their ideas. The nature of creative work means that this may not be an insignificant loss. It is better to have a community of high performers than not and such people should be retained or attracted whoever they work for, but thought needs to be given to how they may best be persuaded to interact with the national community.

The 'floating elite' is, almost by definition, internationally minded. The Australians among the high-flyers are not noticeably racist nor even particularly nationalistic. They do not seem interested in the 'Bilby culture' (the Easter Bunny has been replaced by the native Bilby, an animal few people have ever seen, permitting local cultural producers to capture rents by starting to delink Australia from the remainder of the English-speaking world). There is a message in the discrepancy of attitude between the truly talented and the rent-seekers, not to mention the Australian media.

The need is to retain, indeed attract, the 'floating elite'. These are the people who will create jobs for others. Bear in mind that a majority of students, including Australians, replying to a big survey by PricewaterhouseCoopers, have said they are interested in international careers. Bear in mind too that a Berlin conference in June 1999 grappled with the phenomenon, now very evident in European labour markets, that working conditions have to cater for transnationals who hold more than one passport, sometimes more than two passports (Radio Deutsche Welle, 10 June 1999). The market for the highly-skilled is international and more fluid than is widely recognized. The mobility of skilled workers is likely to be increased by the modern habits of staying single or marrying late, which are now such prominent behaviours among the tertiary educated. Moreover, I know women who have taken jobs with overseas, notably American, companies not only because the pay is higher but because they believe too many Australian firms are still chauvinist; they say that this is improving but are not prepared to wait 10 or 15 years until the climate has completely altered. Whether their impressions are accurate or not does not constitute the main point – as with much else in life, perception is what counts.

Once again I have seen no specifically Australian data but evidence from Canada shows a large increase in the outflow of educated managers and professionals to the United States, unrequited by an equivalent inflow (*Financial Times*, 16 October 1998). In 1994 Canada lost 18 per cent of its cohort of university-educated graduate managers, 14 per cent of its doctors and scientists, and 40 per cent of its nurses. Managers could earn an extra C$7400 by moving to the USA and, according to Canadian business lobbies, pay less tax. But Canadian business has too restricted a view if it seeks to explain the exodus solely in terms of income incentives and tax disincentives; it needs to acknowledge the greater excitement of working in the USA and do what it can to compensate. Freedom and opportunity as well as high take-home pay must be offered by firms anywhere that wish to compete in the world market for the highest quality labour.

The literature of the history of science contains ample clues as to the personal characteristics and working conditions most conducive to originality. It is important for instance to avoid squandering resources on bureaucratic solutions like the placebo of science parks, since the firms in them prove no more innovative than those outside (*The European*, 20 July 1998). Within a company, autonomy in the workplace is the best lure. Provision needs to be made for individuals (and not merely lab-bench scientists) to have 'bootlegging' time, like the 15 per cent of working hours that 3M grants to its employees for working on projects of their own. Few people will come up with much of commercial worth while 'bootlegging' but the one who invents something like 3M's Post-it notes will pay for all the others. Offering a contract of the type Microsoft offers to programmers, requiring them to keep up their hobbies, is another imaginative device.

Cars are black, said Henry Ford, and managers are grey. It is hard to expect managers, or at any rate administrators, to cope easily with the free-floating world that is striving to be born. They are likely to be formalists, drawn from among the majority of humankind who feel they have nothing original to say or whose creative days are over. CEOs and boards, more than managers, will have to be the ones responsible for setting firms free. What can be expected of them?

THE ROLE AND COMPETENCE OF BOARDS AND CEOS

The formal educational attainments of Australian CEOs and board members may be less to the point than the quality of their imaginations but education does mean something and the picture is not encouraging. Only eight of the CEOs of the top 50 firms have an MBA, 15 have no tertiary qualification at all, and most of those who do are engineers or accountants with a sprinkling of natural scientists, altogether a far from diverse or balanced population (*Australian Financial Review*, 1 May 1999).

Are individuals of this type capable of passing with flying colours the examination that a more integrated world economy is setting them? There is reason for doubt in the case of some of the largest firms, which have made such a poor fist of going global. In 1998 it was said of BHP, long Australia's biggest corporation, that, 'the management is discredited and the board demoralised ... the past 10 years have been a write-off ... BHP's attempt to go global during the past decade has basically wholly backfired' (*Australian Financial Review*, 1 August 1998, and letter 8 August 1998). Confidential internal documents cited in the NSW Parliament in 1997 revealed that BHP preferred to employ 'young, educated, physically fit Anglo-Saxon males', which is no way to train up a workforce for global circumstances (*The Australian*, 8 May 1997). On top of heavy losses, BHP wrote down assets worth \$2.7 billion in 1997–98 and \$3.3 billion in 1998–99 (*The Australian*, 26 June 1999).

Fosters, despite initially unbridled enthusiasm, lost over \$80 million in China in four years. Telstra's investments in seven countries, dating from the heady days of 1993–95, seriously underperformed, leaving the company 'without a credible strategy for growth abroad'. As for Westpac, it had a bad debt charge of $2.8 billion in 1992. An American had to be brought in to curb its unrealistic global ambitions. Although Australians do head some leading corporations in the USA, there were simply too few senior Australian executives of the requisite experience and quality able or willing to meet the challenges of deregulation and 'globalization' at home in the early 1990s. Moreover, external affairs managers only then began to be appointed from outside industry, as had been the practice for years in the USA. When the external affairs manager at BHP secured a board seat in 1997 it was the first time one had done so in a top 20 Australian company.

Several American CEOs were brought in to shake up the cultures of leading firms. At the peak period four of the top seven Australian firms were run by Americans, and three more were in the top 20. It is not good news that only the advent of serious problems brought about these appointments, although in fairness it should be added that boards were finally acknowledging the need and also that some of the Americans, notably Dennis Eck at Coles, made their mark by releasing the considerable talents of existing Australian managers (*The Australian*, 12 February 1997; 13 February 1999; 10 May 1999).

One reason for the slow and painful adjustment to international standards was beyond reasonable doubt the lack of diversity at board level. This is what gave them, as Les Coleman commented, 'a locker room subtleness [subtlety] towards differences in thought and behaviour' (*The Australian*, 29 April 1998). Fifteen individuals are said to occupy 10 per cent of the board seats in the top 100 firms (*Australian Financial Review*, 6 June 1998). Internationally comparative data are hard to find but a study by John Onto and Christopher Thomas and one at the University of Southern California fill some of the gap.[18] Only 28 per cent of the boards of public companies include a woman (cf. 69 per cent in the USA), and only a tiny proportion contain a member of a racial minority (51 per cent in the USA) or a foreign national (17 per cent in the USA). Slightly more recent evidence shows that women occupy only 10.7 per cent of board seats in Australia's 300 largest companies, while 63.1 per cent of companies have only single board seats open to women (*The Australian*, 20 July 1999).

If the analysis is restricted to Australian companies with at least 10 per cent of their assets offshore, only 7 per cent of board members prove to be foreign nationals and these include New Zealanders. Sixty-seven per cent of directors live in the city where the company has its headquarters and the chairman of one leading bank actually said, 'if I had my choice, all members of my board would be from Melbourne'. CEOs have recently been hired at younger ages (only 9 per cent of the chief executives of top companies are now aged 60 or more) (*The Australian*, 29 July 1999). But boards still seem to be dominated by the elderly. In 1998 the average age of the 64 board members of Amcor, BHP, Boral, CSR, Pacific Dunlop and WMC was 59 years. Clear strategic thinking and a taste for radical change are not common at that time of life. Among smaller companies the situation seems healthier. Probably the nimbleness of the Australian economy during the Asian Crisis was due substantially to small firms in a wide range of industries and export trades.

Another reason why the performance of leading corporations may be less than visionary is that no great penalty attaches to failure on the part of individual CEOs. This, of course, does not apply only in Australia. A letter in *The Economist* (29 May 1999) points out that chief executives can act primarily, and not necessarily illegally, to maximize their personal benefits for three to five years before the harmful effects on a company are evident. If one leaves with $10 million rather than $15 million or $20 million, so what? The diminishing marginal utility of real income must have set in long since for all except the pathologically greedy. Other directorships will still be available. A means is needed to index total compensation to real performance.

A ROLE FOR GOVERNMENT

In many respects Australia is less a single country than a collection of small societies half-isolated from one another by distance and states' rights, and physically very distant from the rest of the world, especially from the cultures that it most resembles. On the bright side, the advent of the Internet has reduced the tyranny of distance and gone some way to combating that other great tyranny, small market size. But keeping up culturally and capitalizing on the intrinsic advantage of belonging to the English-language world is bound to take an effort.

Corporations must save themselves, which is difficult given the hierarchical structures of the larger ones and the conditioning to which the current generation of senior executives has been exposed. As it happens, the fact of steep hierarchies in the larger firms may be a perverse advantage: if a lively CEO is appointed he or she can stir things up, or rather down, throughout the organization. The final question I want to ask is, however, broader than the individual firm. What role should government play in trying to support business?

Government should try to make Australia attractive to mobile factors of production by reducing what Kasper has called in an important paper 'ITO' costs (information, transaction and organization).[19] Given the assumptions in the present chapter about the swelling international competition for highly-skilled labour, associated changes must include the improvement of education. I would start by attempting to raise the literacy rate and purify the teaching of

English. Showing real seriousness in that respect would have pervasive effects. But this is a difficult area to reform given a teaching profession mostly too young to have learned the relevant skills. The difficulty is said to be compounded by the emergence of a cohort of barely teachable young people but that may be a defence mechanism. There are no bad soldiers, only bad officers.

Plenty of other reforms need to be introduced in syllabuses and teaching practices, up to and including at the level of higher degrees. This is where the half-false analogy between business and education does harm, since it delivers institutions into the hands of pedestrian administrators and sanctions the use of myopic cost-benefit measurement that tends to divert resources from genuine scholarship. The red-tape and crass quantitative measures employed in the evaluation of publicly-funded research are inimical to innovation, sometimes risibly so, and appear to satisfy few ends other than those of an uninformed and self-serving bureaucracy.[20]

A proper aim of policy would be to improve the quality of education, which is not to say that the solutions automatically lie in expanding the public sector of education. Realistically, however, public education will persist and it is clear that not only the funding available to it but also its current standards are inadequate. Morale is ultimately more important but Australian educational and R&D expenditures (the latter at 1.6 per cent of GDP being only about half the South Korean ratio) are well below acceptable international levels. There are plenty of plans to improve the quality of Australian education but no guarantee that they will be carried out – the situation is bedevilled by the division of responsibility between the Commonwealth and the States – and, even if they are successful, the gestation period for educational investments is a long one. In the meantime, businesses would be wise to be self-reliant and devise ways to employ available skills more effectively.

RESISTING CULTURAL PROTECTIONISM

As or more important than positive policies are some things government ought not to do. Government should no more cosset particular industries or, worse, individual corporations in the creative sphere than in older sectors of the economy; and it should definitely stand up and be seen to resist the wave of cultural protectionism sweeping across the world. This is no 'threat' from globalization but a threat from the opposite direction: cultural closure. The arguments advanced for the protection of culture and the cost of transfer payments to producers that would ensue seem identical to those adduced for manufacturing industries.

Campaigns to protect national cultural producers have provided a fresh cause and new allies for the greying Green movement, which may go to show that the non-governmental organizations (NGOs) have been more astute than business in noticing where the new springs of wealth are going to be. A combination of NGOs, notably from Canada but linked around the world via the Internet, has arisen to fight the battle for cultural protection. It has piggy-backed on the community's vague fears about 'globalization'. In concert with the French bureaucracy, the NGOs scored a victory when they forced the abandonment of the Multilateral Agreement on Investment (MAI).[21] 'The sovereign right of governments to give way to sectional pressures is not a principle worth defending', declares Henderson (p. 55) as he recounts such absurdities as the way French films are protected though they can be defined as such only because they receive French subsidies. The sectional interests nevertheless won hands down over the feeble government proponents of the MAI.

If French culture cannot reasonably be defined, neither can Australian culture. No mechanism such as the market exists that is able to resolve conflicts among the various claims and definitions put forward by producer interests. All that remains is a set of assertions and a perpetual lawyerly squabble over the artificial details of written precedent. Proceeding down the culturally protectionist path could lead only to a scramble for subsidies for local producers and a thicket of tariffs, quotas or local content laws to exclude overseas competitors and shelter those not willing to compete. Public support tends to be enlisted by appeals to preserve the fugitive, chameleon-like concept of 'national identity'. Such are the nationalistic antagonisms already engendered that *The Australian*'s art critic has been attacked merely for daring to compare Australian art with that of other countries (*The Australian*, 14 March 1998; but see letter 16 March 1998).

Contrary to their triumph over the MAI, the protectionists lost when it came to the 'Blue Skies' case relating to the entry of New Zealand television films to the Australian market. The CER was already in existence and the ruling of the courts was that its provisions must be read to include cultural products, meaning that those from New Zealand could not be kept out. Lamenting the consequent throwing of the Australian television industry to the Moloch of New Zealand competition, Senator Vicky Bourne, Democrat spokesperson for Foreign Affairs, claimed on ABC radio that this threatened not merely the 'cultural identity' of Australians but their human rights. (Her declaration was immediately followed by a programme on Jane Austen.)

The Chairman of the Australian Broadcasting Authority, David Flint, Dean of Law at the University of Technology, Sydney, did not go quite so far. He protested merely that 'national identity' had been 'sacrificed for trade obligations' (*The Age*, 29 April 1998). Subsequently he recommended *changing the rules* about what was admissible, while still satisfying international treaty obligations, from 'Australian produced' to 'Australian subject matter', a legalistic device certain to hamper foreign competitors. As the *Australian Financial Review* remarked in a leader on 1 May 1998, Australians would be permitted to listen to Joan Sutherland but not to Kiri Te Kanawa.

Most unfortunately, the Federal government announced that it regretted the Blue Skies decision, adding that although this would have to be lived with, Australian culture would be protected in future. It went on to proclaim that local content quotas already protected the 'world class' (yet preternaturally vulnerable!) Australian television networks from any new competition for the next decade. Beneath this sop to producers must lie the assumptions that Australian consumers and voters will either submit supinely to having their freedom of choice restricted or can be manipulated into agreeing to this through appeals to blind nationalism and what Henderson calls 'do-it-yourself' economics. No *bona fide* defence of a definable Australian culture is to be found here, only its shadow. The issue is not about a chimerical 'national culture' or 'national identity', much less about any genuine or defensible 'human rights'. The struggle is for the rents that come from excluding trade competitors and for the votes that accrue from appealing to an unthinking insularity.

Ample evidence and powerful argument exist that *public* interest in the arts has always been better served by market competition than by government intervention.[22] The role of government should be to refrain from intervening to promote or protect sectional interests and industries, old or new. The case of Japan, though once held to demonstrate the exact opposite, shows the failure of industry policy and the '1940s System', as Japanese scholars themselves now recognize. The effect of protection is an especially serious one in a small market like that of Australia where efficiency can be quickly lost if producers are shielded from the need to meet competitive pressures. Government ought to leave the market as free as possible in cultural spheres as in traditional industrial ones. It should concentrate on improving the general business environment rather than respond to the self-interested demands of lobby groups.

CONCLUSIONS

International economic integration in the service sector seems set to continue, give or take the efforts of protectionists to frustrate it. The theme of this chapter has been that demand has reached a stage when special opportunities and returns will attach to cultural services. This has immense implications for the labour market. In addition, more firms headquartered in Australia will find they have to engage in trade and undertake part of their work overseas. The record so far has not always been good. Large firms in traditional industries have not always succeeded in 'going global' profitably. Although some companies in the creative service industries have performed well, negative signs like the 'exodus' of new IT firms are apparent even there.

Structural change in most economies, especially developed economies, will increase the competition for high-quality labour. Australia is not well placed to increase the supply of such labour beyond present levels. Among the changes that will be required are, in the background, the improvement of education and, in the foreground, the encouragement of individual creativity. Neither government nor corporations seem to recognize these needs clearly or show willingness to offer the conditions that talent will demand. Those who manage creative workers will have to become more imaginative and adaptable and so will the boards that oversee the managers. Without changes in the business culture and company structures, the most gifted individuals will not be as productive as they might be nor will they necessarily remain in Australia. Businesses must take seriously the tasks of attracting and managing creative labour if they are to do better in the export trade and import substitution.

NOTES

1. Robert D. Atkinson and Randolph H. Court, 'The New Economy: How Is It Different?', *Issues in Science and Technology*, **XV** (3), 1999, 86-7.
2. Department of Foreign Affairs and Trade, *Trade in Services, Australia, 1997-98* (Canberra: DFAT, 1999), pp. 64-5.
3. Australian Coalition of Service Industries, *The Australian Service Sector Review, 1998* (Melbourne, 1998), p. 33. Although this report acknowledges that an attraction for departing professionals is the opportunity to learn new skills and not merely to earn higher pay, it does not notice the implicit inconsistency that the more internationally competitive are the graduates educated in Australia the more likely they will be to leave. Nevertheless it does correctly conclude that, 'a key issue for Australian business and professional service firms will be to try to attract those professionals back to enrich Australia's talent pool'. Well-educated Australians are already more prone to emigrate than, for example, Americans, Britons, the Dutch, Germans, Irish, Japanese or Norwegians. IMD, *World Competitiveness Year Book*, (Lausanne, 1999), t. 8.13, p. 494.
4. World Trade Organisation, *Annual Report* (1998), p. 71, table III.77; *The Australian Service Sector Review*, op. cit., 11.
5. D. Crowe, 'Exodus: Why Australia's IT Champions are Leaving the Country', *Australian Financial Review* (29 May 1999), pp. 23-5; see also *The Australian*, 9 July 1999.
6. David Martin Jones and Michael L.R. Smith, 'Advance Australia - Anywhere', *Orbis*, **43** (3), 1999, 457.
7. Charity A. Dorgan, *Gale Country and World Rankings Reporter* (New York: Gale Research Inc., 1995), p. 83.
8. Various, *Book of Australian Facts* (Sydney: Reader's Digest), 1992, p. 49.
9. House of Representatives' Standing Committee on Employment, Education and Training, *The Literacy Challenge: A Report on Strategies for Early Intervention for Literacy and Learning for Australian Children* (Canberra: Australian Government Publishing Service, 1993), p. 167.
10. Clive James, *Falling towards England* (London: Picador, 1986), p. 167.

11. In England phonics has become the norm again after 30 years of 'child-centred' pedagogy during which the under-performance of schoolchildren worsened further relative to continental Europeans; test scores have been rising again for five years (*Financial Times*, 10 July 1999). In New Zealand, after the damage the wholeword fad has done to the teaching of English, phonics enthusiasts may at last be coming 'out of the closet'. See the speech of 24 September 1998 by Roger Kerr, 'Restoring Sanity to Education' reprinted in New Zealand Business Roundtable, *Turning Gain into Pain* (Wellington: NZBR, May 1999), pp. 209–16.

12. I am informed that standards of accuracy in the teaching of other languages have also slumped, at least in Victoria.

13. H.G. Da Souza (UNESCO), Conference on 'Cultural Responses to Globalization', EU–Japan Fest, Stockholm, November, 1998; Briefing by H.E. Mr Peter Grey, Centre for the Practice of International Trade, Melbourne Business School, 9 June 1999; *Financial Times*, 10 November 1998; *International Herald Tribune*, 12 November 1998; Industry Commission *Annual Report, 1996–97* (Canberra: Commonwealth of Australia, 1997), pp. 7, 9.

14. It will indeed be apparent that I am speaking mostly of large corporations. The weaknesses of management and governance have shown up most clearly there, as they have in large-scale projects such as those relating to Collins' class submarines. Smaller firms seem less inward-looking, perhaps because they are disproportionately run by the foreign-born: one-third of current small business operators were born overseas, a proportion 50 per cent higher than that of immigrants in the population.

15. I owe this point to Professor Peter Hart of the University of Reading.

16. *TechWeb Technology News*, 5 July 1999.

17. For compelling evidence of the role of Chinese and Indian entrepreneurs in creating jobs and high-technology exports in the USA, see AnnaLee Saxenian, 'Silicon Valley's New Immigrant Entrepreneurs', Public Policy Institute of California Home Page, June 1999. In the USA as a whole, entrepreneurship rates are as high as 18 per cent for Korean immigrants and 15 per cent for Greek immigrants, while the rate of self-employment among immigrants is higher than for the native-born (*Business Week*, 29 May 1999).

18. John Onto and Christopher Thomas, *Corporate Governance and Globalising Business: Reconciling Competing Pressures* (Melbourne: Melbourne Business School, 1997); and David Uren, 'Anemic Boards Need New Blood', *The Australian*, 7 March 1998.

19. Wolfgang Kasper, *Institutional Innovation to Enhance International Attractiveness*, Economics and Management Discussion Paper, 1/93 (Campbell, A.C.T.: Australian Defence Force Academy, 1993).

20. Dallas Hanson *et al.* (1999), 'Management of Basic R&D: Lessons from the Australian Experience', *Prometheus*, **17** (2), 1999, 187–97. For a powerful argument that private funding has been a more effective means of promoting scientific research, see Terence Kealey, *The Economic Laws of Scientific Research* (Basingstoke: Macmillan, 1996).

21. Henderson, David, *The MAI Affair: A Story and Its Lessons*, Pelham Paper Number Five (Melbourne: Melbourne Business School, 1999).

22. Tyler Cowen, *In Praise of Commercial Culture* (Cambridge, Mass.: Harvard University Press, 1998).

11. The case for supermarkets: the Australian experience

PERIODS OF CHANGE

The central fact about the history of grocery retailing in developed countries is that the trade has constantly striven to provide shoppers with more choice. It has succeeded abundantly in doing so. The number of items offered to the Australian consumer has grown from about 400 soon after the Second World War to 40 000 or more now, a rise of over 100 fold. Although this chapter will recount the stages of the increase, the magnitude of the change virtually speaks for itself. Add in the calculation that the price of a standard basket of groceries has been reduced by one-quarter over the past 25 years and vast gains for the consumer are utterly undeniable.

The opening section of this history describes a number of landmark changes in Australia over the period since 1914. The continual evolution of supply and demand is traced from the days of hawkers and small corner stores to the present, when it is scarcely fanciful to describe the newest supermarkets as Aladdin's caves. The early history sets the scene for sections on developments since the Second World War. The story is carried to the brink of the major change now expected in direct selling as a result of widespread public use of the Internet. Specific evidence is drawn from the records of Coles Myer, a company formed from the two long-established ones whose names it incorporates and now one of the largest supermarket chains.

The retail trade has accommodated and even anticipated enormously changing consumer preferences. These preferences have been shaped and reshaped by massive forces, particularly in the latter part of the century, involving many factors including technology (universal motor cars and refrigerators, the computer) and a domestic revolution that has released women to play a huge role in the paid workforce. The Australian public has become extraordinarily diverse and more demanding with respect to the range of foodstuffs it wishes to buy, a range which it seems to wish to see constantly expanding. At the same time consumers have become intensely sensitive to matters of food quality and food safety, while expecting competitive prices and opening hours that suit their multifold convenience.

The kaleidoscopic diversity of goods and types of store makes many general observations hazardous, as do differences among the states, among suburbs and between city and country. The retail grocery trade perpetually faces the operator with the predicament of whether to add value to products, to compete on price, or try to strike a balance. Different firms at the same time, and the same firm at different times, have explored all the possibilities. There will be exceptions to any generalization that attempts to pin down so much variety. For all that, the main trends and active behaviour of the industry remain clear.

Since everybody shops, everybody has an opinion about shopping. People tend to base their estimates of how much change there has been on the difference from the style of shopping in their own formative years. Someone who can remember only as far back, say, as the 1970s will take for granted facilities that someone else who can recall the 1940s will consider the result of a modern revolution. Both are likely to have rosy-tinted impressions of corner shops – youngsters because such things will seem quaint, their elders because memories tend to soften with age. The historical information here helps to present the clean, convenient and well-filled modern store in a more objective light.

In the late 1990s the trend towards supplying greater choice is continuing at a rate and with a profusion that earlier generations would have thought pure science fiction. The 1990s stand out as a decade of astonishing improvements. From the retailer's side, however, the process of development remains, as it has always been, a matter of trial and error. Although the dominant theme of the century has been waves of expansion in the size and complexity of stores and range of products, the offerings set before customers are subject to the technological limitations prevailing at any one time and occasional ill-judged ventures by companies. But even innovations that are subsequently abandoned benefit the consumer since they denote an industry eager to make sure that it reflects the wishes of the community.

During the twentieth century the retail food industry has been subject to extraordinary pressures, of which we can pick out three main types:

1. External shocks, such as two World Wars and the Depression.
2. The evolution of socio-economic structures that have raised incomes, altered household arrangements out of recognition, and increasingly replaced stay-at-home housewives with a cohort of independent, educated and working women.
3. Changes in the public mood when people have tired of some shop formats and unexpectedly spurned certain products (an example is lard and a format is a type of store layout).

The industry has been obliged to react to these pressures. Yet it has not remained a passive responder, it has actively created surges of innovation. Here it will be insisted that the continual probing to discover which new ideas the consumer will take up has been socially desirable: the consumer has been the gainer overall. Successful retailers, past and present, have usually gone out of their way to find novelties from which the public may make its selection. In a competitive industry, the consumer has nevertheless been the one to make the decision about what to buy and where to buy it.

Home delivery was the first truly major transformation. It started early in the century, when it began to supplement reliance on local shops. The home delivery era persisted into the 1950s, until the onset of the second great transformation. That was the rush to create suburban self-service stores, precursors of the establishment of large modern supermarkets that was soon to overlap it. This development extinguished the occupations of door-to-door delivery men, apart from a few milk and bread roundsmen: 'recollections of such tradespeople were smashed to bits, like the prices, by the supermarket'.[1] Australians rapidly voted with their feet, or rather their cars, for the convenience and low prices of the supermarket.

The four subsequent decades of the supermarket era have been characterized by repeated increases in size and alterations of format, as well as astonishing extensions of the range of products on offer. Yet, rather than the simple trend to gigantism that this suggests, the average size of Coles stores is falling a little at the end of the 1990s. The company is establishing a new format of 'Express Stores' in central business districts in order to serve the current trend towards inner-city living and the homeward rush of commuters who, though they have disposable income, see themselves as 'time poor'. This means that there is more to the history of growth than meets the eye. During most decades the retail grocery trade has certainly expanded in one shape or form but it is instructive to note the more defining feature: willingness to adapt to what the market wants.

At the end of the millennium the plain fact is that consumers want *everything*. To quote the American super-retailer, the late Sam Walton of Walmart, 'as a consumer, you want everything: a wide assortment of good quality merchandise; the lowest possible prices; guaranteed satisfaction with what you buy; friendly, knowledgeable service; convenient hours; free parking; a pleasant shopping experience'.[2] Modern Australian consumers have all these expectations.

THE 1920s

From the very start of the twentieth century retailing has remained in flux.

Australia has always been an exceptionally urban society and at the start of the period much of the population lived in what are now inner suburbs, with shops within an easy walk. Households were also surprisingly self-sufficient: photographs of backyards in the early part of the twentieth century show dense rows of rabbit hutches, chicken runs, vegetable plots and fruit trees. But already, and especially after the First World War, this world of small localities was in the process of being replaced by a new one dominated by suburban living and home delivery.

As suburbs developed around Australian cities, even low-income households came to rely on shops that took orders and delivered to the home via a cart. Low weekly earnings and shortages of cash necessitated frequent, small purchases. In addition, suburbs with quarter-acre blocks were well spread out. Visits to distant shops were a chore, especially in rain or hot weather. Suburban houses did not at first contain any advanced means of refrigeration but possessed Coolgardie safes, and later ice chests, and built-in pantries that had to be restocked often. Hence perishable items like milk, ice and bread were delivered daily. The 'rabbito' and the fish seller sold from door to door. A mythology has built up around deliveries of this type, romanticizing the visits to make them seem the highpoint of the lonely housewife's day. Perhaps they were for some, though for others the practice must have been a mild irritant. 'The greengrocer would always interrupt lunch, whenever we had it', Michael Symons recalls, 'and after hiding away in his tall green van, crunch down the gravel drive with his filled deal box.'[3]

Retailers thus followed their customers out to the spreading suburbs, so to speak, by means of delivery carts, waggons and eventually vans. In addition many city retailers established branches in the new suburban shopping strips. Customers in this era bought a familiar range of brands and grew to expect plentiful food, though by later standards the variety within many lines was limited. Advertising permitted manufacturers to speak directly to consumers and there were early grumbles about the de-skilling of grocers. These men (they were almost always men) ceased to blend teas, for example, and instead filled orders for prepackaged brands. The positive side of this development was that it made entry into retail grocery easier for people who had not served the long apprenticeship necessary to become master grocers.

The 1920s was a decade of particular expansion and experimentation. In terms of formats, the firm of Grace Brothers experimented with a cash-and-carry food department in Sydney as early as 1920 and a Brisbane chain did so in various Queensland centres in 1923, although in the event cash-and-carry did not spread far beyond variety stores. Nor did turnstiles find much favour, though they were in use in a few self-service groceries in Victoria as early as 1926.

As an example of product change, a greater range of breakfast foods became available in the mid-1920s and the consumption of bread actually started to fall. Even pre-wrapped bread was offered as early as 1928 though it did not catch on; housewives tore the paper open to see what they were getting. The future had not quite arrived.

THE 1930s

The Depression of the 1930s reined in the experiments and accelerating changes of the 1920s. The real income of most families grew only slowly, for some it did not grow at all, and for the unemployed it fell. Income per head had been $1046 in 1914, it recovered during the 1920s from a wartime fall, but only to $980, and fell back to $934 in 1933 (in dollars of 1966-67). By 1939 it had only just regained the level of 1914. A refrigerator then cost ten times as much as an ice chest and, as it happens, ten times the average male's weekly wage. In any case during the 1930s the looming fear of unemployment inhibited large expenditures.

Methods of retailing groceries during the interwar period – home delivery and the corner store – are easily romanticized. Assistants in small shops worked long hours and seldom had holidays, sick pay or morning and afternoon breaks for tea. The corner store was often cramped, poorly equipped, and heaped with goods that left only a tiny space for selling. This crowding of shop space persisted into the 1950s. During the Depression years price mattered so much that product quality was often sacrificed. A number of grocers did introduce cash-and-carry shopping because there were districts in which it was no longer advisable to extend credit nor profitable even to continue home deliveries.

THE 1940s

From the customer's point of view the 1940s was another rude shock. 'Austerity menus' were the order of the day. 1942-44 were really hard years. By 1944 consumption per head had fallen below that of 1939 for poultry and game, tomatoes and citrus fruits, meat, milk and milk products, sugar, and oils and fats. The least fall was 7 per cent for oils and fats, for poultry and game it was as much as 32 per cent, and for meat as a whole 16 per cent. Admittedly, the consumption of cereals, potatoes and eggs rose but the tightening of belts and restricting of food choices was obvious. Despite the cut in meat consumption, American servicemen stationed in Australia were scornful of local tastes that continued to glory in meals of 'meat and potatoes' and skimped, relatively speaking, on fruit and salads.

The war years slowed, even halted, the redesigning of grocery shops for self-service, a trend that had originated in the USA in 1916 and dominated that country during the 1930s. Rationing, commodity shortages and price controls persisted for years into peacetime. In New South Wales price controls were not finally abandoned until 1955. The period was a dour one. In a savage attack on the costs of the Protectionism then ruling, Robin Boyd pointed out that Australian manufacturing was supplying kitchen equipment that was ten years behind that of the USA.[4] Whereas in the nineteenth century Australians had imported every latest gadget, once local manufacturers took over 'the housekeeper sometimes had to wait many years before new labour-saving devices were offered her'.

Under-equipped kitchens were not ready for a revolution in culinary habits. It comes as no surprise, then, that retailing was also said to have 'stood still' during this period, though in fairness this did not apply to the whole product range. The likely future was becoming clearer with the post-war introduction of prepackaged frozen foods and meat, Nestlé's introduction of cans of strained vegetables for babies, and frozen Chinese meals which were first sold in 1949 – from ice-cream cabinets. The 'war lag' of ten years affected formats most. Not until 1949 were the food departments of many department stores converted to self-service, while the first, or almost the first, fully self-service grocery opened in Sydney no earlier than 1950.

THE 1950s

Home delivery persisted into the early 1950s: at that date 'our milkman still leapt the fence before dawn to fill the billy', recollects Symons.[5] A majority of shops had old-fashioned premises when the decade opened. Housewives queued while the grocer and his assistants scurried about filling each order. Counter displays offered the only opportunity for impulse buying; the assistants were said not infrequently to be too tired to make suggestions about what to buy.

Yet the early 1950s were marked out by the entry of self-service stores and more and more prepackaged food. The decade was an increasingly prosperous one, with suburban living customary and car ownership becoming the norm. Annual income per head, which in 1939 had been $1045, rose after the war, reaching $1179 in 1947 and moving well up to $1627 by 1961 (all in 1966–67 dollars). More women were working. They had less time to shop, though television advertisements increasingly made them aware of what was available (the first television with commercials came to Sydney in September 1956). Seventy-three per cent of metropolitan homes owned a refrigerator in 1952, when the cost was still some six times the average male weekly wage. Ninety-three per cent of all Australian households owned one by 1956. A week's perishables could safely be kept. These developments facilitated large family purchases, preferably made in a single store. Self-service meant that shopping was carried out rather briskly by choosing for oneself rather than standing at a counter for assistance or waiting at home for a series of delivery men, for which fewer customers were able to afford the time.

Already in 1954 there were 766 self-service stores in Australia and by 1957 the *Australian Financial Review* was reporting that food retailers were converting to self-service at the rate of 40 per month. By the end of that year there were 1700. Regional shopping centres were also first opened in 1957 in Melbourne, Sydney and Brisbane. Summer 1958 saw a staggering leap of 25 per cent above the number of self-service stores that had existed in 1957: by February there were 2126. Associated innovations appeared in the form of equipment such as turnstiles and trolleys. In 1958, a survey of 9000 Melbourne housewives found that 61 per cent did indeed prefer self-service to either counter service or home delivery.

The industry was responding eagerly to their preference. The 1950s was the decade of the self-service-cum-supermarket transformation. Coles and Woolworths were trialling self-service in 1956. It immediately became popular through, as Coles found, permitting the customer to choose 'exactly what she desires'.[6] Coles soon decided that it was 'past the stage of experimenting'. It leap-frogged the phase of conversions to self-service by establishing big, purpose-built, free-standing, suburban supermarkets. These were of course in essence large-scale self-service stores, though with a full range of products that included meat, bread and vegetables. The first was opened in North Balwyn, Victoria, in March 1960 and there were eight by 1962.

These big supermarkets were one-stop shops with a full range of merchandise, pre-packed meat, fruit and vegetables, and cakes cooked daily on the premises. They were recognizable predecessors of modern stores that contain their own delicatessens (and perhaps successors of the Coles café back in 1924). It might not have been possible, however, to anticipate that by the late 1990s Coles would employ 30 chefs and rebuild the Grace Brothers department store in Sydney to house *four* restaurants.

Widespread availability of cars was vital to the upsurge of supermarket shopping in the late 1950s. The weight of an average family's food and beverages was about 50 kg per week, which could be carried conveniently only in one's own vehicle. As the following table shows, the density of car ownership more than doubled during what may be termed the mass entry phase of supermarkets, or what one author calls, more picturesquely, the introduction of 'carpark shopping'.[7]

Table 11.1   Population per car (to nearest whole number)

1921/22	55
1929/30	11
1945	9
1957	7
1968	3

Source: Greg Whitwell, *Making the Market: The Rise of Consumer Society* (Ringwood, Vic.: McPhee Gribble, 1989), pp. 14, 46.

THE 1960s AND 1970s

The affluence of the 1950s continued in the succeeding decades. Income per head rose from the $1627 of 1961 to $2398 in 1974 (again in 1966–67 dollars). The Cost of Living index published by the Commonwealth Bureau of the Census had to be replaced because it no longer reflected reality. In 1962 the quarterly Consumer Price Index was introduced, supplemented from 1973 by a monthly index of food prices.

For the moment we need touch only lightly on the 1960s and 1970s, noting four other important tendencies:

1. The growing technological richness of the grocery environment, symbolized by the earliest fully computer-controlled warehouse, which Davids opened in Sydney in 1972 (only one A & P warehouse in Toronto was earlier).
2. The rise of 'banner groups' and other arrangements whereby independent retailers sought to meet the low prices charged in chain supermarkets by combining their purchases – a knock-on gain for the consumer.
3. The prevalence in the 1970s of waves of amalgamations when one chain of stores took over another – which can likewise be seen as a consumer gain because it greatly facilitated the opening and shutting of outlets to match shifts in the distribution of population.
4. Complaints that mass production and supermarket selling had impaired the quality of some foods.

The criticisms of supermarket foods deserve to be looked at in a little more depth. Considerations of price were said to be ousting those of flavour. Supermarkets were blamed for requiring growers to supply unblemished, regularly-shaped fruit, waxed to look more attractive. Orchardists grew few varieties of apple other than Granny Smiths, Delicious and Jonathans. Tomatoes were grown large to reduce handling costs, uniform to fit foam trays, and tough to last well on the shelf. Battery chicken were said to be bloated and tasteless. In 1981 the consumer magazine *Choice* reported that it was unable to buy commercially a genuine free-range chicken anywhere in Australia.

Nevertheless diets were already becoming more varied than the 'meat and potatoes' that Americans had deprecated during the war. The annual consumption of beef and veal, which had been 64 kg per head in 1938–39, was down to 40 kg by 1970–71. By contrast, the annual consumption of dressed poultry was sharply increasing at the end of the 1960s (9 kg per head in 1968–69 and 11 kg in 1970–71). Whatever the truth about their palatability, the sale of dressed and frozen poultry really took off in 1963. It was greatly encouraged by the adoption of home freezers (by 1978 one in three households owned a freezer) and, ironically, by the public's inability to buy red meat at convenient times as a result of restricted trading hours. The consumption of other frozen foods and fruit juices also jumped from the 1960s.

Cheese is said to be 'the barometer of social changes'.[8] A survey of 1966 revealed the dismal fact that 40 per cent of Melbourne housewives had never tasted any variety of cheese other than cheddar. In 1976 a state premier actually supported a ban on imported cheese with the pronouncement that, 'just because a few migrants want their spicy tucker, I fail to see why the Australian community as a whole should suffer'.[9] Immigrant 'New Australians' were not going to put up with this restriction and the remainder of the population also decided to reject such bigotry. In reality, gouda, ricotta, fetta and mozzarella were all being manufactured and sold in Australia by 1976.

THE 1980s

The 1980s saw a general introduction of electronic aids to selling. Front-end scanning originally appeared in an independent grocer's in Sunshine, Victoria, in 1980; this was adopted by Coles in 1982 and by other chains during the next two years. It made the check-out much faster and more accurate. Format changes were also evident. Coles opened its big new-look Super K stores in the 1980s, with twice the floor space of its largest 1960s stores.

Nevertheless the 1980s was a relatively dull decade, not to be compared with the tentative excitements of the 1920s or the boom in remodelling retail outlets of the 1950s. The public may have become jaded and tired of bland, mass-produced food, even though the supply was reliable and cheap. The buying of cheese and freshly-ground coffee went into a decline. Self-service meant the end of the grocer as a surrogate family retainer, an expert who would personally guide the customer's choice. One critic objected to 'bread stacked in anonymous aisles, peas frozen in plastic and pineapples ... entombed in cans'.[10] According to him, supermarkets had become impersonal, unpleasant and even unreal. Although this was not borne out by his own figures – he cited a survey in which 54 per cent of shoppers found them pleasant or better as against 15 per cent who found them unpleasant or worse – articulate opinion was turning to a negative view of supermarkets.

That there was some truth to accusations of a lack of flavourful foods, or at any rate some sign that more discriminating consumers did exist, was witnessed by the founding of gourmet and food magazines. These promoted fashions in food as other magazines promoted them in clothes. Large supermarkets were meanwhile placing constant quality, regular supply and level prices at the top of their concerns. Interested in long shelf-life, they emphasized tinned, dried and frozen foods. They were driven by the efficiencies of their operating systems and were drifting away from a customer focus, or rather the discriminating customer was drifting away from them. They had succeeded beyond all expectations at mass selling yet gave the impression of being unadventurous in layout or offerings. The improvements they had brought, the reliability, convenience and lower prices, were not enough for the more complex society evolving in Australia. The trade had run fast but society had run faster.

Part of the problem at this period was slack competition in the industry. Each of the supermarket groups could point to a period when it has not kept pace with consumers' expectations and its patronage has fallen off. For Woolworths the worst decade was the 1970s, when the company actually lost money. Coles then rode high, until in the 1980s it began resting on its laurels, which led to sales falling off, market share shrinking, profits falling, and innovation being stifled. During the 1980s Woolworths became the leader in supplying fresh food. For Coles a new approach awaited the 1990s, a period which was to seize a place in the front rank of innovative decades.

THE 1990s

In interviews today, senior managers at Coles tend to make much the same striking observation: during the 1990s 'people have changed', employees and customers alike. This is an intangible but nevertheless fundamental matter, the other half of what has been called, 'Coles Myer's near revolutionary push to test new retail concepts'.[11]

The sea-change in consumer attitudes may perhaps be attributed to the greater availability of information, assisted in part by the Internet and undoubtedly spurred by the spread of higher education. People possess more information and demand still more. They ask to be treated as individuals. They are intolerant of risks to their health and accordingly expect scrupulously clean stores, absolute concern with food hygiene, and new-style 'look-in' delis where they can observe the preparation of meals taking place. The market is virtually fragmenting into a mosaic of specialized tastes, though this is overlain by a good deal of exploratory buying as consumers test the range. A far more extensive variety of goods and services is demanded than in the past.

A shift in the composition of the Australian population, ethnic, educational, occupational, is taking place. It is easy for businesses to be overtaken by the rapidity of this change, which, as we shall shortly show, has made the nature of consumers immensely complex. Social complexity tends to start as a city phenomenon, assimilating Australian society to the norms of urban areas in all the developed countries. But the change in rural consumers is marked too. One feature of modernity is that the rural–urban gap narrows. Country people are immediately informed about new lifestyles; television and greater personal mobility see to that. Their kitchens possess domestic equipment entirely adapted to modern living and modern cuisines.

Responding to this post-modern marketplace, and also to the downward pressure on sales and profits during the late 1980s, Coles changed its culture. This is abundantly clear in the range of goods on sale, as we scarcely need to reiterate. Less apparent, but equally dramatic, is the altered environment of the workplace. Casual workers have less place in the modern retail environment and have been sharply reduced nationally, from 60 per cent of the workforce in 1994 to 38 per cent in 1998.

The company also undertook a fundamental shift in its operations. Firstly came a centralization, particularly of buying, which since about 1991 has taken place at the national level instead of at the level of six state companies. Best practice now spreads more easily among the states. The economies of scale that result can be passed on rapidly in lower prices. 'We are in the infancy of the supply chain', one buyer commented in 1999. He promises further gains from working closely with suppliers and farmers, helping them with their business plans and supporting applications for bank loans.

Hard on the heels of centralization, about 1994, came another development, which sounds contradictory: localization. However this means localization-in-centralization. Store managers continue to reap the benefits of centralized purchasing but have been freed to customize a proportion of their offerings to the demographic features and purchasing habits of their store's trading area. Formats have proliferated, such as 'Express' stores, 'Fast and Fresh' convenience stores, and 'Let's Eat', with its ingredients for gourmet meals and individual advice on how to prepare them. These developments are intended to suit some of the many distinct social groups in the community. The trade has taken a long step forward from the environment of mass consumption that prevailed 15 or 20 years ago.

INFLUENCES ON CONSUMPTION

An outline history of consumers during the twentieth century might be organized around any number of variables. Prominent among them would be the evolution in the size and composition of population, immigration, workforce and household; the shift in where people live; and the overall rise in purchasing power. The analysis might be elaborated to emphasize the growing role of women in the workforce, supposing them (correctly) to be the chief decision-makers in grocery buying. The story would need to be further refined to take account of other consequences of rising incomes, such as the way car and refrigerator ownership became universal, and the modern ability to indulge tastes for such diverse categories as health foods, convenience foods and exotic foods, each of which the retailer is called upon to supply.

Above all, a history of consumers would need to recognize their increased diversity in ethnic and other respects, their greater education and wider experience of the world. These factors have produced an explosion of tastes. As a former head of the Australian Centre for Retail Studies concluded his own historical sketch, 'more than any other industry, retailing encapsulates society, delivers its standard of living and mirrors its aspirations'.[12]

THE STRUCTURE OF POPULATION

Australia's population has grown in every period but from the standpoint of retail markets the essential features relate less to total size than to changing composition. Let us select some indicative facts about the population since the Second World War. The age composition has changed. People are living longer. The proportion of those of 65 years and over is growing while that of 15 and under is shrinking. The already high urban proportion continues to increase. In 1986, 85 per cent already lived in towns of over 1000 people and this reached 89 per cent by 1996. Capital city shares of state populations have grown.

At least as significant has been the surge in immigration. From a record low of 766 persons per year entering Australia in 1936–40, the number shot up after the war to 60 998 in 1947–60 and to well above 200 000 in 1968–69 and subsequent years. During the 1960s the intake continued to derive largely from traditional and culturally similar, though not identical, sources in Britain, Ireland and New Zealand. It was however diluted by flows from other

European countries, notably Italy, Greece, Germany and The Netherlands. Asian immigration, once suppressed by the 'White Australia' policy, became more evident in the 1980s, and the origin of Australians today is the whole wide world.

The market implications of a country of immigrants are worth considering at some length. Immigrants have had an enormous influence on Australian creativity and made a massive difference to tastes. An illustration is the soaring sales growth taking place throughout the industry in 1998 in Mexican foods, spaghetti sauces and Indian foods, while the most dramatic increase in sales among all so-called ethnic foods is dry pasta (27 per cent up on 1995).

The initial effect was nevertheless not the liberating one now so evident. Immigrants often sought out small shops like those to which they were accustomed and which could be relied on to specialize in ethnic foods not initially available in larger stores. Immigration actually helped to reduce average meat consumption, mainly because in no other country (except the USA) did people expect to eat nearly as much meat per head as was eaten in Australia. Immigrants from Mediterranean countries were less enamoured of potatoes than was the existing population, and consumption fell. Nor were they great tea-drinkers. Sales of tea fell (coffee consumption passed that of tea in 1979). There was no gross 'Hollywood effect' whereby eager immigrants outstripped local levels of consumption, as sometimes happened in the United States. But immigration started to diversify the Australian diet and cuisine.

How far cuisine was transformed is clear when we contemplate the typical café meal of the early 1950s: steak and chips, white bread and butter, ice cream with passion fruit or rock melon, and a cup of tea. White bread and perhaps brown: as a single instance of the change that had just begun, the Riga Bakery opened at Bankstown in 1949 to supply immigrants' more varied tastes. By 1982 it was selling 80 varieties of bread to a large clientele. The Italians added pasta and the Vietnamese added rice.

The more confident and prosperous second generation of immigrant communities widened the Australian diet dramatically and began the process of melding ingredients that has already produced a distinctive 'Mediterrasian' cuisine in Australia. The many sociological influences on the formation of taste are not readily separable, though the consequences are plain and a major role for immigration is beyond dispute. Immigrants are exploratory people. They have often moved, if only from country to town, before finally leaving their home countries. A surprising number, including many of British descent, came to Australia after experiencing a spell in some other Commonwealth country. Even immigrants arriving directly from English-speaking countries were likely to be more adventurous than those who had stayed at home, a trait which spilled over to experimenting with foods.

The population was in any case rapidly becoming mixed. Whereas the proportion born in Australia had fallen to 80 per cent by 1971, this still fails to bring out the extent of cultural mixing. Only 61 per cent had both parents who were Australian born. Add to this in-built mixing the swelling influences of television, higher incomes, higher education, diverse role models, travel abroad by Australians and the stream of tourists coming in, besides the remarkable opportunity of sampling unfamiliar foods in Australia's own ethnic restaurants, and one gets the correct picture of cultural ferment. The sheer numbers and combinations of national or ethnic foods for which someone in the community already possessed a taste brought home to food retailers what they could do by way of stocking a far wider array of goods. When they diversified the supermarket 'Offer', as the trade calls what it sets out for sale, this produced its own 'demonstration effect'. People who had seldom contemplated trying exotic foods were brought face-to-face with infinite possibilities.

Meanwhile a gender revolution was taking place. The share of women in the workforce doubled in 50 years (Table 11.2), with all that this implies for female independence, personal income, and buying habits.

Table 11.2   *Percentage of females in the workforce (to nearest whole number)*

1947	22	1971	32
1954	23	1987	40
1961	25	1990	41
1966	28	1998	43

Source: Whitwell, op. cit., p. 22; Australian Supermarket Institute, *The Way We Shop: Grocery Shopping in Australia* (Sydney: Australian Supermarket Institute, 1998), pp. 32–3.

The proportion of married women at work climbed even more steeply. In 1947 it was only 4 per cent but by 1971 it had already reached 21 per cent.

Households fell in size, being 2.7 persons on average in 1996 as opposed to 3.5 exactly 30 years previously. The very striking pattern of changes over 25 years is shown in Table 11.3. By 1998, 55 per cent of households were made up of only one or two people, a fact of considerable significance for purchasing habits.

Related trends have been delayed marriages, single-parenting and childlessness. In this respect, more than any other, people tend to suffer from 'assumption drag' in that they still think in terms of 'traditional' families comprised of couples with children. In reality the number of such families has continued to shrink during the 1990s, whereas the number of one-parent families and families with no children has gone on rising.

Table 11.3   Household sizes as percentages of all households

Number of residents	1971	1996	Percentage change
1	13.6	22.1	+8.5
2	26.5	32.5	+6.0
3	18.0	16.8	−1.2
4	18.7	17.0	−1.7
5	12.2	8.1	−4.1
6 or more	11.1	3.7	−7.4
Average	3.3	2.7	−18.2

Source: ABS Economic and Demographic Statistics.

DINKS, that is to say couples with double incomes but no kids, comprised 30 per cent of households in 1986 but an astonishing 40 per cent by 1998. With so many women, especially married women, working, so many childless couples, so many single parents, and so many households with a high leisure preference and the means to indulge it, the opportunity costs of time have soared. The average age of first births has risen, giving more people the chance to establish a consumer lifestyle before starting a family. The implications of all these tendencies for spending on ready-prepared, convenience foods are enormous.

Consider the following information about freshly-prepared meals, first those designed to be heated and served at home – they rose from 9 per cent to 14 per cent of meals over the period 1996–98 alone. Next consider ready-to-eat hot meals, that is meals like pizza or hot chicken that do not even have to be heated – one-third of metropolitan grocery shoppers bought such a meal in a single week in 1998. Moreover 44 per cent of shoppers expressed interest in the category and the market is expected to boom. Supermarkets sell the lion's share of ready-to-eat foods.

The average time spent on preparing a meal is said to have fallen from 30 minutes in the 1970s to 10 minutes in one generation. The 1990s have emphatically not seen any more time spent on average on food preparation, however long dedicated gourmets may spend in the kitchen. But over the period from 1992–97 a 31 per cent increase was reported in the average time spent actually *consuming* food and drink. Much of this time must be lavished on eating and drinking as a pastime and in order to socialize. It shows an evolutionary jump, perhaps even a revolutionary jump, in the Australian consumer's interest in food.

As the twenty-first century begins the market is characterized by small, autonomous, busy and often quite well-to-do units. These units – these people, these consumers – have more diverse points of reference and lifestyles than any previous generation. None of this is astonishing, though it may be useful to point out once more the perils of assumption drag: Australian reality has far removed itself from the image in the minds not merely of foreigners but often of its own residents. The point may be grasped by remembering that the economy no longer rides 'on the sheep's back.' Revenues from tourism are perhaps six times greater than those from wool. The value of manufactured exports is approximately equal to that of the export of farm goods. An enormous input of science and technology enters the production of the 'elaborately-transformed manufactures' that figure increasingly in exports, just as more and more technical knowledge enters the financial services and information technology sectors.

The workforce that engages in these activities, or at any rate in their leading sectors, is far better educated than before. It is white collar, with diplomas, degrees and advanced degrees, and tastes that are correspondingly advanced. With the relaxation of restrictions on trading hours in some states, it is as though a blanket has been lifted that was smothering the public's preferences and making them appear more uniform than they really were. Surveys of shoppers now distinguish between morning, afternoon, evening and 'night owl' groups. Time of day actually exhibits more of a pattern than day of the week, though young working males and people with high incomes do tend to favour Saturday shopping and young, wealthy single males prefer Sunday. The emphasis on the relative youth of these groups suggests that such habits will go on growing. Unsurprisingly, then, late evening and late night shoppers, who constituted 5 per cent of all shoppers in 1990, had become 9 per cent of the whole by 1996. The market has broken up into ever more varied, demanding and fickle elements – a retailer's nightmare or a retailer's dream, and undoubtedly a retailer's challenge.

RESPONSES FROM RETAILERS

For simplicity's sake, the attention that grocery retailers have given to the demands of customers may be dealt with under three headings, product range, store size and new technology. It is obvious that the list of relevant topics could be extended and each could be greatly elaborated, but there is no need to gild the lily. These headline categories are sufficient to demonstrate the vigour of the response.

Product Range: The 'Offer'

The array of product lines on display in supermarkets has been expanding for decades. The fact cannot be gainsayed. There has been a 100-fold increase in 50 years. The 'Offer' is at an all-time high and is still expanding. Coles has 'densed up' its shelves and so reorganized its stores that the customer can see 'product' around all 360 degrees. Part of the reason for this is that space was at a premium in existing stores, at least until layouts were amended. The Coles store at Donvale, Victoria, as a single example, now carries over 40 000 different lines and although it is a large and newly-renovated store, it is neither the largest nor the newest! No doubt about it, then, the 'Offer' is a treasure house beyond any historical precedent.

Yet when we try to trace the path by which this cornucopia has come into being the task becomes formidable, although not quite impossible. There are three types of issue. Firstly, there are issues of measurement and definition that make it hard to compare past and present offerings. Admittedly, we may discount the so-called 'churn' whereby some line or other is always being discontinued while new ones are added. Census-takers are always obliged to count populations that are changing; a cut-off date can be chosen and the items on the shelves counted at that point. The existence of 'churning' is simply further evidence of consumer sovereignty. If consumers never wanted anything different, grocers could still put forward the limited offerings of past decades.

Can we simply count items on the shelves? Consider a pot of marmalade. Is this a single item – one SKU or stock-keeping unit? Perhaps not, since it is possible to buy orange or lemon marmalade. Is a pot of orange marmalade, then, a single SKU? Again, perhaps not, since it is possible to select fine cut or thick cut. (And, as it happens, to select many further sub-varieties, quite apart from choosing different sizes of pot and among the products of different manufacturers.) Surely, though, the warehouse can tell us what degree of splitting or lumping is involved, what definitions are actually being used at a given date? Maybe so: but the problem in writing a history is that past figures on SKUs do not specify the definitions then used. We cannot be sure that the same distinctions were being made throughout the industry at all periods, though the data from Coles Myer which form a substantial part of Table 11.4 are more secure.

A second question is what benchmark period should we choose? Which previous period is the appropriate contrast with the profusion of the late 1990s? After all, no one would be surprised to be told that a store today contains infinitely more lines than in 1915, or the Depression, or the period of regulation and price control that lasted until the mid-1950s.

As it happens, the answer to a third question determines the answer to the second. What actual historical information can we use? The answer is precious little, and what there is does not stretch far back into the past or refer to many years or runs of years. Nor does the vague classification of types of store for which numbers of lines are sometimes cited incline one to believe that like is always being compared with like.

However the numbers are clearly not random; even the brief table (Table 11.4) makes it plain that the 'Offer' has swollen over time, that the intro-duction of supermarkets was responsible for an enormous extension of choice, and that the scale of recent changes has been positively gargantuan. It should also be taken into account how much value is now added to many of the lines on sale by way of the cleaning, packing and preparing of food, increasingly food that is fresh. Items on offer are more numerous than formerly. They are also different. They are better.

Table 11.4   Grocery product lines on offer

Date or period	Class of store	Number of lines
1947	Traditional grocery	400
1950s	Coles 200–700 square metre stores	1200
1960s	Coles standard stores (1000–1500 square metres)	1500–2500
1970	Typical supermarket	*c.* 8000
c. 1980	Traditional grocery	under 1000
	Average supermarket	10 000–15 000
1996	Australian Supermarket Institute figure	25 000
1990s	Coles supermarkets of 2500–4000 square metres	15 000–25 000
	Coles large supermarkets (5000 square metres)	35 000–40 000

Source: Various, including Coles own data.

Store Sizes and Formats

The most straightforward measure of the capacity of retail stores is floor area. At any given date stores of a range of sizes were being built, typical ranges are cited in Table 11.5. The figures amply demonstrate the upward trend in modal (the commonest) size of store ever since the late 1950s. However stores are increasingly being designed to suit particular locations, often inner city ones, and are no longer necessarily expanding in sheer area. All sorts of formats exist to sell groceries, from food barns (warehouses) and half-case stores to delis and convenience stores (like the 7 Elevens that first opened in Oakleigh, Victoria, in 1977).

The figures of supermarket floor area can give only an impression of how this has grown, because, while there is now an international standard definition of a supermarket in terms of selling area and commodities sold, 'these technical definitions do not necessarily correspond at all to the manner in which retailers have, in the past, utilized the term "supermarket"'.[13]

In addition, the 'densing up' of stock on the shelves during the 1990s needs to be taken into account – in other words, floor area in square metres under-represents the scale of recent developments.

Table 11.5   Coles Myer stores (floor space in square metres)

Small grocery-only stores	
1958–1963	200–700
Standard supermarkets	
1960–1966	1000–1600 (a few larger)
1966–1971	2000–2400 (a few larger and smaller)
1971–1980	2000–3000
1980–1985	2400–3000
1985–1990	3800–5000
Extended range stores	
1964–1970	most 3000–3500
1971–1980	most *c*. 3000
1980–1984	most 3200–3800
1984–1990	most over 4500
1991–1998	most 2500–3500
1999	two 5000
Express stores in CBDs	700–1400

Source: Construction Department, Coles Myer.

Technological Innovation

Little is more obvious than that the task of providing food at the retail level involves a substantial feat of logistics. As many as 55 or 60 separate operations may be needed to take a fresh grocery item from the field to a distribution centre, process it, wrap it, and put it on the shelf. To carry out many of these operations, modern companies depend on advanced technologies. Products could not be assembled on the present scale, kept in good condition, kept track of, priced, wheeled to the check-out, or scanned and sold without a mass of equipment. Much of this equipment is very new. All of it is constantly upgraded, to say nothing of the 'permanent revolution' that takes place in computer software.

We need pick out only a handful of the technologies in use, because (once more) it takes only a few to reveal how much the industry has progressed during present lifetimes. As an indication, let us consider the matter of wrapping. There is a long history of using all sorts of paper, including greaseproof paper, for this purpose. The Depression and war years commonly obliged retailers to use old newspapers, which was not popular with customers and was abandoned as soon as possible. Although cellophane had been introduced as early as 1910, tougher forms of plastic film had fortunately become available by the time self-service was generally adopted. Cellophane would have been too fragile for extensive use by customers doing their own wrapping (early customers were inclined to wash it for re-use). Another important innovation in wrapping, this time in the late 1950s, was the continuous perforated roll of transparent plastic that allowed customers to serve themselves with fruit and vegetables.

Two types of modern technology seem absolutely outstanding. One is refrigeration: without it no one could hope to assure product quality and freshness through Australia's summer or, in the Queensland tropics, at any time of year. The ravages of heat, moisture and insects that had made canning food an attractive option made refrigeration a compelling one. It is interesting to note that when Hordern's Food Hall in Sydney was remodelled in 1932 refrigerated cases 200 feet long were installed for cooked and pre-cut meat. And as an example of the speed of change that was possible when there was a good thing going, it is even more interesting to note that the New South Wales Pure Foods Act had to be amended in 1934 because so many retailers not registered as butchers had already caught on and were selling meat from refrigerators in forms only legally permitted to butchers.

The other obviously significant technology is computerization, which is much more recent. Woolworths first installed an IBM computer for which it had paid £250 000 in 1961. The first fully electronic grocery ordering system was established by the Foodland banner group in 1974. The industry has moved on apace from those points, especially since the universal adoption of barcoding. The thousands upon thousands of individual items sold every day could not have been monitored, re-ordered and accounted for with any previous technology. Coles was the first grocery chain to install the electronic funds transfer system, EFTPOS, and now provides this service at all 6000 checkouts. The most astonishing feature is the almost explosive use of this as a banking service: every year customers withdraw a total of $2 billion in cash.

Another attractive innovation is easily forgotten. This is air-conditioning. Cool air made entering shops a pleasurable, or at any rate a highly acceptable, activity for customers, especially when many fewer homes and cars were themselves air-conditioned. Some leading clothing stores in Sydney had been air-conditioned by 1935 but once again the war slowed or deferred a desirable development. Retail stores in general did not begin to be air-conditioned until the 1950s. Since then air-conditioning has become the norm and is simply taken for granted. It is as good a marker as any of the extent of progress.

CONCLUSIONS

In an advanced country, retail grocery is always evolving. Consumer tastes change, and, as we have seen, never faster than at the present day. The possibilities of unheard-of additions to grocery offerings also constantly expand. Methods and technologies continually alter and facilitate the giant game of risk-taking that supplying the market involves – one in which a sizeable section of the community is nevertheless willing to participate.

The risks that retailers undertake to match supply and demand are socially beneficial. Whatever goods are stacked on the shelves, the customer is free to walk away from them. Successful supermarkets do not necessarily capture all of a locality's trade. Specialist shops may flourish next door to them. During the twentieth century, free choice has been hampered in Australia only during the Depression, wartime, and the aftermath of the Second World War. There was a short spell during the 1970s and 1980s when the supermarket chains failed to grasp the growing elaboration of their customers' tastes. Subsequently, stores have made big efforts, akin to those in earlier experimental decades like the 1920s, to anticipate and even lead demand.

There are four ways of anticipating the market: sheer experimentation; intuition or casual observation, which is not to be scorned since retailers themselves are customers and members of society; trend-spotting via demographic data and opinion surveys; and imitating the overseas industry. The last point warrants comment. Almost all the retail pioneers in Australia visited the United States and Europe, including Britain, to study retailing. G.J. Coles himself did so before first opening his shop in 1914. The USA and Britain are larger but culturally congruent societies. The size of their markets and retail trade means they are understandably likely to innovate first. Overseas tours by supermarket managers have continued and over the years many American practices, in particular, have been introduced as a result. Australian grocers do their own community a service when they introduce 'best practice', whatever its geographical origin. They are creating positive externalities for the consumer. Other countries, even some rich ones in the OECD, have not invariably developed retailing to a comparable pitch. The Mom-and-Pop stores in Japan are cramped. The shops in Germany that are nicknamed *Tante Emma Laden* (Aunt Emma Shops) are like squeezing back into the Australia of the 1950s. The German Shop Closure Law of 1956, though relaxed a little in recent years, is recognized as the source of 'massive inconvenience to millions'.[14] The actual improvements to formats, display and business methods being made in Australia in the 1990s have persuaded foreign grocers to visit the country on fact-finding tours. Groups of grocers from all over the world visit the Coles Express Store in central Melbourne. It is understood that another company is building what is virtually a replica Coles Express Store in Auckland, New Zealand.

During the Depression of the 1930s Coles continued to sell at the lowest possible prices, earning the name of 'the stores that helped reduce the cost of living' – as Collins remarks, 'when it was sorely needed'.[15] The extraordinary expansion of the 'Offer' has not cost the consumer more. In real terms, food in Australia costs less than it did 25 years ago. Coles calculates that in 1972 it took the average wage earner almost four and a half hours to earn enough to buy a basket of 15 food items, whereas by 1998 buying the same basket took only three hours and twenty minutes – a fall of 26 per cent.

The next big change may be direct selling, which is already being introduced overseas, for example in New Zealand and some Asian countries; Woolworths has introduced it in Sydney. Coles Myer, too, is developmg selling over the Internet. Customers are able to order electronically, sorting their grocery lists whichever way they like – by nutritional content, cost per kilogramme, or from recipes, that is to say, building up meals by clicking on the ingredients. The software, which has been devised in association with the American company, Peapod, can of course retain the lists and refill orders automatically, until such time as the customer wishes to add or delete an item.

Since the order is known in advance, produce can be delivered to the customer's home fresh from the market. Home delivery will however be very different from the old days; a single delivery will be sufficient and there will be no need to wait for a succession of boys bicycling up the driveway. Coles has arranged to employ part of the Australia Post fleet of vans; software in each van will calculate the best route to the next customer's address.

Writings on the history of retailing occasionally contain grumbles about the very notion of choice. This may be fashionable in some quarters of social science but in the palatial realm of supermarket retailing it seems distinctly perverse. As with worries about the deskilling of grocers and housewives by early self-service stores and supermarkets, the proof of the pudding is clear from the industry's subsequent record and the consumer's reciprocal willingness to embrace the available choice. There was nothing more skilful in the grocer of 1950 supplying and the purchaser selecting his or her groceries from 1000 or 1500 lines than there is today in providing or choosing among 40 000. 'The infrequent supermarket shopper is becoming harder to find', remarks A.C. Nielsen's 1998 survey, *The Way We Shop*. Almost one-third of grocery shoppers claim to visit a supermarket three to six times per week. No one could take this to mean that consumers dislike the spread that has been placed before them. Tastes in food have been globalized.

ACKNOWLEDGEMENTS

This account has been compiled from a number of sources, including material supplied by various divisions within the Coles Myer company. Laurie Giuseppini, Steve Johns, Ken Reading and Jon Wood were particularly helpful in explaining the work of their departments. Outside the company Kerrie Evans of the Australian Centre for Retail Studies cheerfully supplied research assistance. The past director of that Centre, Michael Collins, and the present director, Alan Treadgold, provided valuable background information, as did Bill Pratt, formerly of Safeways Australia.

NOTES

1. Michael Symons, *One Continuous Picnic: A History of Eating in Australia* (Adelaide: Duck Press, 1982), p. 177.
2. Sam Walton, *Sam Walton: Made in America, My Story* (New York: Doubleday, 1992), p. 173.
3. Symons, op. cit., p. 177.
4. Robin Boyd, *Australia's Home* (Harmondsworth, Middlesex: Penguin, 1978), p. 255.
5. Symons, op. cit., p. 177.
6. Kim Humphery, *Shelf Life: Supermarkets and the Changing Cultures of Consumption* (Cambridge: Cambridge University Press, 1998), p. 111.
7. Symons, op. cit., p. 181.
8. Robin Walker and Dave Roberts, *From Scarcity to Surfeit: A History of Food and Nutrition in New South Wales* (Kensington, NSW: New South Wales University Press, 1988), p. 12.
9. Neil Raphel and Murray Raphel, 'What's Up Down Under', *Progressive Grocer*, **71** (10), 21 October 1992, 21.
10. Symons, op. cit., p. 187.
11. *Australian Financial Review*, 16 January 1999.
12. Michael Collins, *A Brief History of Retailing, Part 2: The Development of Australian Retailing (1800-1990)* (Caulfield East: Monash University, n.d.), p. 22.
13. Humphery, op. cit., p. 213.
14. John Ardagh, *Germany and the Germans* (London: Penguin, 1991), pp. 208-9.
15. Collins, op. cit., p. 15.

12. Global integration and global prospects

INTERNATIONAL NEWS

In the developed countries public awareness about the remainder of the world is falling away. Just when the global economy has been becoming more integrated than at any time since before the First World War, less and less interest has been shown in foreign news. During the 1990s, television offerings by major networks in the so-called 'Anglo-Saxon' countries were cut back. Sometimes they were reduced to little more than headlines and stories of scandal and tragedy keenly interesting to the participants but of little wider importance. The personalities of announcers have become selling points. Even the BBC World Service competes for listeners by filling time on air with popular entertainment. It is barely a coincidence that the United Nations has established a roster of singers and actors to promote its causes. Expertise about global problems has taken a back seat in favour of being a 'star' – and 'stars', adroitly sensing public taste, tend to endorse fashionable and sometimes dubious remedies for the world's ills. 'Better Red than Expert', as an older slogan had it.

Seriousness admittedly still persists on German and Japanese news channels, and round-the-clock reporting, like that on CNN, has become widely available. Yet it is said with some justice that the most attentive audience for information about international affairs is among business people, who have wider markets at stake than before. The general public shows less concern about the plight of foreigners and aid has fallen as a percentage of national budgets. Among the reasons for this we can probably discount the influence of economists who point out that aid and debt relief reward the wrong behaviours. Rather, cynicism has developed about corruption and the anomaly of giving aid to militaristic states.

Why should international awareness have slumped at all, let alone during a phase of rapid economic integration? The middle classes in the developed countries are richer than ever before and more likely to have travelled overseas. They have more formal education. Many of them meet foreigners in the course of their work. We might therefore have anticipated a *rising* interest in international affairs. Perhaps this has not happened because, whereas concern with the outer world used to be sustained by the threats implicit in international affairs, the level of threat has seemed to recede. Wars and disasters do take place but, as far as the Western public is concerned, they happen off-stage. Fewer people have any personal experience of war. The Vietnam War was the last conflict in which numbers of young men from Western countries risked their lives in foreign fields; since then most wars have been policing or peace-keeping operations involving only tiny proportions of the younger age-groups. These operations have taken place in an atmosphere where any loss of life has become unacceptable. This unmartial attitude matches the modern insistence that goods in the shops should carry absolutely no risk. It is not inconsistent with the concern shown nowadays by the Green movement for the environment and the welfare of all species.

THE BACKLASH: WHAT NEXT?

Yet the 'greenies' are graying. To 18 year olds their movement, which for almost a generation has been the dominant focus of political protest, must now seem a cause associated with ageing baby-boomers. Conceivably the way that the Green candidate, Ralph Nader, took votes away from Al Gore in the US presidential election of 2000 may herald a third wave of environmentalism, so *The Economist* of 18 November 2000 surmised, but there was little sign of this over the preceding period. The membership of many environmental organizations was falling. Their officers, whose livelihood depends on subscription income, responded by differentiating the product. One organization began to specialize in this type of issue, another in a different type. All of them need continual scares to attract and retain public support. But they have been almost too effective at getting their message across for their own good. In many countries the regulations they insisted on have been incorporated in routine legislation.

For several years I have therefore taxed my students with the question, 'What Next?' – what will come after the environmental movement? Had one been able to forecast in 1970 just how influential the movement would become, one could have made money by persuading companies and governments to act ahead of the trend rather than limp along behind it. Any argument with a profit motive has a chance of appealing to the business school students whom I teach. Hence I ask them to identify the next great cause and make money out of their prescience. For a long time there were no very compelling suggestions in response to my challenge. Classes offered much the same ideas every year. The issue of privacy was the most often mentioned, that is to say a campaign against making data on individuals available on commercial and government computers. I did not think this would run; the topic may appeal to graduate students but seemed unlikely to bring youth as a whole into the streets. The students themselves found the whole topic only mildly interesting. They often have first degrees in science or engineering and are somewhat apolitical by temperament. In addition they grew up in the tepid 1980s and 1990s, when little of urgency seemed to be happening in the public sphere.

However, after a couple of decades in which such attitudes have prevailed, a fresh minority has unexpectedly arisen to protest about – everything and anything. These activists have turned the tables on authority by organizing via the Internet and ensuring that unelected NGOs (non-governmental organizations) have been accepted as legitimate policy-making bodies. Democratic accountability has been shunted aside. Companies, governments and international bodies have been willing to cooperate with the larger NGOs, which they see as the respectable face of a protest movement too powerful to ignore and all too likely to target individual firms and institutions that stand in their way. Between 1990–94 the proportion of EU foreign aid (taxpayers' money) that was channelled through NGOs rose from 47 per cent to 67 per cent. The proportion of World Bank projects in which NGOs were involved rose from under 50 per cent in 1994 to over 70 per cent by 1999. Government representatives on the board of the World Bank made only feeble protests at this usurpation of their legitimate role.[1]

As a result, the 'New Millennium' collectivists, as David Henderson calls them, may become influential enough to frustrate policies that would otherwise help solve the world's problems.[2] The pivotal year for the resurgence of 'protest' was 1997. Thereafter, activists above 50 years of age were joined by a fresh cohort of college-age people. Protest reasserted itself with a bang at the riots outside the WTO meeting in Seattle in 1999, followed by violence at meetings of the World Economic Forum. Although a shift towards post-materialist values was evident throughout the 1990s, and was meticulously documented by Ronald Inglehart, no one had really predicted the specific protests or the level of violence that was about to emerge, including the police forces and security agencies whose job it is to monitor such things.[3]

The protests were an unintended consequence of the very success of capitalism that the activists seek to subvert. Capitalism, trade and business have created a plenitude of wealth and leisure. Most adults in the Western world have twice the leisure they would have had a century ago and some of them have taken to expending this on – protest. What are we to conclude about people so eager to bite the hand that feeds them? The incoherence of many of their views implies that the common thread among them is not so much a new political programme (though most of them are 'for' government control and interventionism) but the creation of an alternative establishment in which they, rather than business people or elected representatives, would have power and prestige.

What's next, then, is Anti-Capitalism or Anti-Globalization. Businesses more than governments are singled out, for instance by 'hackivists' who seek to interfere with their computer files and websites. 'I am talking about ... dismantling the transnational corporation itself', one Filipino protester told the crowds outside the World Economic Forum meeting in Melbourne.[4] 'Anti-Capitalism' is a cause that is unlikely to reach its final goal, short of a push from world economic catastrophe, but its indeterminacy turns out to be its strength. As a cause it can mean anything. Interviews with protestors show them to be uninformed about economics and international affairs, and muddled or at odds with one another about what it is they want. None seems to grasp, for example, that the WTO is a voluntary body without global powers of its own. I have spoken to people who say they are 'against international trade' but who have never thought to read a book on the subject. But they have nevertheless found a protean 'cause' that may run and run.

The most unfortunate aspect is the 'treason of the clerks', that is to say the almost complete absence from the popular press of rebuttals by professional economists, who prefer to write for one another rather than explain the errors of the 'do-it-yourself economics' wheeled into battle by the New Millennium Collectivists. There may be cases of market failure where tariffs, industry policy and other interventions are justified, at least technically. History's experience is that government failure is more evident, not to say harder to eradicate. One problem with specific interventions is that they build up coalitions which remain as advocates for trade distortions. Another is that it is hard to enforce sunset clauses. Worse would be to give way to the unfocused and insatiable demands of anti-globalization crusaders.

MODERN ATTITUDES

The Asian Crisis of 1997 resurrected fears of a global slump. It brought normally sanguine people up with a jolt. The previous financial shock in 1987, which was in any case quickly contained, is already too remote to influence the current generation of students. Has 1987 faded so soon? Even teachers, who each year face an audience a further step more distant from themselves in age, are often surprised when they realize how recent their pupils' upbringing has been. Sometimes they are astonished to find what experiences the latest cohort of students no longer shares with them.

For some years my pupils have been candidates for an MBA or for a Master's degree in International Economics. The MBAs have a median age of 29 and have usually worked in business for half-a-dozen years, often outside their own countries. Each cohort is highly international – I have taught someone from Tibet and someone from Andorra. Almost all come from business or professional families. They grew up in cities or comfortable suburbs. Personal circumstances and experiences have a big impact on expectations and world-view. For instance my students are scarcely cognizant of the fact that the village-dwelling proportion of the world population is still very big and has only just now shrunk to half the total. They know little about crops or livestock and little about the natural environment, except that it is required of them to look on it approvingly.

I tease the students about being 'People of Plenty' (after the title of an American book which explored the implications of prosperity) and 'Children of Stability' (because none has ever suffered war).[5] Few, if any, have ever known hunger or a world without electricity. They bring lap-tops and mobile phones to class and for the rest of their careers they intend to keep in touch with one another by e-mail. Although they grasp intellectually any point I can make to them, they have seldom thought how short a time it is since such gadgets and activities could be taken for granted. They are surprised when I tell them that I watched the moon landing in 1969 as the guest of Sir Kenneth Swan, whose father invented the incandescent bulb. As far as they are concerned, electric light and power have always existed and, what is more, are virtually free goods.

Another unstated assumption on their part is that economic well-being will continue unchecked into the indefinite future. Further assumptions are that all people are rational maximizers who will negotiate or trade their way out of problems and that developed countries will not go to war, whatever martial antics our ancestors so puzzlingly got up to. I hope they are right but unfortunately the fact that many people have lately been growing up in peaceful and prosperous parts of the world does not guarantee that old kinds of trouble will never recur.

There is no doubt that my students belong near the top of the 'Golden Billion' who live in the developed world or the richer cities of the developing world. They are part of a particularly small segment of highly educated, well-travelled and ambitious people. According to the *Financial Times* (27 May 2000), there are about 20 million global citizens or what it calls 'cosmocrats', of whom about 8 million live in the USA. These are affluent people whose tastes are commonly thought of as American. They follow the international news: the combined circulation of *Time*, *Newsweek*, *The Wall Street Journal*, the *Financial Times*, the *International Herald Tribune*, *Business Week*, *Forbes*, *Fortune* and *The Economist* does indeed total about 20 million. Most 'cosmocrats' take an international flight at least once a year (10 million Europeans and 5 million Americans). Their relationships and expectations are open-ended compared with those of their village ancestors or the bulk of their contemporaries on earth. They are a small proportion of humanity but we should note how very recently and how very fast, by any historical standard, this group has expanded and become international in its connections and sympathies.

The near future is likely to be a difficult time for the world as the gap between the wealth, assumptions and aspirations of the cosmocrats and the rest sets up frictions in world politics. History takes place in the lag periods while trends are working themselves out. It is an almost permanent condition of disequilibrium. Generalizing the prosperity of the cosmocrats to the rest of humanity, so many of whom are still poor, rural and illiterate, ensures that the future will not be easy. Nevertheless, getting this far was probably the hardest part. We have accumulated a body of experience about how to generate economic growth.

HOW NEW IS THE MODERN WORLD?

Young people are inevitably coming across many things for the first time and tend to think them new because in their own experience they are. They thus commonly mistake the appearance of novelty for its reality. The trick is to judge what is really new and what is a re-run of old tendencies in modern dress. For example, how new is globalization? International trade is certainly very old. Walt Rostow tells us that an Athenian citizen in the time of Pericles could dine off food and lounge on furnishings from as far afield as Carthage, the Black Sea and Persia.[6] The ancient world did not however provide such a variety of goods to ordinary folk. Rostow's fortunate Athenian was a member of a tiny minority. In that sense the expansion of the modern international economy *is* new, though we should not forget that there was also a striking episode of globalization in Victorian times.

The late nineteenth century witnessed rapidly falling transport costs (railways, steamships) and costs of communication (the telegraph, popular newspapers), and an altogether greater degree of international economic integration than the current generation has experienced. This surprises many people, yet in 1914 the ratio of world trade and foreign investment to world GDP was higher than it was again until the 1980s. The strains that these earlier changes brought about inspired collectivist and Protectionist reactions. Agriculture began to be protected against cheap foreign imports before the First World War in almost every European country except Britain and Denmark. Between the wars protectionism became a plague. The war itself, the interwar depression and the rise of virulent nationalisms, fascism and communism were all in part flawed adaptations to open markets.

Since the Second World War governments have recreated a liberal trading order piece by piece. They were helped by a fresh impetus from technology, especially in respect of moving capital and information around the world.

Multinational companies took the opportunity to establish operations across borders. As is well known, trading volumes soared 18 times between 1950-98, far ahead of the five-fold increase in production. The 'gains from trade' have been enormous as firms and industries in different countries have been enabled to specialize in what is to their best advantage. But the process of adaptation to new international competition is never perfect and this has helped to fuel the recent bout of protests and protectionist impulses. Economists who only a few years ago boasted that the battle for Free Trade was won may have been intellectually correct but were naive if they thought there would be an end to calls for Protection. The calls are revived whenever a fresh wave of economic change becomes too stressful.

New technology is at least as influential as trade in bringing the pressure of open competition to bear on firms, industries and regions. Rustbelts are not just aspects of modern experience. Trade expansions and technological development have altered the geographical distribution of economic activity since at least the Decline of Venice in the seventeenth century. They lead to deep shifts in industrial structure. The two greatest and most general examples have been the transitions from agriculture to manufacturing and from manufacturing to the service sector. The world is now in the midst of the second of these shifts, which is well advanced in some countries while others struggle to catch up. Globalization is a larger and more rapid episode in an old resorting process, and the fact that the process is regionally out-of-phase helps to arouse the old conflicts on a grander scale. Losers and those who fear losing may always outnumber people confident of winning. It is never easy to persuade people who seem likely to lose from competition that the good of the greater number is at stake. Economists, bureaucrats and politicians have done an unsatisfactory job of explaining the processes to the public.

RESHAPING THE WORLD

Three powerful forces reshaping the world are all arguably newer than globalization, though each still represents some intensification of an earlier trend. All fall into the category of 'swell of the ocean' changes that work beneath the surface and at first attract little attention from politicians and business executives. These forces have broken the surface now. They are information technology, the education of women, and the current form of demographic change.

Information Technology

The dust of contention has not yet settled with respect to information technology. Argument continues as to whether the computer, the Internet and e-mail have created a genuinely 'new economy', even in the United States. Sceptics point out that so far the main productivity gains are to be found in only one sector, the manufacturing of computer equipment itself. There is nothing as profound here, they assert, as the changes brought about early in the twentieth century by electric power. Others urge that it is early days and procedures so widely affecting transactions and the flow of information will come to have systemic effects: business-to-business commerce aided by computerized searches for the lowest price, together with e-commerce retailing to customers, must, the enthusiasts think, give the economy a revolutionary boost. It is hard to come to a judgement as yet, though this is one of the subjects where the journalistic appetite for gloomy predictions is less marked than usual. Most people are excited about the effects of IT and there are big incentives to come to a quick conclusion. The market will pay for a plausible argument, however premature.

Whatever the ultimate productivity implications, the lifestyle effects of access to the Internet and e-mail do already look enormous. It is conceivable that the IT 'revolution' will have relatively minor economic effects yet bring major social and political repercussions. This possibility leads me to retain the catch-all term 'globalization' rather than the more respectable 'international economic integration'.

Too much of the discussion about the effects of IT has centred on the developed world, especially the United States. Too many general theorems have been advanced on the basis of Western experience alone. The effect of cheaper information on more rigid economies may turn out to be proportionately greater. In India, peasants who have never previously been able to penetrate officialdom and obtain useful data are now able to search the Web for crop prices and also check that no one has tampered with the land records. We may even see some societies become information rich before they have undergone the changes in industrial structure that the West has experienced. No one knows the implications of changing the 'order of events' in this way, although a possible model is the existence in the nineteenth century of highly literate and well-educated but still relatively poor countries like Scotland and Sweden. They took some time to catch up with the industrial leaders in GDP per head but the essential fact is that they had put themselves in a position to join the group of rich countries. Knowledge is power. Another aspect of open access to information is the way it desperately frightens authoritarian regimes such as the authorities in China, who are fast buying software from complaisant Western companies in order to link their police databases and scan huge numbers of messages for keywords objectionable to their regime. Fortunately work of this type is not attractive to the most creative minds in IT.

One feature of the IT scene is, in a phrase used by the international chairman of Andersen Consulting, the 'extraordinary war for talent' that is being provoked. This serves to highlight the emerging stresses in global labour markets. Several countries are courting India in the apparent belief that the current shortages can be overcome by hiring English-speaking programmers from Bangalore. The ethics of draining a developing economy of its own scarce talent have dropped out of consideration. The global market for programmers is so tight that the Philippines, South Africa and Eastern Europe have similarly been targeted. The supplicant countries include Singapore, Germany, Ireland, South Korea and Britain, and their search for talent is being carried out at the highest, Prime Ministerial, level. Britain and Germany have already faced down domestic opposition to immigrant labour and eased visa entry requirements for skilled workers. Countries like China and Japan, where a surge in investment in IT in 1999–2000 has highlighted the shortage of programmers who are fluent in English, have likewise joined the hunt. The problem with this undignified scramble, which turns a fierce spotlight on the failure of manpower planning and deficiencies in education in country after country, is that India estimates its own skill requirements to be greater than its home supply. Currently India's IT sector employs 280 000 people but expects to need a workforce of 2 200 000 by 2008, despite the fact that its engineering colleges can offer only 33 000 places per year.[7]

When it comes to education in computer science or even basic computing skills, a lapse in official policies throughout much of the world is that the female half of the workforce has been neglected. Where women do get access to the Internet they often become markedly entrepreneurial, because the Web is gender-blind. Most of them however have far less access than males; nothing else can be expected of less-developed countries where even simple literacy is denied to girl children. Western countries themselves are only just reaching the point where as many women as men go to college and there is still a tendency to place computer science among subjects that are 'too hard for girls'. The consequences of this distortion are now blowing back into the faces of politicians who have not been brave enough to confront prejudice and discrimination.

Female Education

If you want to change the world, educate women. There is no guarantee that this will at once raise their official or public status (consider Japan) but in the long run it will surely do so. The signs are clear that fertility will come down at an early stage, once women gain more choice over child bearing. Nothing has been more marked than that economic growth is associated with declining fertility rates, though the link may not be what at first appears. A fascinating indication that something other than a simple income effect may be at work appears in Susan Cotts Watkins' study of Europe, which shows that completed family size fell after 1870, converging on two adults and two children (ideally, so to speak, a 'pigeon pair', one for you and one for me).[8] This was the case regardless of income level, religion or language, leading the author to suggest that norms concerning the most desirable family size were being communicated informally from woman to woman – in other words that there was a sociological mechanism at work distinct from the relationships ordinarily measured by economists.

Modern parallels may be found in a number of non-Western regions. The Maghreb (North Africa) is a case in point. Until very recently the standard assumption was that there was a specifically Islamic behaviour pattern holding birth rates high, but in countries of the Maghreb this has not proved to be true.[9] The birth rate has fallen fast. The suggestion has been made that this is an unintended consequence of the movement of labour to work in Europe. Emigrants send money home and, furthermore, when they return home to visit they put pressure on their families to spend some of the remittances on educating girl children. Given the conflicts surrounding Muslim immigrants to Europe, and the fact that Muslim women are returning there to the traditional practice of covering their heads in public, it may seem surprising that they have picked up the liberal Western attitude to female education. But they have done so and the fall in birth rates in much of North Africa is one unexpected outcome. Certain other Islamic countries, on the other hand, remain extremely conservative. Female illiteracy (the inability to read or write) is as high as 58 per cent in Egypt and 71 per cent in Pakistan, figures with obvious consequences for the quality of the workforce and continuing high fertility rates.

Demographic Structure

Shifts in demographic structure are among the greatest of forces at work in the world. Whereas the *bête noire* of the 'doomsayers' of the 1960s and 1970s was over-population, serious demographers have understood for the past 15 or 20 years that world population growth is ebbing and, less certainly, that it may actually go into reverse within a couple of generations. Almost more important for the present is that the rate of change differs across the world: it is 'regionally staggered'. Fertility rates have fallen almost everywhere, but first and most in a number of developed countries. The age profile there is altering fast. Italy and Japan, for instance, are conspicuously ageing countries, where the proportion of the population over 60 or 65 years of age is rising rapidly and the share made up by teenagers is falling. Unless a great deal more immigration is permitted, the population of Italy will fall by 16 million by

2050. It is no good pretending that the consequences of falls like this can be left to solve themselves, which has been the usual attitude among politicians. They have failed to provide for an appropriate future supply of labour and have also let pension schemes go unfunded, paying current pensioners out of current tax revenues instead. With the dependency ratio altering unfavourably (though the declining number of dependent children does soften the blow), it may become politically intolerable to raise enough taxes from a shrinking workforce to continue this just-in-time practice.

The labour supply available in the industrialized world will shrink fast. Shortages of particular skills like computer programming are only the thin end of the wedge. In countries with ageing populations labour is likely to become scarce over a far broader front. Already there is a conflict between business and government regarding immigration policy. Governments incline to resist increases in the rate of immigration because of costs to the public sector and because the less educated sections of the voting public (who see themselves facing direct competition for jobs and housing) are often fiercely opposed to the arrival of strangers. Despite that opposition, fewer and fewer people in the developed countries are willing to take DDD jobs (dirty, dangerous and dull), even in times of high unemployment.

Those who resist immigration have already lost much of the argument in the 'Anglo-Saxon' world. A significant part of the high rate of economic growth in the United States has been attributed to the cheap labour of an army of immigrants: 20 per cent of the US population is now comprised of immigrants and their children. At the end of August 2000, non-Hispanic whites became a minority in California, having been as much as 80 per cent of the population in 1970. By 2010 whites will become a minority in London. The demographer who calculated this wished to remain anonymous because merely reporting the facts may be seen by hotheads as 'racist'.[10] Meanwhile business becomes increasingly concerned about shortages of labour.

A geopolitical problem also looms. Whereas the nineteenth century was Europe's century and the European share of world population rose, the pattern has since reversed itself. Ninety-eight per cent of world population growth in the next quarter of a century will be in developing nations. The world share of population in the industrialized countries or the democracies, however one defines them, is falling fast. International power and prestige now depend more on wealth and military technology than on the number of foot soldiers who can be fielded, but population size still counts. What may count most of all is the gradient between demographic growth in the less-developed world and the slowdown, soon to be actual shrinkage, in the developed world. This has already blown strong currents of illegal migration into Western countries from as far away as Afghanistan and South Africa. Barring some astonishing improvement in rates of productivity growth, with workers producing far more than they are currently expected to do, an inflow of labour will unavoidably be needed. Tensions over managing who gets in and who is kept out will continue to roil world affairs. Without extraordinarily rapid economic growth to absorb the growth of the labour force in the remainder of the world, the rich countries will remain the destinations of choice for energetic or desperate people. Nothing else can be expected when we observe that the GDP of Spain is 12 times that of Morocco and 40 times that of Nigeria.

A CONVERGENCE OF ATTITUDES

It would be facile to think, as some Westerners seem to do, that rising incomes will lead people living elsewhere in the world to adopt the behaviours of 'modern' people in the developed countries. We are perhaps passing through the middle of a sequence of reactions to modernization. An earlier generation of non-Western intellectuals was strongly influenced by things Western. They mastered the West and could move freely in it and at the same time in their own world. This was true even of the radical nationalists who grew up in late colonial times and devoted their careers to securing independence for their countries. A subsequent generation became more choosy, inclined to adopt Western, or global, technology but without adopting the 'modern' lifestyles of the West.

The affluent Third World young are often nationalists and traditionalists, even fundamentalists – witness the resurgence of Islamic and Hindu fundamentalisms. This is quite alien to Western expectations; I can see my Western students struggling to grasp the fact, which is hard for them to do because the non-Westerners in class with them are among the most Westernized of their age group. But it has to be remembered that many able young people in many societies are staying home and studying their own religious traditions.

For a generation or two Western intellectuals have tended to be agnostics or atheists who cannot imagine that any educated person would not abandon religious adherence in the way they themselves have done. They have put their trust in 'secularization theory', which urges that education and rising incomes will cause religion to fall away as a kind of superstition. This theory has proved wrong within Western society. Religion proves not to be an 'inferior good' which is abandoned when income rises. In terms of foreign policy, the expectations have been even more disastrously wrong. Imagine, for instance, the foreign policy implications of failing to understand the strengthening of Islam, yet that is what a number of Western advisers did. None of this need mean that the instincts of my Western students will prove wrong in the longer term and that, with successful economic growth and further urbanization, the children of the present non-Western generation may not yet come to change in the expected 'modern' direction. In the meantime we are likely to have to live with a generation that is increasingly suspicious of the West and inclined to reject many of its ways.

HEARTENING TRENDS

The usual means of deciding whether the world is becoming a better place is to compare the income received by the richest fifth and poorest fifth of the entire population. Utterly wrong reports about this appear almost daily and are cited by the highest authorities. The gap between the top and bottom fifths is said to be widening fast. In so far as there is a source for these statements, it is the *Human Development Report, 1999*, which originated from the United Nations Statistical Commission. This report was severely criticized by Ian Castles, Vice President of the Academy of the Social Sciences in Australia, and as a result has since been admitted by the UN statisticians to contain 'material errors' – the kind that distort the picture being drawn. The UN statistical team now admits that the fifth of the world's population living in the highest income countries receive 60–65 per cent of the world's income, not 86 per cent; that the gap between the richest and poorest fifths is not 74 to 1 but 16 to 1; and that this gap is 'not unequivocally widening'.[11]

Big gaps in the global scorecard remain to be closed, obviously, yet to pretend the direction of change is negative, either through ignorance or political malice, can only get in the way of policies to improve conditions still further. There can be no doubt that by any past standard the world is vastly better off and, for the moment, more peaceful than it has ever been. At the upper end of the distribution, historically unimaginable wealth has been spread throughout society. In the United States over 98 per cent of people have electricity, telephone, and a flush toilet.[12] Over 70 per cent own a car, VCR, microwave, air conditioner, cable TV, washer and dryer. The incidence of disease, the quality of the air and the productivity of American agriculture have all improved.[13] These achievements would be less impressive if they were confined to the rich countries, but in reality gains were made almost everywhere during the last 40 years of the twentieth century. In low-income countries, life expectancy at birth, which is probably the most telling statistic of all, reached 56 in 1992 from only 42 in 1960. Enrolments in primary schools rose and literacy improved (even female literacy). Installed telephone lines and the number of calls, including international calls, are expanding almost too fast to keep track. The economic basis of these changes in the Third World has been a huge rise in exports and a shift in the type of products made and exported. Low-yielding primary commodities, which constituted 90 per cent of all Third World exports in 1960, had fallen to the 20 per cent to 60 per cent range by 1994. The share of manufactured exports, which are better earners, has increased. In short there has been a manufacturing revolution, with all this implies for the spread of skills.

Economic growth is good for the poor. In the fastest growing countries poverty has fallen the furthest and pollution been reduced the most, while literacy and life expectancy have risen the highest. There has of course been stress from structural change as economic activities have relocated themselves. Some people adapt to change, others would like to halt or reverse the process, partly because they overreact to short-run or regional impacts and do not care to consider the whole picture. It is difficult to stand aside from the vast churning of change while one is living through it and hard to perceive the underlying processes clearly. The imagination may easily fail and the malevolent will ride in to exacerbate the confusion. Yet the statistics, properly presented, leave no doubt that the gain has been very widespread indeed. The political and institutional conditions giving rise to this outcome are, in essence, those that have produced similarly benign results in the past; it is the modern consequences that have outclassed all historical precedent.

Protestors of the anti-capitalist and anti-globalization persuasion have, overall, no rational leg to stand on. We can only suppose that their bitterness derives from something other than the facts – from an exaggerated rise in expectations combined with personal ambition on the part of their leadership. Stridency may be heightened by the frustration aroused not only by the failure of many of their predictions but from a static level of support in terms of gifts of money and volunteers' time.[14] This stasis has intensified competition among the various campaigning groups. Their desire to stop the economic clock is deeply reactionary, though naturally they assert at the tops of their voices that they are the radical and progressive ones. This is like the note in the curate's sermon: 'weak point – shout'.

In a situation where fewer and fewer people express an active interest in foreign affairs, unrepresentative small groups may get their way if they are vocal enough. Politicians respond to electoral threats and squeaky wheels, not to the unthreatening silent majority and certainly not to academic researchers. This is 'Skaggs' Law'.[15] The anti-globalization protestors may not in the end succeed in bringing down the house about our ears but they give comfort to nationalists who find economic integration disconcerting. As a result, deluded or timid governments and firms may hesitate to open their economies or face up to competition from other businesses precisely when it would pay to speed up change and reform. Many governments are happy to be given an excuse to avoid the conflicts that the opening of trade initially tends to create. Some firms and industries are always happy to lobby for special protection against foreign competitors.

For decades the tide has been slowly running against the protectionists but this may now be changing. Two authors who have completed a large study of nineteenth-century globalization make a depressing prediction. After noting that journalists typically extrapolate the immediate past into the immediate future, and thus forecast continued international economic integration, they beg to differ. History, they find, says no; there will be a backlash.[16] No scientific law says the backlash must succeed in closing down multilateral free trade. That is a matter of political will. But there is ample evidence that the prediction of a new backlash is correct. 'What's next' is anti-globalization or anti-capitalism. It is characteristically accompanied by misrepresentation of the functions of the WTO and cheered on by some who should know better.[17] Sadly, as I have noted, economists seldom lift their voices to drown the roar of protest or laugh it out of court.[18] The world, as opposed to the Establishment of New Millennium Collectivists, cannot benefit if the train that has brought us such a long way is thrown into reverse. The effort to expand international trade and investment needs to go on; the results so far justify this opinion and no other. Retreat can only damage the chances of people from the poor world joining my students and creating still more 'Golden Billions'.

NOTES

1. *The Economist*, 4 February 2000.
2. See David Henderson at www.iea.org.uk.
3. Ronald Inglehart, 'Globalization and Postmodern Values', *The Washington Quarterly*, **23** (1), Winter 2000, 215–28.
4. *Financial Times*, 11 September 2000.
5. David M. Potter, *People of Plenty: Economic Abundance and the American Character* (Chicago: University of Chicago Press, 1954).
6. W.W. Rostow, *How It All Began: Origins of the Modern Economy* (New York: McGraw-Hill, 1975).
7. *Financial Times*, 23 April 2000.
8. Susan Cotts Watkins, *From Provinces into Nations: Demographic Integration in Western Europe 1870-1960* (Princeton: Princeton University Press, 1991).
9. Keith Sutton, 'Demographic Transition in the Maghreb', *Geography*, **84** (2), 1999, 111–18. Writing about the relationship of Islam to trends in fertility in general, and after observing that, 'the unambiguity of the Islamic scriptures, and the eternal nature ascribed to them, may be an impediment to the adjustment of Muslim behaviour', Coleman nevertheless concludes that changes in this 'may depend substantially on political, rather than specifically religious, developments'. David A. Coleman, 'Religion, Reproduction and Risk: Measuring Survival and Growth', in Eric Jones and Vernon Reynolds (eds), *Survival and Religion: Biological Evolution and Cultural Change* (Chichester: Wiley, 1995), 240–41.
10. *The Observer*, 3 September 2000.
11. The assessment of Castles' criticisms is at http://www.un.org/Depts/unsd/statcom.htm.
12. *Policy Analysis*, 15 December 1999.
13. The most convenient source on these indicators is Julian Simon (ed.), *The State of Humanity* (Oxford: Blackwell, 1995).
14. *Financial Times*, 20 September 2000.
15. James M. Lindsay, 'The New Apathy', *Foreign Affairs*, September–October, 2000, 2–8.

16. Kevin H. O'Rourke and Jeffrey G. Williamson, *Globalization and History: The Evolution of a Nineteenth Century Atlantic Economy* (Cambridge, Mass.: The MIT Press, 1999), p. 286.

17. See for example an attack on the WTO by a philosopher, Peter Singer, in which he urges (without demonstration) that 'free trade is too important to be left to the economists'. ('How are your morals?', in Dudley Fishburn (ed.), *The World in 2001* (London: *The Economist*, 2000), p. 76.

18. There are honourable exceptions. See for example David Robertson, 'Civil Society and the WTO', *The World Economy*, **23** (9), 2000, 1119–34.

Bibliography

Allen, Robert C. (1999), 'Tracking the Agricultural Revolution in England', *Economic History Review*, **52** (2), 209–235.

Anderson, J.L. and E.L. Jones (1988), 'Natural Disasters and the Historical Response', *Australian Economic History Review*, **XXVIII**, 3–20.

Anderson, J.R. (1980), *Cognitive Psychology and its Implications*, San Francisco: Freeman.

Annan, Noel (1996), *Changing Enemies: The Defeat and Regeneration of Germany*, London: HarperCollins.

Ardagh, John (1991), *Germany and the Germans*, London: Penguin.

Atkinson, Robert D. and Randolph H. Court (1999), 'The New Economy: How Is It Different?', *Issues in Science and Technology*, **XV** (3), 86–7.

Australian Coalition of Service Industries (1998), *The Australian Service Sector Review 1998*, Melbourne.

Ayittey, George B.N. (1989), 'The Political Economy of Reform in Africa', *Journal of Economic Growth*, **3**, 4–17.

Barraclough, Geoffrey (1967), *An Introduction to Contemporary History*, Harmondsworth, Middlesex: Penguin.

Basu, K., E. Jones and E. Schlicht (1987), 'The Growth and Decay of Custom: The Role of the New Institutional Economics in Economic History', *Explorations in Economic History*, **24**, 1–21.

Bellah, Robert N. (1957), *Tokugawa Religion*, New York: The Free Press.

Bellerby, J.R. (1956), *Agriculture and Industry: Relative Income*, London: Macmillan.

Berger, Peter (1984), 'Can the Caribbean Learn from East Asia?', *Caribbean Review*, **XIII**, 7–9.

Borgstrom, Georg (1972, second revised edition), *The Hungry Planet*, New York: Collier Books.

Boserup, Ester (1965), *The Conditions of Agricultural Growth*, London: Allen and Unwin.

Bowers, John and Paul Cheshire (1983), *Agriculture, the Countryside and Land Use: An Economic Critique*, London: Methuen.

Boyd, Robin (1978), *Australia's Home*, Harmondsworth, Middlesex: Penguin.

Brown, R.A. (1994), *Capital and Entrepreneurship in South-East Asia*, New York: St Martin's Press.

Chabal, Patrick and Jean-Pascal Daloz (1999), *Africa Works: Disorder as Political Instrument*, Oxford: The International African Institute/James Currey.

Chan, S. (1987), 'Comparative Performance of East Asian and Latin American NICs', *Pacific Focus*, **2**, 35–56.

Chang, K.C. (1983), *Art, Myth, and Ritual: The Paths to Political Authority in Ancient China*, Cambridge, Massachusetts: Harvard University Press.

Choi, K.I. (1971), 'Technological Diffusion in Agriculture under the Bakuhan System', *Journal of Asian Studies*, **XXX**, 748–59.

Clower, Robert (1973), 'Snarks, Quarks, and Other Fictions', in Louis P. Cain and Paul

J. Uselding (eds), *Business Enterprise and Economic Change*, Kent, Ohio: Kent State University, pp. 3-14.

Coleman, David A. (1995), 'Religion, Reproduction and Risk: Measuring Survival and Growth', in Eric Jones and Vernon Reynolds (eds), *Survival and Religion: Biological Evolution and Cultural Change*, Chichester: Wiley, pp. 240-41.

Collins, Michael (n.d.), *A Brief History of Retailing, Part 2: The Development of Australian Retailing (1800-1990)*, Caulfield East: Monash University.

Cowen, Tyler (1998), *In Praise of Commercial Culture*, Cambridge, Massachusetts: Harvard University Press.

Cowen, Tyler (1998-1999), 'Is Our Culture in Decline?', *Policy*, Summer, 31-4.

Crane, Nicholas (2000), *Two Degrees West: An English Journey*, London: Penguin.

Crosby, Alfred W. (1972), *The Columbian Exchange: Biological and Cultural Consequences of 1492*, Westport, Connecticut: Greenwood Press.

Crowe, D. (1999), 'Exodus: Why Australia's IT Champions Are Leaving the Country', *Australian Financial Review*, 29 May, 23-5.

Cummings, E.G. Bruce (1984), 'The Origins and Development of the Northeast Asian Political Economy: Industrial Sectors, Product Cycles, and Political Consequences', *International Organization*, **38**, 1-40.

Deng, Gang (1993), *Development versus Stagnation: Technological Continuity and Agricultural Progress in Pre-modern China*, Westport, Connecticut: Greenwood Press.

Department of Foreign Affairs and Trade (1999), *Trade in Services, Australia, 1997-98*, Canberra: DFAT.

Diamond, Jared (1993), *The Rise and Fall of the Third Chimpanzee*, London: Vintage.

Dillon, P.J. and E.L. Jones (1996), 'Environmental Consumerism in the United Kingdom: Some Reflections on Managerial Responses and Educational Needs', *European Journal of Agricultural Education and Extension*, **3** (2), 107-8.

Dorgan, Charity A. (1995), *Gale Country and World Rankings Reporter*, New York: Gale Research Inc.

Drucker, Peter (1987), 'Japan's Choices', *Foreign Affairs*, **65**, 923-41.

Easterly, W. and R. Levine (1997), 'Africa's Growth Tragedy: Policies and Ethnic Divisions', *Quarterly Journal of Economics*, November, 1203-50.

Eggertsson, Thrainn (1997), 'The Old Theory of Economic Policy and the New Institutionalism', *Lectiones Jenenses*, **12**, 1-42.

Eggertson, Thrainn (1999), *Norms in Economics - With Special Reference to Economic Development*, Discussion Paper, 10-99, Jena: Max-Planck-Institut.

Elvin, Mark (1984), 'Why China Failed to Create an Endogenous Industrial Capitalism', *Theory and Society*, **13**, 379-91.

Fox, Frank (n.d. [1913]), *Our English Land Muddle: An Australian View*, London: Thomas Nelson.

Freeman, Richard B. and David L. Lindauer (1999), *Why not Africa?*, NBER Working Paper No. 6942, Cambridge: Massachusetts.

Fukuyama, Francis (1998), Response to Sebastian Mallaby on "America in Asia's Mirror"', *The National Interest*, **52**, 25-6.

Fukuyama, Francis (1999), *The Great Disruption*, New York: Free Press.

Gellner, Ernest (1988), *Plough, Sword or Book: The Structure of Human History*, London: Collins Harvill.

Gerschenkron, Alexander (1962), *Economic Backwardness in Historical Perspective*, Cambridge, Massachusetts: The Belknap Press.

Goldsmith, Raymond (1987), *Premodern Financial Systems: A Historical*

Comparative Study, Cambridge: Cambridge University Press.

Goldstone, Jack (2000), *Europe's Peculiar Path: Would the World be 'Modern' if William III's Invasion of England in 1688 had Failed?*, Mimeo, University of California, Davis.

Goudsblom, J., E. Jones and S. Mennell (1996), *The Course of Human History: Economic Growth, Social Process, and Civilization*, Armonk, New York: M.E. Sharpe.

Gress, David (1998), *From Plato to NATO: The Idea of the West and its Opponents*, New York: The Free Press.

Grigg, David (1974), *The Agricultural Systems of the World: An Evolutionary Approach*, Cambridge: Cambridge University Press.

Grin, François (1996), 'The Economics of Language: Survey, Assessment, and Prospects', *International Journal of the Sociology of Language*, **121**, 17–44.

Hall, Ivan P. (1997), *Cartels of the Mind: Japan's Intellectual Closed Shop*, New York: W.W. Norton.

Hanson, Dallas et al. (1999), 'Management of Basic R&D: Lessons from the Australian Experience', *Prometheus*, **17** (2), 187–97.

Harrison L. and S. Huntingdon (eds) (2000), *Culture Matters: How Values Shape Human Progress*, New York: Basic Books.

Havinden, M.A. (1961), 'Agricultural Progress in Openfield Oxfordshire', *Agricultural History Review*, **IX**, 73–83.

Hayek, F.A. (1960), *The Constitution of Liberty*, London: Routledge and Kegan Paul.

Henderson, David (1998), *Industrial Policies Revisited: Lessons Old and New from East Asia and Elsewhere*, Pelham Paper Number Three, Melbourne: Melbourne Business School.

Henderson, David (1999), *The MAI Affair: A Story and Its Lessons*, Pelham Paper Number Five, Melbourne: Melbourne Business School.

Hicks, Sir John (1969), *A Theory of Economic History*, Oxford: Oxford University Press.

Hillaby, John (1983), *Journey Home*, London: Paladin.

Ho, Ping-ti (1955), 'The Introduction of American Food Plants into China', *American Anthropologist*, **57**, 191–201.

Ho, Ping-ti (1956), 'Early-ripening Rice in Chinese History', *Economic History Review*, **9**, 200–218

Holloway, Simon (1996), *The Historical Atlas of Breeding Birds in Britain and Ireland: 1875–1900*, London: T. and A.D. Poyser.

Honey, John (1997), *Language is Power: The Story of Standard English and its Enemies*, London: Faber and Faber.

House of Representatives' Standing Committee on Employment, Education and Training (1993), *The Literacy Challenge: A Report on Strategies for Early Intervention for Literacy and Learning for Australian Children*, Canberra: Australian Government Publishing Service.

Howell, Llewellyn D. and Donald Xie (1996), 'Asia at Risk: The Impact of Methodology in Forecasting', *Management Decision*, **34** (9), 6–16.

Humphery, Kim (1998), *Shelf Life: Supermarkets and the Changing Cultures of Consumption*, Cambridge: Cambridge University Press.

IMD (1999), *World Competitiveness Year Book*, Lausanne: IMD.

Inglehart, Ronald (2000), 'Globalization and Postmodern Values', *The Washington Quarterly*, **23** (1), 215–28.

James, Clive (1986), *Falling Towards England*, London: Picador.

Jones, David Martin and Michael L. R Smith (1999), 'Advance Australia – Anywhere', *Orbis*, **43** (3), 443–60.

Jones, E.L. (1968), *The Development of English Agriculture, 1815-73*, London: Macmillan.

Jones, E.L. (1981; second edition with new introduction, 1988), *The European Miracle: Environments, Economies, and Geopolitics in the History of Europe and Asia*, Cambridge: Cambridge University Press.

Jones, E.L. (1990), 'The Real Question about China: Why Was the Song Economic Achievement not Repeated?', *Australian Economic History Review*, **XXX**, 5–22.

Jones E.L. (1992), 'Culture, Environment and the Historical Lag in East Asia's Industrialization' in J. Melling and J. Barry (eds), *Culture and History*, Exeter: University of Exeter Press, pp. 75–91.

Jones, Eric (1994), 'Asia's Fate: A Response to the Singapore School', *The National Interest*, **35**, 18–28.

Jones, E.L. (1994), 'Patterns of Growth in History', in John A. James and Mark Thomas (eds), *Capitalism in Context*, Chicago: University of Chicago Press, pp. 15–28.

Jones, E.L. (1995), 'Culture and Its Relationship to Economic Change', *Journal of Institutional and Theoretical Economics*, **151** (2), 269–85.

Jones, Eric (1995), 'Technology, the Human Niche and Darwinian Explanation', in Eric Jones and Vernon Reynolds (eds), *Survival and Religion: Biological Evolution and Cultural Change*, Chichester: John Wiley, pp. 163–86.

Jones, E.L. (1996), 'The European Background', in S.L. Engerman and R.E. Gallman (eds), *The Cambridge Economic History of the United States I*, Cambridge: Cambridge University Press, pp. 95–133.

Jones, E.L. (1996), 'Venetian Twilight: How Economies Fade', *Journal of Economic History*, **56** (3), 702–5.

Jones, Eric (1998), 'Globalism and the American Tide', *The National Interest*, **53**, 16–19.

Jones, Eric (1998), 'East Asia's Achilles Heel', *Agenda*, **5** (1), 119–21.

Jones, E.L. (2000), *Growth Recurring: Economic Change in World History*, Ann Arbor: The University of Michigan Press edition, with new introduction.

Jones, E.L. (2000), 'Time and Chance in the Old World Economies', *Journal of Economic History*, **60** (3), 856–9.

Jones, Eric L. (2000), 'The Case for a Shared World Language', in Mark Casson and Andrew Godley (eds), *Cultural Factors in Economic Growth*, Berlin: Springer, pp. 210–35.

Jones, Eric L. (2000), *Australia's Economic and Strategic Prospects*, Osaka: Kansai Economic Research Center [in Japanese].

Jones, E.L. (forthcoming), 'Environment: Historical Overview' and 'Natural Resources: Overview', in Joel Mokyr (ed.), *The Oxford Encyclopedia of Economic History*, New York: Oxford University Press.

Jones, S.R.H. (1988), *Economic Growth and the Spread of the Market Principle in Later Anglo-Saxon England*, University of Auckland Working Papers in Economics, no. 48.

Junning, Liu (2000), 'Classical Liberalism Catches on in China', *Journal of Democracy*, **11** (3), 48–57.

Kagan, Robert (1998), 'What Korea Teaches', *The New Republic*, 9 March.

Kasper, Wolfgang (1993), *Institutional Innovation to Enhance International Attractiveness*, Economics and Management Discussion Paper, 1/93 Campbell,

A.C.T.: Australian Defence Force Academy.

Kasper, Wolfgang (1994), 'The East Asian Challenge', in Helen Hughes *et al.*, *Australia's Asian Challenge*, Sydney: Centre for Independent Studies, pp. 17-34.

Kasper, Wolfgang (1994), 'The Stillbom Tiger Cub', *The Independent Monthly*, November, 70-71.

Kasper, Wolfgang (1998), 'The Open Economy and the National Interest', *Policy*, Winter, 21-6.

Kealey, Terence (1996), *The Economic Laws of Scientific Research*, Basingstoke: Macmillan.

Kerr, Roger (1999), 'Restoring Sanity to Education', reprinted in New Zealand Business Roundtable, *Turning Gain into Pain*, Wellington: NZBR, pp. 209-16.

Kindleberger, Charles (1995), *The World Economy and National Finance in Historical Perspective*, Ann Arbor: University of Michigan Press.

Krugman, Paul (1994), 'The Myth of Asia's Miracle', *Foreign Affairs*, November-December, **73** (6), 62-78.

Krugman, Paul (1996), 'A Country is not a Company', *Harvard Business Review*, January-February, 40-44, 48-51.

Krugman, Paul (n.d.), 'Two Cheers for Formalism', formal.html@web.mit.edu.

Kuhn, Thomas S. (1962), *The Structure of Scientific Revolutions*, Chicago: University of Chicago Press.

Kuran, Timur (1997), 'Islam and Underdevelopment: An Old Puzzle Revisited', *Journal of Institutional and Theoretical Economics*, **153**, 41-71.

Lal, Deepak (1998), *Unintended Consequences: The Impact of Factor Endowments, Culture, and Politics on Long-Run Economic Performance*, Cambridge, Massachusetts.: The MIT Press.

Landes, David (1990), 'Why Are We So Rich and They So Poor?', *American Economic Review*, Papers and Proceedings, **80**,1-13.

Landes, David (1991), 'Rethinking Development', *Dialogue*, **21**, 66-71.

Landes, David S. (1998), *The Wealth and Poverty of Nations*, New York: Norton.

Levi, John and Michael Havinden (1982), *Economics of African Agriculture*, London: Longman.

Lewis, Bernard (1998), *The Multiple Identities of the Middle East*, London: Weidenfeld and Nicolson.

Lin, Justin Yifu (1990), 'Collectivization and China's Agricultural Crisis in 1958-1961', *Journal of Political Economy*, **90**, 1228-52.

Lindsay, James M. (2000), 'The New Apathy', *Foreign Affairs*, September-October, 2-8.

Lingle, Christopher (1997), *The Rise and Decline of the Asian Century: False Starts on the Path to the Global Millennium*, Barcelona: Sirocco.

Llosa, Mario Vargas (2001), 'The Culture of Liberty', *Foreign Policy*, January-February, also available at www.foreignpolicy.com.

Macomber, J. (1989), 'East Asia's Lessons for Latin American Resurgence', *The World Economy*, **10**, 469-82.

Maddison, Angus (2000), in Ian Castles (ed.), *Facts and Fancies of Human Development*, Canberra: Academy of the Social Sciences in Australia, Occasional Paper 1, pp. 1-22.

MAFF (2000), *England Rural Development Plan 2000-2006*.

Martin, John (2000), *The Development of Modern Agriculture: British Farming since 1931*, New York: St Martin's Press.

McBride, Edward (2000), 'Survey of Turkey', *The Economist*, 10 June.

McCrone, Gavin (1962), *The Economics of Subsidising Agriculture*, London: Allen and Unwin.

McEvedy, Colin (n.d.), *The Penguin Atlas of Modern History*, Penguin: no place stated.

McEvedy, Colin and Richard Jones (1978), *Atlas of World Population History*, Harmondsworth, Middlesex: Penguin.

McGurn, William (2000), 'The Gang of Three: Mao, Jesus and Hayek', *Policy*, **16** (3), 35–7.

McNeill, W.H. (1980), *The Human Condition: An Ecological and Historical View*, Princeton: Princeton University Press.

Mead, Walter Russell (2000), 'The End of Asia', *Foreign Affairs*, November–December, 156–61.

Mennell, Stephen (1996), 'Introduction: Bringing the Very Long Term Back In', in Johan Goudsblom, Eric Jones and Stephen Mennell, *The Course of Human History: Economic Growth, Social Process, and Civilization*, Armonk, New York: M.E. Sharpe, pp. 1–13.

Minami, Ryoshin (1986), *The Economic Development of Japan: A Quantitative Story*, Basingstoke: Macmillan.

Mokyr, Joel (1990), *The Lever of Riches*, New York: Oxford University Press.

Mokyr, Joel (2001), 'Eurocentricity Triumphant', *American Historical Review*, **104** (4), at http:/www.historycooperative.org/journals/ahr/104.4/ah001241.html (10 January).

Morawetz, David (1981), *Why the Emperor's New Clothes Are Not Made in Colombia: A Case Study in Latin American and East Asian Manufactured Exports*, New York: Oxford University Press.

Morishima, Michio (1982), *Why has Japan 'Succeeded'? Western Technology and the Japanese Ethos*, Cambridge: Cambridge University Press.

Morris, Cynthia Taft and Irma Adelman (1988), *Comparative Patterns of Economic Development 1850–1914*, Baltimore: The Johns Hopkins University Press.

Munz, Peter (1994), 'The Two Worlds of Anne Salmond in Postmodern Fancy Dress', *The New Zealand Journal of History*, **28** (1), 60–75.

North, Douglass C. and Robert Paul Thomas (1973), *The Rise of the Western World: A New Economic History*, Cambridge: Cambridge University Press.

O'Rourke, Kevin H. and Jeffrey G. Williamson (1999), *Globalization and History: The Evolution of a Nineteenth Century Atlantic Economy*, Cambridge, Massachusetts: The MIT Press.

O'Rourke, Kevin H. and Jeffrey G. Williamson (1999), *The Heckscher–Ohlin Model between 1400 and 2000: When it Explained Factor Price Convergence, When it did not, and Why*, NBER Working Paper, 7411.

Olson, Mancur (1982), *The Rise and Decline of Nations*, New Haven: Yale University Press.

Olson, Mancur (1987), 'Diseconomies of Scale and Development', *Cato Journal*, **7**, 77–97.

Onto, John and Christopher Thomas (1997), *Corporate Governance and Globalising Business: Reconciling Competing Pressures*, Melbourne: Melbourne Business School.

Perkins, Dwight (1969), *Agricultural Development in China 1368–1968*, Edinburgh: Edinburgh University Press.

Perkins, Dwight H. (1975), 'The Persistence of the Past', in Dwight H. Perkins (ed.), *China's Modern Economy in Historical Perspective*, Stanford: Stanford University Press, pp. 1–18.

Pomeranz, Kenneth (2000), *The Great Divergence: China, Europe, and the Making of the Modern World Economy*, Princeton: Princeton University Press.

Porter, Michael E. (1990), *The Competitive Advantage of Nations*, New York: The Free Press.

Potter, David M. (1954), *People of Plenty: Economic Abundance and the American Character*, Chicago: University of Chicago Press.

Raby, Geoff (1996), *Making Rural Australia: An Economic History of Technical and Institutional Creativity, 1788-1860*, Melbourne: Oxford University Press.

Raby, Geoff (2000), 'Reforming Agricultural Trade', in Oldersma, Harry (ed.), *From Havana to Seattle and Beyond: The Quest for Free Trade and Free Markets*, The Hague: Sdu Publishers, pp. 127-35.

Redding, S.G. (1990), *The Spirit of Chinese Capitalism*, Berlin: Walter de Gruyter.

Robertson, David (2000), 'Civil Society and the WTO', *The World Economy*, **23** (9), 1119-34.

Rodriguez, Richard (1981), *Hunger of Memory*, Boston: David R. Godine.

Rosenberg, Hans (1943), 'The Economic Impact of Imperial Germany', *Journal of Economic History*, Supplement 3, 101-7.

Rosenberg, Nathan (1976), *Perspectives on Technology*, Cambridge: Cambridge University Press.

Rostow, W.W. (1975), *How It All Began: Origins of the Modern Economy*, New York: McGraw-Hill.

Russell, Nicholas (1981), 'Who Improved the Eighteenth-century Longhorn Cow?', *Exeter Papers in Economic History*, **14**, 19-40.

Sack, P.L. (1974), 'The Triumph of Colonialism', in P.L. Sack (ed.), *Problem of Choice: Land in Papua New Guinea's Future*, Canberra: ANU.

Sen, Amartya (1990), 'More Than 100 Million Women are Missing', *New York Review of Books*, 20 December.

Sen, Amartya (1998), 'Asian Values and Economic Growth', UNESCO World Culture Report, *Culture, Creativity and Markets*, Paris: UNESCO, 40-41.

Simon Julian (ed.) (1995), *The State of Humanity*, Oxford: Blackwell.

Simpson, John (1999), *Strange Places, Questionable People*, London: Pan.

Singer, Peter (2000), 'How are Your Morals?', in Dudley Fishburn (ed.), *The World in 2001*, London: *The Economist*, p. 76.

Smith, T.C. (1959), *The Agrarian Origins of Modern Japan*, Stanford: Stanford University Press.

Sowell, Thomas (1985), *The Economics and Politics of Race*, New York: William Morrow and Company.

Sutton, Keith (1999), 'Demographic Transition in the Maghreb', *Geography*, **84** (2), 111-18.

Symons, Michael (1982), *One Continuous Picnic: A History of Eating in Australia*, Adelaide: Duck Press.

Taagepera, Rein (1978), 'Size and Duration of Empires: Systematics of Size', *Social Science Research*, **7**, 108-27.

Tracy, Michael (1964), *Agriculture in Western Europe: Crisis and Adaptation since 1880*, London: Cape.

van Bath, B.H. Slicher (1960), 'The Rise of Intensive Husbandry in the Low Countries', in J.S. Bromley and E.H. Kossmann (eds), *Britain and The Netherlands*, London: Chatto and Windus, pp. 130-53.

Van Bergeijk, Peter A.G. and Nico W. Mensink (1997), 'Measuring Globalization', *Journal of World Trade*, **31** (3), 159-68.

Various (1992), *Book of Australian Facts*, Sydney: Reader's Digest.

Walker, Robin and Dave Roberts (1988), *From Scarcity to Surfeit: A History of Food and Nutrition in New South Wales,* Kensington, New South Wales: New South Wales University Press.

Wallraff, Barbara (2000), 'What Global Language?', *Atlantic Monthly*, November, 52–66.

Walton, Sam (1992), *Sam Walton: Made in America, My Story*, New York: Doubleday.

Watkins, Susan Cotts (1991), *From Provinces into Nations: Demographic Integration in Western Europe 1870–1960*, Princeton: Princeton University Press.

Watson, A.M. (1974), 'The Arab Agricultural Revolution and its Diffusion, 700–1100', *Journal of Economic History*, **34**, 8–35.

Webb, W.P. (1952), *The Great Frontier*, Boston: Houghton Mifflin.

Wilhelm, R. (1982), *Chinese Economic Psychology*, New York: Garland.

Wilson, A.T. (1978), 'Pioneer Agricultural Explosion and CO_2 Levels in the Atmosphere', *Nature*, **273**, 40–41.

World Bank (1980), *World Development Report 1980*, Washington, DC: The World Bank.

World Trade Organisation (1998), *Annual Report*, Geneva: WTO.

Wright, Robert (2000), *Nonzero: The Logic of Human Destiny*, London: Little, Brown.

Yamamura, Kozo (1980), 'The Agricultural and Commercial Revolution in Japan, 1550–1650', *Research in Economic History*, **5**, 85–107.

York, Robert and Paul Atkinson (1997), *The Reliability of Quarterly National Accounts in Seven Major Countries: A User's Perspective*, Paris: OECD, Economics Department Working Papers, no. 171.

Index